TEA with HEZBOLLAH

Sitting at the Enemies' Table, Our Journey Through the Middle East

TED DEKKER and CARL MEDEARIS

DOUBLEDAY RELIGION

NEW YORK

CD
DOUBLEDAY

Library of Congress Cataloging-in-Publication Data
Dekker, Ted.
Tea with Hezbollah; sitting at the enemies' table,
our journey through the Middle East / Ted Dekker and Carl Medearis.—1st ed.
1. Middle East—Description and travel.   2. Arab-Israeli conflict.
I. Medearis, Carl.   II. Title.
DS49.D375 2010
956.05'4—dc22   2009028137

ISBN 978-0-307-58827-2

Printed in the United States of America

Design by Debbie Glasserman

10 9 8 7 6 5 4 3 2 1

First Edition

Contents

TEA with HEZBOLLAH

1

Into the Lion's Den

A JOURNEY INTO MADNESS

THE FIRST CLUE that I had thrown myself into the mouth of madness should have been clear before the Middle East Airlines 767 took off from Jeddah, Saudi Arabia, with hardly a soul aboard besides me, the lowly writer, and Carl Medearis, the fearless trailblazer who sat beside me, trying to look at ease.

Correction. The first clue should have come five days earlier when I received the call that the Hezbollah had just stormed the parliament buildings in Beirut, had declared their own form of martial law, and were killing dissenting party members who'd taken up arms. A full-scale war had broken out in the very city Carl had talked me into visiting on this quest of ours.

Tanks and military vehicles, hundreds of them, were rolling down the streets. Citizens were fleeing. Hezbollah had seized control of the airport and stopped all flights. The American State Department had just issued a travel advisory, essentially prohibiting travel into the region.

I remember the call vividly. I was standing in a small luggage shop in my hometown of Austin, Texas, trying to decide whether the exorbitant price they were suggesting I pay for Tumi bags was worth the extra coin. I could buy a good Samsonite suitcase for a third the price.

It was then my cell phone chirped and I stepped out of the shop, glad for the distraction.

"Have you heard the news?" Carl asked in his ever-nonchalant voice.

"What news?"

"Lebanon's at war."

"Huh. Really?"

"The airport is shut down."

"Wow. Really?"

"Many are reported killed."

"Seriously?"

You see, my own use of those words, *really* and *wow* and *seriously*, should have sealed the deal for me. Going to Beirut at a time like this was ill-advised. And going to Beirut to have tea with the top leaders of the Hezbollah, of all people, was now just plain absurd.

"What about Saudi Arabia?" I asked with as much bravado as I could muster. I was the apprentice here, playing the role of adventurer-in-training, and it was important that I didn't start squealing like a frightened child.

"Well, this *is* the Middle East," Carl came back casually. "Samir just evacuated his children on a private plane. He's adamant that we cancel the entire trip."

Samir. One of Carl's many friends in the Middle East, but unique in that Samir knows and is trusted by everyone. A linchpin for this trip, he was responsible for many of our appointments. If he said cancel, clearly we canceled.

My partner wasn't panicking, so I followed his most admirable example. I glanced back through the window where my wife, Lee Ann, was talking to the clerk about the Tumi bags. Naturally we wouldn't be needing either Tumi or Samsonite—the world was coming to an end.

"What about Syria?" I asked.

"Yeah, well, the road from Lebanon into Syria is blockaded with burning tires."

"Seriously?" Again that word. "So our meeting with Assad's government—"

"Is now probably out of the question."

"What about the West Bank? The Hamas?"

"Yeah, crazy, huh? Same with the bin Laden brothers in Saudi Arabia. The whole region could erupt. This is big news."

"What does Chris think?" Chris is Carl's Greek goddess, his marriage partner who has given him three children and traveled the world at his side with superhuman grace. That's my take.

"Yeah, she thinks the trip is dangerous."

Now that I think about it, I did take notice of those early clues that traveling through the Middle East to ask "never before asked questions" of Islam's most influential ideologues and America's "enemies" was a misguided mission. In fact, I distinctly remember feeling buckets of sweet, cool relief washing over my body as Carl broke the news.

The trip was off. I felt jovial! I was liberated from the fear that had nagged at me for many months as Carl slowly but surely put together this unprecedented trip.

Honestly, I never really thought he'd pull it off. Without fail, my mention of the trip to publishers or people of influence would garner the same coy smile. "Yeah, good luck with that." Who'd ever heard of such a thing? I mean, it's one thing to sit in a coffee shop in downtown Denver and dream about the ultimate trip to the most dangerous parts of the world, but the list of people whom Carl wanted to meet amounted to a delusional dream. Or a nightmare, depending on your perspective.

Did I say delusional? Add impossible to that. No one from the State Department could get the meetings Carl was going after. In fact, no one but Carl Medearis could land them, but more on that later.

As the months stretched into a year and the appointments began falling into place, I tried to back out a dozen times. Finally, two days before we were scheduled to leave, God Himself had reached down and mercifully rescued me from almost certain death. Not to mention an overpriced luggage purchase.

Being the puppy in tow of the great mastiff, I put on a brave face. "So, what do we do?" I asked.

"Well, we wait and see."

"Wait for what?"

"For things on the ground to change. Could all be fine tomorrow."

I'm here to tell you that nothing was fine tomorrow. I'm still not sure what—besides foolishness—put me on a flight from Denver to Cairo two days later.

And I'm even less sure of what absurd notions could possibly have persuaded me to board the first flight into Beirut four days later, following a week's upheaval that had sent souls far braver than me either running for cover or to their graves.

Yet here I was, cranking open the vent over my head to dry the ribbons of sweat seeping from my forehead, never mind that the cabin was already freezing. Samir Kreidie, the wealthy Muslim businessman in Saudi Arabia who'd helped to set up the trip, was returning to Beirut with us. Indeed, without his help, the trip would have been impossible—many of the muftis and clerics we would meet agreed to do so only because of his unshakable reputation as a powerhouse of reconciliation.

But Samir himself, only days earlier, had insisted the trip was now far too dangerous.

Such is the Middle Eastern mind-set. I suppose when you spend your whole life dodging bullets, the threat of a sniper on the corner doesn't keep you housebound for long. Better to run rather than walk, naturally, but you can't let dissenters with machine guns make you a prisoner in your own house.

On the bright side, Carl, Samir, and I had virtually the whole jet to ourselves. It turns out that the owners of Middle East Airlines know Samir well. We'd canceled our flights from Saudi Arabia to Beirut a few days earlier on my urging, during a time when all three of us possessed our full share of good sense. Rebooking would normally have been impossible at a time like this, but a single call from Samir and we were on. Such is the power of a man who spends the day talking to heads of state on his flip phone.

And business class to boot. Wonderful. The staff was excellent, as was the food. It was certainly better than any service I'd experienced in the United States. The stewardesses all knew Samir—no surprise there.

But the essential facts remained: One, Beirut was a city besieged by the Hezbollah. Two, we were on the first flight in after a week's closure. Three, according to reports, anywhere from dozens to hundreds had been killed in fighting around the city, and the Lebanese army controlled the streets only by lining them with tanks and machine-gun placements.

Four . . . I mean, please. Anything could happen. Anything.

Sometimes I feel like hugging Carl and slapping him on the back. The kind of guy who would befriend a starving grizzly bear, he is loved by all, and I do mean all. Other times I feel more like locking him in the bathroom and making a run for it. Both his love and his bravery are greater than mine.

Sweating bullets at thirty thousand feet and headed into the lion's den better known as Beirut, I was feeling the bathroom might be a good idea. But I had nowhere to run. I was committed.

No longer interested in stewing in my own fears, I turned to Carl. Thankfully, the seats in business class are large, because Carl—a good Nebraska boy with blue eyes and a smile that won't quit—stands six foot two and is built like the grizzly bears he befriends.

"So you really think this is a good idea, huh?"

"Teddy, Teddy, you worry too much." His standard answer. I don't find it remotely comforting and I don't even try to smile.

"Seriously, Carl." There's that word again. "I got a bad feeling about this."

"Samir wouldn't have agreed if it wasn't safe," he said.

I looked over at the wealthy Lebanese businessman who made his home in Jeddah, Saudi Arabia. He grins and winks. Honestly, this is a man who could make the most hostile enemy lower his gun and settle down for a cup of tea. Being with him coaxes a perpetual smile from all in his presence. I'd just spent two days smiling.

But that was before this flight.

I politely forced a smile and remembered that Samir went to extraordinary lengths to get his family out of Beirut just days ago. I'd lain awake each night since then with visions roiling inside my head of gunmen bursting into my hotel room.

We'd already been to Egypt and met with perhaps the most powerful ideologue in the Muslim world. We'd spent three days in Saudi Arabia meeting with those who shaped Saudi thought, and we'd sat down with Osama bin Laden's brothers.

I'd heard countless nerve-wracking accounts that testified to the frailty of human life in this part of the world: the time when the CIA had kicked Carl and his family out of Lebanon for their own safety; the time when he was kidnapped at gunpoint in Iraq and very nearly assassinated; the time when Bonnie, one of his coworkers from the United States, was shot in the face and killed, south of Beirut. And this was just Carl—everyone we met had a dozen similar cautionary tales of death or near death.

This was only the beginning of our trip. Ahead lay the gravest dangers, the West's greatest perceived enemies, the making and un-making of war: Beirut, Baalbek, southern Lebanon, Syria, the West Bank.

I've had my encounters with danger, naturally. I was born in the jungles of Indonesia, where my parents spent their lives as mis-sionaries among headhunters. The father of one of my best friends was killed and consumed by the cannibals in the valley next to ours. He was one of two missionaries who were eaten by the locals when I was a child. I saw war and destruction, and I've had more than my share of close encounters with death.

But that was my life before I turned twenty. Since I've been living as an adult in America, the danger I've faced has been of my own making—the dark antagonists who populate my novels.

Now I was facing real danger again, and it made my blood run cold. Honestly, I was having difficulty remembering exactly why we were subjecting ourselves to this madness.

"Carl, remind me again exactly what we hope to accomplish with all of this," I said, turning back to my friend of fifteen years.

"Well . . ." For the hundredth time we rehearsed our ambitions.

It all started nearly two years earlier when Carl Medearis, the man with a thousand stories and ten thousand friends, had lunch with one of those friends, Ted Dekker, the man who has befriended his computer keyboard. It was a pleasant day in July and we sat in an outdoor patio at a Hard Rock Cafe on the Sixteenth Street Mall, downtown Denver. Our wives, Chris and Lee Ann, were deep in a discussion about traveling abroad; Carl and I had each other's ear.

"Tell me, Ted," said my good friend, "what is one thing Martin Luther King, Gandhi, and Jesus have in common?"

I thought for a moment. "They were all murdered?"

"Actually, that's right. And they all died for the same message, at least in large part. So, what was that message?"

"Tell me."

"To love your neighbor. Even if they're the enemy."

I nodded. "They make us all look like hypocrites. Is it really possible to love your enemy?"

We both fell into a few moments of introspection. Then Carl looked up with bright eyes.

"Why don't we find out?"

"Okay."

"Seriously." That word. "Why don't we go to this country's greatest so-called enemies and ask them what they think about this scandalous teaching."

"The Middle East?"

"Not just the Middle East. The Hamas, the Hezbollah. The greatest minds and influencers in Islam."

"And ask them what they think of Martin Luther King, Gandhi, and Jesus?"

"Well, it's a thought. The parable of the Samaritan is probably the most famous teaching on loving your neighbors. Muslims revere Jesus, who gave the teaching. We could start with that."

He actually was serious.

"So we go together, sit at the table of our greatest enemies." I paused. "We're talking about one of the most complicated regions of the world, brimming with violence. Huge divides between Muslims, Jews, and Christians. Bus bombs, terrorism, massive loss of life . . . You honestly think anything we hoped to accomplish with a trip to the Middle East would really do anyone any good?"

"It would do me good," Carl said. "And it would do the people we talked to good. Talking is always good."

"You're talking about the people who blew up the Twin Towers! Thousands of our soldiers and citizens have lost their lives at the hands of Muslims. They want to push Israel into the sea, for heaven's sake. Talking would do no good."

He shrugged. "Maybe not. But it would be one heck of trip. Imagine it."

"I am, that's the problem. My imagination is pretty good and I'm imagining nothing but trouble." Pause. "You really think you could set it up?"

"It will be difficult, but yeah, I think I can."

"We sit with these so-called enemies, ask them what their favorite joke is, and what they think of the parable of the Samaritan, which teaches us to love our neighbors even if they are our enemies. And we do it all to discover if anyone really can love his enemy. That about it?"

"Pretty much, yes. And in writing about it all for an American audience, we would be sitting Americans at the table with their enemies. We'll let them decide what to do with this radical teaching that got Martin Luther King, Gandhi, and Jesus killed. I would be willing to go out on a limb for that."

He stared at me and his lips slowly curled into a daring smile. When Carl talks about going out on a limb, it brings to my mind the time he went out on a limb in Iraq and was kidnapped at gunpoint. I have no desire to follow Carl out on his limbs.

"Sounds dangerous." But man, imagine the book. "You could really pull off meetings like that?"

"If I could . . . Interested?"

I let my mind go. The idea suddenly sounded irresistible, in part because it seemed so impossible. A protected fantasy.

"Maybe. If you could, maybe I could. Maybe. *If* you could."

As it turned out, he could. And he did.

It took Carl a year to talk me from a *maybe* to a *yes*. It took another year to line it up. And a third to write the book.

Though Carl and I are about as similar as the mastiff and the puppy, we do share some basic points of connection. We both used to live in Colorado, where we first met eighteen years ago. We've both lived in predominantly Muslim communities (Carl in Lebanon, me in Indonesia) for many years. We both realize our views of the world are colored by our own experiences and as such are subject to change.

We are both Christian. We both cringe at being called Christian, because in both of our worlds, Christians are the bad guys who either slaughter civilians or destroy civilization in the name of God.

We both have a personal, profound belief that there is purpose in this world that has little to do with rules and regulations and has everything to do with faith in God. We both believe that whether you are Christian or Muslim, the teachings uttered by Jesus in the

Middle East two thousand years ago are utterly life changing. We both believe that over the centuries those teachings have been misunderstood and misappropriated by most of those who claim to revere them, both in America and abroad, Christian and Muslim.

And we have both developed a fascination with the one teaching that Jesus himself claimed was second only to his instruction to love God, namely to love your neighbor as you love yourself. Carl was right—Martin Luther King and Gandhi were both killed in large part due to their message of hope based on this one teaching.

But who is willing to follow Martin Luther King today? Who will turn a cheek to the enemy's batons as Gandhi did? Who will love the heretic as Jesus did?

Two thousand years ago the world was torn by conflicting beliefs and terrible political struggle. The Romans occupied Palestine and subjugated the Jews, among many others, stripping them of their rights in the same way that today invites war. Into this world was born a man who came with a message so offensive that most followers abandoned him two years after he went public with his outrageous teachings: to love rather than revolt against the Romans who subjugated them. Even more extreme, to love heretics, such as the Samaritans, who were viewed as the Great Satan, blasphemers, so deceived and evil that they could hardly be counted as human.

Love your neighbor as you love yourself. This was his cry in the wilderness. When those who had given their lives to following God asked him what he meant by loving your neighbor, Jesus did what he frequently did.

He told them a fictional story.

Like all good tales, his story had a strong antagonist, a killer who took a man, pummeled him within an inch of his life, and left him for dead. And it had a strong protagonist, a man who went out of his way to nurse the victim back to life after others refused to help the dying man.

But what really cooked the goose of those who heard the teaching that day was the twist at the end of the story. In this story, you see, the protagonist wasn't the pious man or the religious leader. The hero of the tale was a Samaritan. A heretic. A bigot. Scum.

It would be like telling a story in which the hero was a Christian among Muslims. Or in the West, a Muslim among Christians. This man, Jesus said, was following the most important teaching. This man was the hero of his story.

So, what is it like to love an enemy? What are our so-called enemies really like, one on one? What are their favorite movies? When was the last time they cried? What is their favorite joke? If we could only take *People* magazine–like snapshots of the very people who make many in the United States cringe.

And what do our "enemies," being deeply religious people, think of this great teaching to love your neighbor, even if that neighbor is your enemy? It's no secret that Muslims believe that even though Muhammad is the last prophet, Jesus is also greatly revered, having lived a perfect life, and destined to return one day and claim his own. What do they think of the parable of the Good Samaritan? Do they follow its lesson as poorly as most American Christians?

The events and people of the Middle East are inarguably crucial to every human being's future, whether or not they recognize that fact. Our presidents are elected and rejected in part because of what occurs in this misunderstood land so far away. Mothers will lose their sons, and daughters will lose their fathers, as ideas and convictions clash in the desert. Countries will stand and fall. It's an important place and its people are even more important. Are they our enemies? And if so, should we love them?

Surrounded by the aroma of food in the safety of a Hard Rock Cafe, Carl and I toasted the ideal travelogue. Assuming it could come together, of course. Little did we know what trouble we were inviting.

First, what this book is not: This is not a religious book that seeks to correct anyone's misguided beliefs, Christian or Muslim. This is not a political book that undermines any one ideology. And it certainly is not a historical narrative that pretends to revise any previous work by far more qualified historians.

Rather, this is a travelogue, albeit one with some fairly major twists.

In the pages that follow we will trace our journey of discovery through the heart of the Middle East with some simple questions for some unique and influential personalities whom most in the United States, including the government, think of as enemies who belong on Most Wanted lists.

We will ask ourselves whether anyone is interested in loving his neighbor. Whether, for that matter, it's even possible to follow this scandalous teaching.

Along the way we will wander through the corridors of little-known history in Egypt, Baalbek, Damascus, and Jerusalem to see just how the teaching of love has fared among enemies over the centuries.

And with each step we take we will seek the Good Samaritan, both figuratively and literally, because we've learned that there are still roughly seven hundred Samaritans alive today.

But as much as these, this is the story of the mastiff and the puppy, boldly and not so boldly going where few have tread. It is the story of fear and misunderstanding, of ignorance and pain, and, above all, it is a story of love.

"Right," I said, peering out the window as the jet banked toward the streets of Beirut lined with tanks below us. "Right," I repeated hopefully. But it didn't feel right.

Carl leaned over. "Streets look deserted. Sophie says there are two tanks guarding the house we're staying in."

"We need tanks? Why's that?"

As we arrived at Samir's house we saw the two tanks stationed outside the building. When we asked why, Sophie said it was for security reasons.

"We're staying with her? What happened to the Marriott?"

"Naw, man. We're their guests—that would be rude. Besides, this will make it more real for you."

I turned back to the window and swallowed, in desperate need of distraction. Maybe I should have bought the Tumi luggage after all.

THE PARABLE OF THE SAMARITAN

On one occasion an expert in the Law stood up to test Jesus. "Teacher," he asked, "what must I do to inherit eternal life?"

"What is written in the Law?" he replied. "How do you read it?"

He answered: " 'Love the Lord your God with all your heart and with all your soul and with all your strength and with all your mind' and 'Love your neighbor as yourself.' "

"You have answered correctly," Jesus replied. "Do this and you will live."

But he wanted to justify himself, so he asked Jesus, "And who is my neighbor?"

In reply Jesus said: "A man was going down from Jerusalem to Jericho, when he fell into the hands of robbers. They stripped him of his clothes, beat him, and went away, leaving him half dead. A priest happened to be going down the same road, and when he saw the man, he passed by on the other side. So too, a Levite, when he came to the place and saw him, passed by on the other side. But a Samaritan, as he traveled, came where the man was; and when he saw him, he took pity on him. He went to him and bandaged his wounds, pouring on oil and wine. Then he put the man on his own donkey, took him to an inn, and took care of him. The next day he took out two silver coins and gave them to the innkeeper. "Look after him," he said, "and when I return, I will reimburse you for any extra expense you may have."

"Which of these three do you think was a neighbor to the man who fell into the hands of robbers?"

The expert in the Law replied, "The one who had mercy on him."

Jesus told him, "Go and do likewise."

2

Squalor at the Gate

EGYPT

REWIND.

Our trip into the Middle East began in Cairo, Egypt, on the thirteenth of May. Some call Cairo the gateway to Africa; some call it the gateway to the Middle East. For Carl and me, it was the place of beginnings. It seemed critical to our objective of meeting with the figures throughout the region who most influence the Middle Eastern mind-set.

Correction. It seemed critical to Carl, which was fine by me, because I rather liked the idea of our first stop being relatively safe. That is to say, Cairo presents a stunning snapshot of the divergent cultures and ideas of the Middle East without Saudi Arabia's religious police or the Hezbollah or the Hamas breathing down our necks.

Another correction. I should say breathing down *my* neck. Carl, being the seasoned mastiff deadened to such small irritations as the barrel of a gun shoved against one's cheek, rarely showed any true concern for life or limb—the operative word being *rarely*, which I will get to.

But apart from Cairo being safer than the destinations ahead of us—namely Saudi Arabia, Lebanon, Syria, the West Bank, and

Israel—there was a perfect reason to begin our quest for the true spirit of the Samaritan in Cairo.

Abdul Fadeel Al Kusi lived there.

Now, please understand that our purpose was to meet with the kinds of ideologues whom people from the West rarely encounter. Therefore, although we had an unprecedented opportunity to meet Colonel Moammar Kadafi in Libya, for example, we passed. We passed on potential meetings with numerous heads of state. Our focus zeroed in on those not commonly heard from in the news. We were after the heart and soul of the region, found among the imams and muftis—the religious warriors, adored by legions on the ground.

Our aim wasn't to uncover an exhaustive history of each of those we met but rather to engage them as two common travelers: to sit and have tea with these perceived enemies and ask the kinds of questions that might give us, and the millions of common Westerners like us, a snapshot of their lives and their thoughts on the greatest teaching of Jesus.

So back to Abdul Fadeel Al Kusi, the first powerhouse of common thought with whom we would have tea. Al Kusi's influence comes primarily through his position as the vice president and dean of academics at the University of Al-Azhar.

Al-Azhar—remember that name. The university is the world's undisputed think tank for Islamic theology, particularly among the Sunni, who account for roughly 85 percent of all Muslims. When Al-Azhar speaks, the world of Islam listens, and does so with rapt attention. The institution has campuses in nearly every country of the world, with an estimated 450,000 students currently enrolled.

One could say that, as the meat-and-potatoes man at Al-Azhar, Abdul Fadeel directs the theology of Islam more than any other person alive today. Now, if you're anything like me, you might already be confused by all the names and positions. After all, this is an ocean away and ever further removed from the everyday life of the average Westerner.

Let me break it down for you. Abdul Fadeel Al Kusi decides who studies what, who, and where. If he leads the students down a fundamentalist path, greater Islam will soon follow. If he preaches moderation, so goes Islam. This one man essentially holds the minds of 450,000 theology students in his hands, and they, in turn, spread the word to the world of Islam.

It is commonly said in the Middle East that Cairo writes Islamic law, Saudi Arabia lives that law, and Beirut fights over that law. Naturally the great mastiff was set upon taking me straight to the fight. But before we headed into the lion's den, we thought it wise to mix with those who form and live the ideology in both Cairo and Saudi Arabia.

It all made perfect sense. Right?

WE ARRIVED in Cairo the day before our set time of tea with the great Abdul Fadeel Al Kusi at the Al-Azhar University, just enough time to acclimate to the Middle East and become fully versed in all of the complexities that have plagued it since long before the time of Christ. I felt a bit like a congressman jetting to destinations abroad to figure it all out and returning with a definitive report that would change U.S. foreign policy.

Only congressmen do it with an armed guard, not by following on the heels of Carl.

We put our bags in the Nile Hilton and met a good friend of Carl's—Andrew, a Canadian like myself who married a beautiful Egyptian woman named Heidi and now lives a humble life of service in Cairo. Andrew has a heart as large as the city he serves. We headed out into the city on foot, thinking a nice boat ride up the Nile River would be a delightful way to spend the afternoon.

Having grown up in Indonesia, and accustomed to worldwide travel, I felt relatively comfortable. After all, what could compare to the daily reality of headhunters staring into our thatched jungle house? What kind of poverty and squalor could be more shocking than the poorest neighborhoods in Jakarta or New Guinea? I've been around the world half a dozen times and seen enough Third World realities to take them in stride. It was the danger ahead that unnerved me, not the conditions in Cairo.

The first thing you notice in any foreign city are the smells. Here in America, if we smell anything offensive, we immediately smother it. We seal up the sewage, ban the smokers, and clean up the exhaust.

Everyone takes regular showers, or if they don't, they at least change clothes regularly. Most people wear deodorant.

Not so in most Third World cities, and Cairo is no exception. The poverty rate pushes 40 percent, and among the poor a second or third pair of clothes is a luxury. Laundry is done by hand, naturally, and then only occasionally. The smells aren't bad once you get used to them, but at first encounter, they are enough to make you blink.

Like the smells, the city itself was quite similar to that of many Third World cities I've visited. People. Lots of people. Millions of people choking the sidewalks and alleys, seemingly headed nowhere for no reason. In fact, there are twenty million of them in Cairo. The only thing that seemed more abundant than people were cars—old, rickety black taxis the size of Mini Coopers, spewing thick, blue smoke that smelled like rotting fuel.

It had been a few years since my last journey abroad, and I immediately found myself asking the same questions I always do. Who are they? I mean, really, who are all these people? They don't even know I exist. I don't know they exist. To each of them, they are the center of their universe, and yet I don't even know who they are and as such I can hardly begin to care.

There, that woman dressed in a brightly colored blue dress—does she have a lover? A child? When she looks at me, does she see an offensive, insensitive rich man? When she looks at Carl strolling along ahead of me, does she see an American criminal?

Or that shopkeeper selling the same useless trinkets every other store seems to be selling, he's eyeing me now. Waving me over to leave some money in his tiny corner of the world. What are his dreams, his fears, his prized possessions?

All things considered, this one man is probably more important to more people than I am, and yet I don't even know his name. Children's lives hang in the balance of how well he does today, selling his useless trinkets on the street, and I have the audacity to walk on past.

These same thoughts and questions have haunted me my whole life. Whenever I wander streets like those in Cairo, I feel hopeless anticipation, like an explorer on the brink of an earth-shattering discovery just around the next bend. But the next bend is always stuffed with the same—more people, more cars, more cats.

Who feeds all these cats?

I stopped on the sidewalk and stared at an emaciated gray cat that limped under a concrete bench, where a litter of four tiny kittens resembling salamanders poked their still blind heads about, sniffing for milk. The cat looked up at me, then back at its offspring, and meowed just loudly enough to be heard above the rattle and honking of cars behind me.

In that moment the world about me was mushrooming with vivid colors and sounds and smells, but my own focus narrowed to this one scrawny cat. She and her kittens would soon be dead; I was sure of it. Yet no one cared.

Why?

"Ted!" Carl was yelling at me. I looked away from the cat and saw that Carl and Andrew had met up with the owner of the *faluka* that would ferry us on our pleasure cruise up the filthy brown Nile. "Let's go, dude. Mohammed, our captain, doesn't have all day."

Actually, Mohammed did have all day. We were his first customers in three days. "Can you ask him whose cat this is?" I asked, walking up with a courteous smile.

Carl asked him in Arabic. Did I mention that Carl speaks Arabic? Well, he used to, anyway, before he was kicked out of Beirut. Now he understands it and speaks it well enough to get by.

"He says it's everyone's cat," Carl said.

"Anyone feed it?" I asked, immediately feeling stupid for asking such a dumb question.

Mohammed chuckled and offered me a smile minus two teeth. One of those *What a dumb American* grins so common throughout the world. He rattled off a long answer.

"He says they can't feed themselves, because the Americans have raised the price of wheat so high that bread is hard to buy. The cat will have to live on scraps, but now people are fighting for the same scraps."

"The wheat shortage," Andrew said.

"What wheat shortage?" I glanced at Carl, who shrugged. *Don't ask me.*

"It's a big problem for millions in Egypt right now," Andrew explained. "Cost of wheat production in the United States goes up, in part because of rising oil prices, and the poor in Egypt begin to starve. Believe me, it's American wheat that's on the minds of most Egyptians, not Saudi oil."

And in the end, the skinny gray cat and her kittens die.

We boarded the faluka, a covered catamaran with cushioned benches around a fixed center table. Andrew had arranged for lunch, an assortment of traditional Egyptian dishes and a few sandwiches in the event the white folk don't take to the native tastes. Mohammed introduced us to his first mate, a toothless man also named Mohammed, who looked to be in his seventies.

His smile was priceless. His language was Arabic.

The Nile is a wide, muddy ribbon of water that wanders past Cairo on its way to the Mediterranean, two hundred miles north. A glance at the region on a Google satellite map will show a swath of green cutting its way through white desert on either side. This is the river's greatest gift. Life.

But aboard the faluka, with Mohammed at the rudder, all I could see was brown. And drifting debris.

We reclined and let the breeze cool us as we nibbled from Andrew's lunch. We quickly offered food to both Mohammeds, but they were wise to our game. "No, better for you to eat now and leave what you don't eat."

They'd obviously taken more than a few Westerners down the Nile and knew that those from the land of plenty never eat more than half of what they buy. Better to take their waste later than to accept a bite or two now.

I was half tempted to overstuff myself so as not to seem so wasteful.

"May I interview you?" I asked our wise captain with the missing front teeth. He looked to be about fifty, and I was curious as to how the teachings of the influential Al-Azhar have influenced the man on the street. Or boat.

"Of course."

I pulled out my recorder. "Good?"

"Yes." He flicked his cigarette overboard. No great concern for pollution in the land of the starving. "Yes." Everyone likes to be asked for his opinion, and there is no shortage of well-formed ones in the Middle East.

Throughout this narrative I will offer you the actual transcripts of interviews we conducted on our quest to search out our "enemies" and their philosophies concerning loving enemies. It somehow seems more appropriate to allow our enemies to speak for themselves, rather than through any filter either Carl or I might inadvertently apply to their words.

We trust you will find each transcript as fascinating as we did, sometimes for what is said, sometimes for what is not said.

TRANSCRIPT

Ted: What is the most important teaching in the *Injil* [Gospels]?

Mohammed: Jesus is the most honored of the prophets. When he was born, his mother was accused of adultery, but God had told her, "Don't be upset." The most important thing that he said was that there would be a prophet called Muhammad and he will complete the message.

Carl: This is the more street version.

Ted: When asked what his most important teaching was, Jesus answered that it was to love the Lord your God with all your heart and to love your neighbor as yourself. Are you familiar with this teaching?

Mohammed: Yes. But what God told Jesus to see was that after him there would come the seal of the prophets, who was Muhammad. God would show this, because all of Muhammad's children died.

Ted: When Jesus said to love your neighbor as yourself, what does this mean to people of God today?

Mohammed: Quite simply, no one loves each other, let me tell you clearly. For example, the guy who owns the boat place wants all the money for his pocket. If he loved others, he would say to be generous to the pilot.

Ted: Should Muslims and Christians love each other more?

Mohammed: In the days of Prophet Muhammad, they used to love each other more than they do now. It should be like that.

Ted: What are the most important issues facing you and the world today?

Mohammed: Number one, to find work. Number two, to be able to eat. Number three, to build a house. Number four, to get married. And number five, to live in peace. I was in the '73 war, but war ruins everything. I just want to find a wife and live in peace.

Ted: What do most of your friends think about America?

Mohammed: America is controlling the whole world. They treat no one fairly, and if I told you anything else, I would be lying.

Surprising to some, perhaps, but theology aside (because there is no shortage of differing opinions on theology), this one interview accurately reflects the sentiments of nearly every layperson we spoke to in the Middle East.

I LAY IN my bed late that night, trying to get some sleep, but a terrible heaviness had invaded me, and fighting jet lag, I simply couldn't force myself to drift off. The four thirty prayer call drifted into my twentieth-floor room, and I yielded to the realization that I would not be sleeping that night.

To any Westerner unaccustomed to the prayer call, it comes as a haunting, mournful tune that reverberates in every nook and cranny for miles. I'm not sure why, but that night, as I lay awake listening to the sounds of pleading for all to honor God, tears filled my eyes.

Perhaps it was the cat. Or the older boat pilot, Mohammed, who'd not yet been able to marry because in Egypt many believe they must prove their wealth by building a house before taking a wife. Perhaps it was the hopelessness of abject poverty that surrounded the Nile Hilton. The average Egyptian makes two-hundred and fifty Egyptian pounds a month—roughly fifty U.S. dollars a month, or just over a dollar-fifty a day. Who was I to sleep in peace on a fluffy white mattress while nearby a father of six begged God on his knees to send rich Westerners like myself by his shop so he could feed his family?

Either way, my tears flowed, as if to cleanse my eyes of all I'd seen that day.

I walked out on the balcony and looked down at the sleeping city, now relatively quiet, and reflected on our first day in the Middle East. Andrew had taken us to see many of the sites Egypt is well known for, everything from the city of the dead (a cemetery), in which the dead reportedly live their afterlife undisturbed, to the great pyramids, in which the pharaohs once did the same. There is a longer written history of Egypt than there is of any other country in the world. Universities honor doctorates centered on two- and four-year periods of the ancient nation's history.

But I wasn't here to report on history or the politics that made that history. I was here to take a snapshot of the Middle East's ideologues. A view from a Google satellite, if you will, with *People* magazine–type questions that are relevant to our pop culture.

A closer view would only get us lost in the trees. We were after a world view.

Still, I couldn't help but dwell on one particular piece of history that I had pried from Andrew's mind as we overlooked a citadel near the city of the dead. We'd just come from another cemetery not far away, built by Christians.

"Another citadel?" I asked. "Muslim, right?" In Cairo, wherever you find a church, you will almost invariably find a mosque next to it.

"Yes," Andrew replied.

"Two citadels a stone's throw from each other, one Christian, one Muslim. How, pray tell, did that happen?"

"Well, my friend. Have a seat on this ledge here and let me tell you how that happened."

THE PROTAGONISTS of Andrew's tale of two citadels are not people but a pair of historic buildings hardly five miles apart from each other, although an eternity apart in nearly every other respect.

Why should a modern reader care about this particular pair of inanimate giants of wood and stone and stucco? Because if you could take a time-lapse photograph of these two iconic hulks, you'd have a snapshot of the bloody, fractious religious history of the Western world.

Egypt is commonly thought of as the land of pharaohs and sun worship or, in modern times, as the defender of modern Islam. But Western Christians often have a hazy understanding of just how much of their own history is bound up in the land of Egypt, movies like *The Prince of Egypt* and *The Ten Commandments* notwithstanding.

In many ways the modern story of Christianity's spread begins with the apostle Mark's journey to Egypt in the early part of the first century A.D. Yes, the very same Mark who gave us the Gospel according to Mark.

Saint Mark's first convert in Alexandria was Anianus, a shoemaker who later became a bishop and patriarch of Alexandria after Saint Mark's martyrdom.

This succession of patriarchs has remained unbroken up to the present day, making the Egyptian Christian, or Coptic, Church one of the oldest Christian churches in existence. Evidence for this age comes in the form of the oldest biblical papyri, discovered in remote regions of Upper Egypt, written in the Coptic script, and more ancient than even the oldest Greek copies of the Bible ordered by Constantine in A.D. 312.

It's no wonder, then, that Egypt is also the home of the Christian monastic movement, founded in the fourth century by Saint Anthony of Egypt. So you see, long before Egypt had heard of Islam, Christianity ruled.

Fast-forward now to the seventh century and our first citadel, actually a squat, round ruin of a fortress deep in what is known today as Old or Coptic Cairo. This maze of narrow, ancient streets is indeed the oldest part of the city. In fact, it is reputed to be the neighborhood where Jesus and his parents lived during their time in Egypt.

It felt strange to imagine that Jesus himself had once raced around the very streets we walked in Old Cairo, Egypt, of all places.

This citadel, whose remains rank as Cairo's oldest original building, is called the Babylon Fortress, although for the last thousand years it has actually served less as a military installation than as an anchor for Christian churches. The most famous, the Coptic chapel of El-Muallaqa, is known as the "Hanging Church" because it literally hangs suspended above the southern tower gate of the fortress ruins.

Why the fortress or its surrounding neighborhood was once called Babylon is something of a mystery, since neither has any known relationship to its namesake several thousand miles to the east. What we do know is that the Babylon neighborhood once straddled the heart of what is now Cairo, back during the years of Egypt's domination by the Byzantine Empire.

Byzantine essentially equals Christian for those like me who feel compelled to reduce the great religious contest of our times. However, calling one adversary Christian and the other Muslim would also be a gross oversimplification. The terms Christian and Muslim mean very different things to many people both in history and in our world today, and as such are not particularly helpful.

A Christian in many American circles, for example, means "right-wing, gun-toting fanatic who hates Democrats." As such, a pacifist Democrat who called himself a Christian in those circles would be lying, albeit unwittingly. To most in this world, American is Christian, just as to most Americans being an Arab means being Muslim. Both labels have only limited usefulness.

I have been called a Christian writer, but I'm not a right-wing, gun-toting fanatic who hates Democrats, not by a long shot. So am I a Christian? Yes and no—it depends on what Christian means to you. The same could be said of Carl. But labels are almost impossible to shed. More on this later.

Egyptian Christians of the Byzantine period had become mired in a complicated and vicious theological dispute that had managed to divide them into hostile factions.

At the time of our historical tale, the nation's Byzantine rulers were labeled as Orthodox Christians who insisted that Christ had one nature, both divine and human without separation—a point of view called *monophysitism.* Egypt's Coptic Christians supported a position called *miaphysitism,* which also held that Christ had only a single nature but retained all the characteristics of both the divine character and the human character.

Don't you just love religion?

Although the Council of Chalcedon had ruled in favor of the Orthodox position, Egypt had remained a hotbed of miaphysite sentiment. This obscure disagreement so consumed the Christians of that age that when the Byzantines took political control of Egypt in 629, their emperor Heraclius began persecuting the Copts, even expelling their patriarch. As a result, many of the nation's Christians professed no sympathy or allegiance whatsoever for their current ruler and were quite happy to take their chances with a regime change.

Into this chaotic, sectarian stew rode the Muslim general Amr ibn al-As, dispatched by Caliph Umar on Muhammad's orders to spread Islam into the land of the pharaohs. He crossed into Egypt on December 12, 639, with an army of about four thousand men on horseback, armed with lances, swords, and bows. The army's objective was this very citadel, which remained key to the conquest of Egypt because of its strategic control of the path to Alexandria.

The Muslims advanced rapidly into the Nile Delta, and in response the imperial garrisons retreated into the Babylon Fortress. For more than a year, the Byzantine Christian soldiers held out, gazing out over their battlements each morning at a sea of encamped enemy troops. But with no victory in sight, they surrendered without bloodshed, impotently handing Egypt over to the Muslim invaders.

It seems that beyond the Byzantine generals' incompetence, the Muslims had received help—from Cyrus, the Christian patriarch of Alexandria. Cyrus had persecuted the local Coptic Christians and helped give birth to an obscure theological heresy. Some even suspected him of having secretly converted to Islam. Many Coptic Christians, tired of being harassed by their so-called Christian brothers, actually helped the invaders. As reward, they indeed found the new rulers to be far more tolerant.

So ended the domination of Christianity in Egypt since the disciple who wrote the Gospel we know as Mark brought his word to the region more than five hundred years earlier.

The Muslims promptly handed down a law forcing all Egyptians to convert to Islam, pay a special tax, or be killed. Most found the tax a small price to pay for complete religious freedom. Likewise, in return for a tribute of money and food for the occupying troops, the Christian inhabitants of Egypt were excused from military service and left free to observe their religion and administer their affairs.

Centuries later, the celebrated Muslim Saladin came to power across Egypt and most of the Middle East. Knowing that Europe was spoiling for a crusade intended to wrest control of his lands away from him, Saladin wasted little time in building a citadel of his own.

According to legend, he chose its site on a limestone spur high above Cairo for its healthy air. The story goes that he hung up pieces of meat all around the city. The samples spoiled within a day everywhere but in the citadel area, where they remained fresh for several days. To this day, the neighborhood is known as the breeziest in Cairo.

Saladin used the most modern fortress-building techniques of that time to construct the original citadel. Great, round towers were built protruding from the walls so that defenders could direct flanking fire on those who might scale the walls. The walls themselves were thirty feet high and ten feet thick.

Saladin also had a well dug in order to provide the occupants of the fortress with an inexhaustible supply of drinking water. Almost three hundred feet deep, it was cut through solid rock down to the water table, its large ramp wide enough so that animals could descend into the well and power the apparatus that lifted the water.

Besides expanding into a sprawling royal palace and administrative complex, the citadel immediately won renown as one of the world's greatest monuments to medieval warfare, as well as a highly visible landmark on Cairo's eastern skyline.

These features would soon come into excellent use. After only a few centuries since their own victory over Christianity, now came the Muslims' turn to blanch at the approach of foreign armies, retreat into their own citadel, and watch the Crusaders surround their positions like an advancing flood.

Despite launching repeated onslaughts against Saladin and his citadel, however, the Crusaders never retook Egypt. The citadel held, and its occupants resisted every attack the invaders could hurl at them. After their dwindling supplies led to a forced retreat, a nighttime attack resulted in a great number of Crusader losses and eventually the surrender of the army. Sultan Al-Kamil, a nephew of Saladin, agreed to an eight-year peace agreement with Europe.

The city of Cairo eventually engulfed both of these citadel hulks in its vast metropolis, erasing the signs of their faiths as well as their strangely linked pasts.

Today, Cairo still plays witness to bloodshed between Coptic Christians and varied Muslim factions. Arcane arguments over theology continue to divide those within the Christian population, just as they do those within the Muslim community. Little has been solved in the millennia since Byzantium was the shining capital of a new Christian emperor.

In fact, if anything, the two citadels of Cairo stand as a mute witness to the unchanging nature of religious conflict, as well as its inability to accomplish much beyond dispatching ever-increasing numbers of human beings into the afterlife.

ALL FINE AND GOOD. But Carl and I weren't in Egypt to walk down history's rubble-strewn corridors with hopes of finding any nugget of truth missed by the thousands of scholars who'd preceded us. Our mission was still to feel the heartbeat of the people in the region where the Great Teacher delivered his solution to the world.

Love your neighbor as you love yourself, illustrated so pointedly through his story of the Good Samaritan.

History had evidently forgotten the teaching, but we were more interested in the present.

For the sake of my host, I donned the one suit I'd brought. Middle Easterners of position are immaculate dressers who hold fashion in high esteem, from what I could gather.

Deprived of sleep, I snatched up my tape recorder and followed the great traveler, Carl, into the waiting car. Our car thrust into gridlocked traffic with a blast of its horn.

I remember Carl and me clacking up the wide white steps of Al-Azhar University like two dignitaries, exhausted but without fear. That would come later in other countries. Here we were greeted as celebrities, and I remember thinking we'd been mistaken for Richard Gere (that would be Carl) and Johnny Depp (an identity I was accused of stealing on more than one occasion on the trip).

Or perhaps they thought we were from CNN.

We were ushered into a beautiful, stately office and immediately offered tea in glasses only slightly larger than shot glasses. Tea is the social staple in the Middle East. It's often served with a few sweet crackers and is poured by the host's servant, always male.

This being the first interview, I felt a bit awkward, but the moment Abdul Fadeel Al Kusi walked in wearing his large, warm grin, any tension I felt melted away. He walked up dressed in a gray suit, and I couldn't help but think he looked very much like Colin Powell. Much has been made about the connection between this establishment and the propagation of Islamic fundamentalism, including the use of violence, to promote its ideals. But like all facilities of higher education, there are always conflicting opinions—I wasn't sure what opinion we would cover today. What I did know was that the opinion of Abdul Fadeel Al Kusi was an important one that influenced millions.

The old Middle Eastern adage came to mind: "Cairo writes Islamic law; Saudi Arabia lives that law; and Beirut fights over that law."

Today we were with the one who wrote Islamic law.

Tomorrow we would fly to meet those who live that law.

And then . . . well, then we would go home, because Beirut was at war.

"Thank you for hosting us, Mr. Al Kusi." I settled in with my questions. "Do you mind if I ask you some plain questions?"

"No, of course not. Please, ask. But before you do, may I say a few things?"

"Yes, of course."

And so he did. I learned then what most journalists learn in this part of the world. Everyone has an opinion on all things religious and political. And they are careful to present their beliefs in a context that is least offensive to any who might happen upon their words. This is very diplomatic, very cordial, and very protracted. Indeed, if I were to include the complete transcripts of each interview we were so fortunate to get, you would be holding a book heavier than your average sledgehammer.

And we weren't in the Middle East for political views, remember. No, we only wanted a slice of the man, enough to see what flows in his veins and no more.

Here, then, is a snapshot of Abdul Fadeel Al Kusi, one of the most powerful men in all of Islam, in his words without any filter or interpretation.

The task of interpreting is left to you, the reader.

TRANSCRIPT

Ted: What kinds of things make you laugh, Mr. Al Kusi?

Abdul: (Glances at his translator and smiles) Laugh? Strange things make me laugh. Unexpected behavior. (He laughs, as if to say, "Such as this.")

I have three sons and one daughter, you know. A pharmacist, a doctor, and a student. My daughter is married. But my grandson, Yosef, who is four, likes to tell me, "Oh, Grandfather, you don't understand many things that even your children understand." Our children do many unexpected things that make us laugh, but in their eyes we are the strange ones.

Ted: What is your favorite joke?

Abdul: Joke? We have many jokes. (Now he grins wide.) I'll tell you a very short one. There once was a judge who summoned a witness and demanded to know his name. "My name is Palm Tree," the witness said. "Palm tree?" the judge cried. "Then are you going to live from blessings alone?" (At this our host slaps his knee and laughs. Something has been lost in translation, clearly.)

Ted: What does your wife do that makes you laugh?

Abdul: (Now chuckling, delighted with these most unusual questions) My wife? My wife is always giving my clothes to my sons by mistake, you know. She can't tell what's mine and what is theirs. And at times they will wear my clothes to make me laugh!

Ted: Do you have any hobbies?

Abdul: Reading. I love to read! My favorite literature is Steinbeck, Shakespeare, the classics, you know? I love music, too, but I have trouble enjoying what my children do. Though I am trying to familiarize myself and my liking with Mozart. I mostly love our old songs.

Ted: What is your favorite movie?

Abdul: Movies? *The Fall of the Roman Empire.* My favorite actor is Richard Gere. We shared a meal once, you know. I am also fond of Sophia Loren. And I love westerns.

Ted: What about Britney Spears?

Abdul: Who? I've never heard of this name.

Ted: What makes you sad?

Abdul: Children in suffering makes me very sad. Orphans make me feel sad. I felt like an orphan the day that my mother died. I pray that orphans in Iraq may endure the tragedy they face. When students are mistreated by teachers, this makes me sad. One of our students fell off a train and lost one leg and one hand because the ambulance didn't come. Her father came, but he was also missing an arm and couldn't help her. This makes me very sad. She's in the hospital now.

Ted: What would you say are Americans' greatest misconceptions of Muslims?

Abdul: Americans only think of Muslims in three ways: One, that they are all terrorists, and this is not true. Two, that Arabs spend all their money on women and wine, and neither is this true. Three, that Muslims are enemies of the West. Again, not true.

Ted: And what are Muslims' greatest misconceptions of America?

Abdul: Yes, well, we are as guilty of misconception. One, that every American is responsible for bad politics. And two, that Westerners are immoral and have no boundaries with women. These are false.

Ted: When asked what his most important teaching was, Jesus answered that it was to love the Lord your God with all your heart and to love your neighbor as yourself. Are you familiar with this teaching?

Abdul: Jesus is a bridge. Mary was the most honored of all women in the Qur'an, which states that Allah purified her and chose her above all women. There is more writing about Mary in the Qur'an than in the Bible—you know this? So both Jesus and Mary are very important to us. As for love, the summary of Jesus' teaching is to love the world. Justice and love for all people. Two mottos that I teach. The first is, Just love; love justice. The second is, Peace for all the world. This is Jesus and this is Islam.

3

To Live by the Law

SAUDI ARABIA

THE FIRST TIME Carl was thrown in jail was in Saudi Arabia, nearly twenty-five years ago. The second time Carl was thrown in jail was also in Saudi Arabia.

I learned this tidbit just before our flight to Jeddah, Saudi Arabia, that night. Needless to say, the fact that Carl shared the story through a smile did nothing to calm my tightening nerves. We were finally leaving the relative safety of Egypt, where laws are written, and heading into the land where people like Carl are thrown into prison. And lapdogs like me? Well, we might just be shot on sight. (Not true, of course, but I have always had an active imagination.)

Carl's courtship of the Middle East began when he was sixteen. He can't put a finger directly on why or how it happened, but he clearly recalls sitting on a bench one night and hearing a voice. *When you grow up, you will love Arabs.* Just that. Not *You will be president* or *You will star in Super Bowl XXXV*, just *You will love Arabs.* Startled at such an absurd notion, he sought for meaning, but understanding wasn't easy to find in the small town of Chadron, Nebraska. The library turned up a handful of books on Arabs, which he quickly consumed, but there were no actual Arabs that he could find in his town.

Preoccupied by the voice, Carl made a critical decision a few years later when he turned twenty: If he was to love Arabs, he would have to *meet* Arabs. And where better than in the Middle East? So he packed his bag and headed to a Dutch humanitarian mission in Yemen to build outdoor toilets. Sounds like a barrel of laughs.

As it turned out, his flight to Yemen went through Jeddah. Being rather naive, and flying all alone, he ran into a minor snag: no transit visa. Every soul brave enough to travel to the mysterious kingdom knows that it's impossible to enter or leave Saudi Arabia without a transit visa.

In a swirl of confusion, Carl found himself hauled off to the airport prison. There, shoehorned into a large cell with a hundred other sweating human sardines suspected of criminal behavior, he became convinced that his life would soon end.

The foul odors of the Jeddah International Airport prison remain with Carl to this day. A large pot of rice was set in the middle of the cell three times a day, but the sole Westerner had neither the nerve nor the stomach to claw his way in for a handful. Two days after his incarceration, he was released and put on a flight to Yemen. But the story doesn't end there. Having successfully built toilets for three months in Yemen, he bid farewell to the humanitarian mission and boarded his flight back to the United States.

Through Jeddah.

Did I say Carl was rather naive back in the day? You guessed it, no transit visa. Another swirl of confusion. Another round of shouts and bustling. And once again Carl found himself in the airport prison. This time his incarceration lasted three days.

So began Carl's long love affair with the Middle East. Hearing the story, I couldn't help but picture a similar fate for us now.

Boarding the flight for Jeddah did nothing to put me at ease. After shuffling from one checkout line to another, and still another, we finally found the right security gate, showed our tickets and passports, and attempted to walk through the metal detector. Carl hummed his way through. Been here, done this, no sweat.

I don't know why the guard stopped me. Perhaps he saw me as an easy target. But he pushed me back and grinned. "Passport!"

I handed him my Canadian passport, wondering why his head was tilted down as if he were looking at my papers while his eyes drilled a hole through my own. A knowing grin twitched on his lips, but I wasn't in the know. He finally nodded and I stepped forward.

"Back! Back!" He stepped in my path, forcing me to retreat. But at the same time he was motioning me with his fingers, as if he wanted me to proceed. Confused, I stepped forward again.

"Back! You cannot pass!" All the while wearing this twisted grin that made me wonder if he might be Hannibel Lecter's cousin. I felt a bit like a puck in a table hockey game, and I began to sweat.

"Can I go?" I asked.

He'd flipped through my passport but didn't seem interested in the visa. His fingers kept egging me on, like a fighter begging me to make the first move.

Carl finally got my attention. "Hey, I think he wants some money," he said in a low voice.

Money? I hauled out my wallet and handed him a bill. He took it and motioned for more, so I gave him all I had.

"Pass!" He stepped aside as though I were a general and dramatically ushered me through.

Everyone behind me got a pass. Evidently they didn't appear to be the rich, naive Westerner kind. For all I know, I was the guard's only catch that night. Was I so obvious? Perhaps I should stop sweating and hum like my mentor, the great adventurer.

We boarded the flight and took off without incident. To my left sat a Saudi businessman dressed in a white *thobe* (a full-length tunic) with a red checkered headdress. He looked at me with a gentle smile, likely thinking nothing but wonderful thoughts, but my mind assumed the worst. Secret police? This was Saudi Arabia, after all, the vast desert land enshrouded in deep, dark mystery—an alternate reality as much as a country, one that holds vast dangers for all who would dare venture into its foreboding airspace, much less set foot on its soil.

Beside me, Carl showed no concern whatsoever. I knew that my imaginings were getting the better of me. Yet my nerves were still screwed tight and I couldn't shake images of doom. This was a land of twenty-four million inhabitants strictly controlled by a monarchy on one hand and the religious police on the other. If the monarchy controls wealth, the religious clerics control behavior through meticulously administered sharia (Islamic) law.

On the books, adultery is punishable by death. Murder and drug dealing will also cost you your life. Stealing will demand the payment of a hand, and drinking alcohol will land you in prison. The country shuts down five times each day when the prayer call wafts over the city from a hundred mosques. The faithful, who must be all, bow in the direction of Mecca, roughly an hour's drive east from Jeddah. Christians are prohibited from participating in any form of worship. If you're a Saudi and attempt to proselytize, the law calls for your death.

This was the land that spawned Osama bin Laden, and we were on the way to sit down with his brothers. Was my nervousness not warranted?

Carl slapped my thigh, jerking me out of my reflection. "Ready, buddy?"

It occurred to me that we were descending. "Sure," I replied. "Just to be clear, though, we head straight to Jordan from Jeddah, right? Beirut and Syria are still out of the picture?"

Beirut. While we'd been floating down the muddy Nile in Cairo, the Hezbollah uprising in Lebanon had worsened. There was talk of a broadening conflict. We were receiving nearly hourly updates from sources who'd fled Beirut, and none were encouraging. Entering the city now would be like descending into a basement full of gunpowder with a lighted match to show the way. You never knew when the bang would come or how much of the neighborhood it would level, only that sooner or later it would all go up in smoke.

"Right," Carl said. "Samir Kreidie says there's no way we can go to Beirut."

"Okay, just making sure we're on the same page here. And Syria is out too."

"Right. The road to Damascus is burning. No way."

"Okay. Okay, good. Promise me you won't let any of your pals from Beirut talk you into coming."

"No, never."

ODDLY ENOUGH, no one paid us much mind as we collected our bags. The expansive airport looked nearly vacant compared to the chaos we'd just left behind in Cairo. No looming threats—so far, so good.

Carl handed the young immigration officer his American passport and said something in Arabic. The man broke out in a wide grin. "You speak Arabic?"

"Yes," Carl replied, and the rest was in Arabic. The Saudi officials were soon laughing loudly, delighted to have an American at their doorstep who actually spoke Arabic. Clearly, this was a rare event. We were quickly waved through.

This time both Carl and I had the right visas. No prison time.

I sat in the back of the Mercedes that Samir had sent to pick us up, staring at the dark sky as we drove into Jeddah. Snapshot, I reminded myself. I'm here for a snapshot. Like taking someone's temperature. I'm not here to uncover what other historians might have missed. I didn't come to explain all things Saudi to America or to shine my brilliant light on the ways others choose to live.

Carl and I had come to have tea with a few select heroes in this region where the great teacher Jesus had delivered his greatest teaching: *Love your neighbors as yourself. Even if they are your enemies.* Most Americans seem to think of Saudi Arabia as an enemy state. That's why we were here.

My first impression of the city at night? Las Vegas. Not nearly as glitzy, mind you, but brightly colored buildings and large glimmering signs rose up on either side of a freshly paved road. Palm trees and manicured landscaping graced the adjacent properties. Mercedes and BMWs ruled new thoroughfares made of six and eight lanes, which—oddly enough—the drivers used, unlike in many parts of the Middle East where lanes are ignored. Lighted Coca-Cola, Marlboro, and IKEA signs abounded. The streets were immaculate, a virtual paradise carved out of the desert.

The city looked to be buzzing at eleven that night—odd because I'd half expected the stiff laws to shut down nightlife. But I would soon learn that nightlife thrives in Saudi Arabia, even more so than in Austin, the live music capital of the world, where I come from. A different kind of nightlife, but no less active.

"Why are there so many people on the street?" I asked our driver.

Andy, who hails from the Philippines, has worked with Samir Kreidie for twenty-five years, returning home to his family once every two years for a two-month visit before returning to make badly needed cash. The Saudi monarchy establishes set wages for the servant class based upon nationality. Bangladeshi servants, for example, are paid only $150 dollars a month, while Filipino servants are paid more than $400, due in part to the ease with which they learn the English language.

"This is when the streets are the fullest," Andy said. "Because it's hot this time of year."

It turns out that the night rules in Saudi Arabia. Many don't retire before four A.M. They might sleep till nine A.M., work till one P.M., when the country virtually shuts down for the afternoon, then go back to work in the cooler evening hours. In short, they take full advantage of cooler late nights and sleep during the hottest part of the day. Smart.

"Where are all the women?" I asked.

Andy just shakes his finger and laughs. "No. Very few women on the street at night. Inside."

True enough, few Saudi women were to be seen outside, during the night or the day for that matter. And following the sharia laws, they venture out only in full black covering. The sight on the street is quite exotic, actually. The men are dressed in modern business suits and jeans, and the few women drift in jet-black abayas that might make a foreigner wonder if they are on their way to a masquerade ball.

One of the mysteries that quickly unveiled itself to us was the unique relationship Saudi Arabia has with its women. To us in the West, the rules that deny them driving rights and demand that they be covered from head to toe in public seem offensive. But don't think for a moment that women don't flex their power in the great monarchy called Saudi Arabia.

Put simply, men may rule the streets, but step through the front doors of most Saudi homes and you'll find a new ruler of this mysterious society. Considering the fact that much of life is lived behind closed doors here, and seeing that many homes are better described as mansions or palaces, it doesn't take long to realize that in many ways women secretly run Saudi Arabia.

We recorded a joke by Ghassan Ma'amari, a businessman in Jeddah, that illustrates this relationship with some humor:

TRANSCRIPT

Ghassan: A man married for twenty-five years thought his wife had a hearing problem. But he didn't want to bring her to the hospital and embarrass her, so he asked the doctor how he could test her hearing. "You go to her and talk to her from forty feet away. Then you move in closer to thirty feet and ask the same question. Move in closer and closer until you are sitting by her, then you will know from how far she can hear you."

So the man went home and called out to his wife from the door, "What's for dinner, dear?" She didn't respond, so he moved closer and asked again. Still no response, so he moved even closer. And when she still didn't respond, he sat by her and asked, "What's for dinner, dear?"

She turned to him exasperated and replied, "For the fifth time, chicken is for dinner!" (Ghassan chuckles.) So, who's really deaf? It depends on perspective. Who has the power? It depends on perspective.

Nightclubs are forbidden, but many homes have lavish entertainment facilities built in. Abayas are required covering for women outside, but in the home, European fashion reigns supreme—everything from the latest designer jeans to chic blouses, skirts, and dresses.

Among the many women we met, whether they be fashion consultants, interior designers, magazine editors, or wives in charge of a twenty-thousand-square-foot mansion and ten servants, women seem to direct the course of men as freely in Saudi Arabia as in the West. Along with the rest of the world, this kingdom seems to bow to the inescapable realization that women are best when they have power. They rule because they are so well suited to rule.

Only a few of the women we asked particularly liked wearing the abaya when they went out. Those who like it said it gave them a sense of anonymity, which is its own kind of power. Most who despised the restrictions on women told us the inconvenience was a small price to pay for the advantages of living in the country. This from women who were well off, were well traveled, and had spent as much time in other parts of the Middle East and Europe as in Saudi Arabia.

I'm not condoning or supporting any policy; I'm only reflecting on my own observations. As in all societies, I'm sure there is plenty of abuse of the system to go around in Saudi Arabia. But as far as I could see, Saudi Arabia is no Afghanistan ruled by a Taliban. Far from it.

In fact, Saudi Arabia's embrace of Western values was what first fomented hatred in the heart of one of its citizens who resorted to terrorism to send a message to the monarchy. His name was Osama and he later introduced himself to the world as the one who brought down the Twin Towers in New York City.

I never quite understood why Osama bin Laden was so incensed at his own country or why he set up shop in Sudan and Afghanistan, but after only two days in Jeddah, the picture became much clearer.

Saudi Arabia wasn't the country I'd feared, at least not down here in Jeddah, the city by the sea.

Samir Kreidie

There's something about stepping into the mouth of the lion and not getting bitten that is exhilarating, and Saudi Arabia is certainly a lion in the mind's eye. Yet here, thousands of miles from the safety of home, we were among friends who smiled warmly and laughed from their bellies.

Even better, the prospect of heading into dangerous Hezbollah and Hamas waters was no longer an option because the airport in Beirut was closed. Life was looking good indeed. At the risk of sounding like a frightened little mouse, I must admit that at this point I was openly wondering at the sanity of the whole trip.

If our primary purpose had been to travel to Egypt and Saudi Arabia, with a stop in Jerusalem, to ask a few friendly neighbors what they thought about loving their enemies, all would have been fine. But the backbone of our journey was to have been through much more dangerous territory, and it now seemed to be off the table. And wisely so.

The whole trip, then, might end up being a wash—a lovely one-week hike through exotic lands with many stories to tell, but not the story we'd come searching for. Never mind the extraordinary effort expended over two years to get the nod to meet with some very important people, the entire voyage was feeling ill-conceived to me.

Unless, of course, we could find a way into Beirut and Syria as planned. More than before, I was now haunted by those looks of horror on the faces of friends I'd shared our intentions with before leaving the United States. "You're what? Are you nuts?"

They were right. I mean, where's the sanity in having tea with the top Hezbollah leaders? With the bin Laden brothers? With the Hamas? Why sit with Sheik Fadlallah when we knew very well that on numerous occasions the United States, Israel, and Saddam Hussein's Iraq had leveled whole apartment buildings in attempts to kill him? Why be forced to dodge flaming tires on the road to Syria? I'm not Leonardo DiCaprio and this wasn't a movie.

Then I met Samir Kreidie and my whole perspective began to change.

In the Middle East, reputation is as valuable as oil and provides no less currency among its many monarchs and heads of state. Within minutes of sitting down with Samir in the Marriott Hotel's brightly decorated lobby, I understood why this slightly built Lebanese businessman had achieved such high standing in the eyes of so many dignitaries. He is a man loosed of the shackles that hold most in a prison of managing expectations, because his own expectations of those he meets are immediately apparent: *I respect and love you first. Then you may respect me, if you wish.*

As I watched Samir and Carl talk and laugh about events that have consumed both of their lives from Washington to Beirut, I could see why these two men had become so close. They were cut from the same cloth, both immediately trusting and transparent, both impossible not to love.

The list of Samir Kreidie's accomplishments in sixty short years on this planet is impressive on any front. Like many in a position of influence in the Middle East, Samir is extremely well educated, possessing a master of science degree in agriculture and a Ph.D. in engineering. He heads or sits on the boards of dozens of foundations and is recognized as president of the Lebanese community in Saudi Arabia. He is on a first name basis with the leadership of many opposing parties, embraced by all regardless of political affiliation. With his wife, Sophie, he has raised hundreds of millions of dollars to give families of war-torn Lebanon their dignity back through housing projects.

But what immediately piqued my interest was Samir's extraordinary love for others. He is a Muslim with roots in Syria and Lebanon, but he now gives of himself for the hope that all of God's children, regardless of their understanding of the God whom they serve, will learn to love each other.

"Excuse me," I said, inserting myself in Samir and Carl's trip down memory lane. "You're a Muslim, right?"

"But of course. And you are Christian, born in the United States. We are what we are."

Made sense. In Lebanon you are born in one of numerous sects or religions and identified as such for life. In most Middle Eastern minds, Americans are Christian, period. Saudis are Muslim, period. What you call yourself has to do with your birthright as much as your theology. Even atheists in the West would be called Christian by many on the street.

Samir smiled and looked at me with laughing eyes. He sat smoking a cigar with legs crossed, dressed in a thin white shirt and loafers, clearly intrigued.

"But you believe in Jesus," I said.

"As should all with half a heart," he said. "It is commanded in the Qur'an and Injil. You know, an interesting story. I once gave a lecture at a university in Lebanon titled, 'I Am a Muslim and a Follower of Jesus.' " He chuckled, anticipating his own story. "The next day the Arabic newspapers wrote, 'Kreidie is a Muslim and a believer in Isa,' the Arabic name of Jesus. Many of my Muslim friends called and congratulated me. They said it was good that I tell the world that Jesus is not only for the Christian but for the whole world. Yes?"

I nodded. "Okay, makes sense."

"However, the second day another newspaper wrote, 'Kreidie is a Muslim and a believer in Yesuah,' the Christianized name for Jesus in Arabic. Now all of my Muslim friends called outraged that I would embrace the Christian doctrine, and many Christian friends called to congratulate me for becoming a Christian."

"Labels," I said. "We have the same problem in the West."

"Labels. I follow Jesus, as should all good Muslims as commanded by the Prophet Muhammad. His teachings are beyond time. But what do you call me? I am a Muslim and will always be a Muslim, but if I use one tiny, tiny word"—Samir focused on a paper-thin space he created between his forefinger and thumb—"I am a Christian. Another tiny, tiny word, and I am a Muslim." He dropped his hand and picked up his cigar.

"It's the heart, not the labels, that allow us to love one another, as taught by Isa, who is Yesuah, who is Jesus."

The comments bring us all back to our quest in this land so close to the birthplace of Jesus; to the search for the Good Samaritan, that despised heretic that Jesus revealed as the true follower. Who was still following, two thousand years later?

Samir was laughing with Carl when Samir's phone rang, perhaps for the twentieth time during those first two hours alone. Everyone wants to speak to Samir—he's that kind of guy. He glanced at his Motorola RAZR casually. This time it was a call he needed to take, the eighth such call.

He glanced at us. "Excuse me." He flipped open his phone. "Hello, hello, Mustafa," he boomed in that endearing voice. "Yes . . . Yes, that is right. No. No, impossible, Mustafa. Please, a million times please, my friend." He snapped the phone closed.

"That was our friends," he said.

"Our friends?"

"You know. Bin Laden."

"Oh? What did they say?"

"Well, they say yes, of course. But we won't know until tomorrow."

I glanced at Carl. "I thought this was all set up."

"So did I. So, what's up, Samir?"

"Don't worry. But these things are not simple."

I feel my pulse start to quicken. "No. Why?"

"Very difficult, Ted. Very difficult." Samir's phone rang again. He saw the number and quickly excused himself. He stepped over to one side, spoke for less than a minute, then returned.

He waved the phone. "That was our friends in Beirut," he said in a soft voice.

"So, how does it look?" Carl asked in equally soft tones.

Samir shrugged. "We'll see. They are trying. So much is up in the air."

I felt like the only one at the table who didn't understand the code language. I glanced around. No one was within earshot. So why the muted voices? Were the secret police listening to our every word? Perhaps the Mutawa, Saudi Arabia's religious police, had been warned that we were in-country and had planted highly sophisticated listening devices in our rooms and on the lapels of passersby.

Of course, they had to be, I thought. The FBI had contacted Carl not long ago and made it clear that they were completely aware of "everything." They knew of any comings and goings to the Middle East, naturally, and Carl was squarely in their sights. We were both aware of the likelihood that some form of authority—be it Saudi, Lebanese, American, or KGB for all we knew—was watching our movements one way or another. My mind began to run wild again, and I was eager to shut it down.

"What do you mean up in the air?" I asked. "What's going on in Beirut?"

"It could go up in flames, my friend," Samir said with a wink. "But they're working on it. With any luck, we may get the meetings you want."

"What do you mean meetings? We're not even going. Right?"

Samir shrugged. "We'll see."

That gnawing fear Samir had sent into hiding was back, and I leaned forward. "No, we can't go. I promised my wife. I didn't come all this way to get killed. We canceled our tickets."

"Right," Carl said. "And I agree, we shouldn't go." He paused. "Not unless we all feel it's perfectly safe."

Safe? What did safe mean in this part of the world?

"Don't worry, Ted. I own a travel agency as well." Samir tapped his cigar on the edge of the ashtray. "But we will not go unless it's a *million* times a million safe." This was said with a huge emphasis on the first *million* and a wave of his hand.

I would soon learn that this humble and trusted servant of the world sees mostly the brightest side of life. Like so many in this part of the world, he seems so used to danger that he sees it as only a passing distraction unless it's right on his doorstep.

Samir is exceedingly expressive, and his dialect is the language of peace, love, and reconciliation. But my own attempt to latch onto his words of confidence was now tempered by a fear that both he and Carl would call in every possible favor to get us to Beirut as originally planned.

"So these meetings aren't set up?" I asked, getting back to the business at hand. "I thought everything was arranged."

"My friend, nothing is set in the Middle East. Everything is day by day. Not until the last moment do we know what will happen the next. But it is a million times safe. Don't worry."

Oh well, that's comforting.

"But you want to write a book, yes? That's why you came here." He motioned to the north. "The book is up there, in Beirut and Syria and Palestine. Here in Saudi Arabia we just want to make you feel welcome and satisfied. Saudi Arabia, as you will see, is one of the safest places in the world. The ruler and the ruled have a loving relationship. Here there are no problems, never, never, never."

I don't want to overplay the nerves that would ride me for the next two weeks straight, but I have to be completely transparent here. I was a walking piano wire every waking moment for days on end. When I ate sweetmeats offered at lavish banquets, I smiled and expressed my great appreciation, but hidden behind my bright eyes was a sense of foreboding. When I sat around a table at the beach listening to Samir's jokes, I would join them all in a belly laugh, but in my gut I felt dread for the road ahead.

There is a reason why so many Saudis were so thrilled to see Americans in their land—so few had come in the last seven years. No, they were all safely at home, comforted by their good sense. I kept telling myself, if I can just survive the next two weeks, I'll be eternally grateful. I can't imagine how a Westerner less traveled than me would have felt.

And yet it was in part *because* of the tension that wound me tight all those days that I began to see the profound beauty in the parable of the Good Samaritan. And no one better personified this teaching than Samir Kreidie. Honestly, if not for Samir, I think I would have headed back then, while I still had full control of my good sense.

But Samir is like a strong elixir of goodness. He is like a narcotic in the best ways, washing away pain and fear and showing the world to be a delightful gift from God to all who will open their eyes.

Now both Carl and I look back at our two days in Saudi Arabia as a vacation by the sea, a time during which we were spoiled by friends and princes alike. On our first afternoon we drove to a members-only beach, hidden behind high walls and protected by armed guards who took one look at Samir and opened the gate. Beyond, we found a lush resort that could compare to any in the Caribbean. Sequestered away from the public, the resort teemed with members who owned one of several hundred villas within its walls. It was a private paradise stripped of all the rules that governed street life. Here the women lounged on beach chairs dressed in bikinis and shirtless men argued politics around tables by an expansive blue pool.

We spent the evening with Samir's children, Danny, Ramy, and Fady, and their wives, who invited friends over to hang out. Inside, we could have been anywhere in Europe and not known the difference. Large plasma TVs, Xbox 360s, torn jeans with studded belts, rock music—it was all there behind the walls where freedom still reigns and women still make the world turn.

We spent hours upon hours discussing politics, religion, and social issues with a wide variety of gracious people from all walks of life who were kind enough to invite us into their homes and spoil us rotten. In a few words, here are a colonel in the Saudi Arabian army and Hussein Shobokshi, an influential media personality.

TRANSCRIPT

Ted: Could you introduce yourself?

Shobokshi: I am Hussein Shobokshi. I went to high school in California and went to university in Tulsa. Then I did my training in New York at a bank. I loved the States. I played football in high school and did some theater in college and played tennis. I still have friends. Now I'm heading a TV show. I also lecture and write various things on Saudi relations, the West, and Islam.

Ted: What would you say is the greatest misunderstanding Americans have of Arabs?

Shobokshi: Americans think the religion of Islam is an odd religion. But Islam is a continuous religion of Judaism and Christianity. We have the same ethics. Americans think Arabs are criminals, not trustworthy, backstabbers. It is, as you say, the flavor of the month.

Ted: And Arabs' greatest misunderstanding of Americans?

Shobokshi: Immoral, no ethics, no high standards, not conservative. Saudis who come back from California and the big cities see this immoral behavior, but the ones who visit or live in the Midwest or South of America come back with a very different conception. It depends where they go in the U.S. and their first impression.

Ted: What makes you cry?

Shobokshi: My daughter, Miriam, will be three in July and she has a very aggressive form of cancer. Her experience has been earth-shattering to me and I've never been the same. She's been through chemotherapy and operations in the United States. Her two doctors are very Jewish and her pediatrician is Irish Catholic.

Colonel: It is a time for crying. Last week I saw on TV a program talking about a mistake in medication. I saw one child who is now thirteen; for eight years he couldn't move. He is dying. The family cannot get the guy who made the mistake. The family only wants the doctor to try to fix the mistake or give them money to send them to a different doctor. I cried because I saw the mother crying. Now I'm going to cry again. Or when you see victims from Africa. It is hard to believe that Americans are throwing their wheat in the ocean and don't want to give it to the poor people just because of the price, yet you blame us for increasing the price of the fuel. Today, if we would like to live in peace, we would have to take away the politics.

Ted: What makes you laugh?

Colonel: I don't think this is a time for laughing. I don't think you'll laugh if you aren't happy. So you have to ask the question the other way: What makes you happy? First, to be successful in your work. To see your family happen. Also to see the good around you. There is nothing special that makes me laugh. It has to be at that moment.

Ted: What do you think is the greatest misunderstanding that American people have of the Middle East?

Colonel: Listening to the American media is their greatest mistake.

Ted: What do you think is Arabs' greatest misunderstanding of Americans?

Colonel: When the people here saw their brothers in Iraq being killed, they did not like America. If they go to America, they find different views, though. I have some American friends, so I understand there are many people against the war in Iraq. I think if we use our minds all the time, there won't be any problems.

The bin Laden Brothers

All the while Samir was on his phone. Did I say Samir knows every-one? It was an understatement. He was always on his phone. Making arrangements. Talking to Damascus. Talking to the bin Laden brothers. Talking to Beirut, which was still off the table.

"So, is it yes or is it no?"

"For the sheik, Yamani, it's a yes, first thing tomorrow. But he is meeting us on his day off, so we must be short." Indeed, in Saudi Arabia, Thursday and Friday are the weekend, and Saturday it's back to work.

"What about the bin Ladens?"

"It's yes. But we have to go now," Samir said. "Immediately."

Our meeting with the two brothers, who have requested to re-main unnamed due to the complicated nature of their brother's sta-tus as both a Saudi citizen and the world's preeminent terrorist, perfectly illustrates the incredible discrepancy between perception and reality. Drop the name bin Laden—brother, cousin, sister, it doesn't matter—and most in the West fear for their lives. So it was with some trepidation that I walked up the majestic marble steps that led to the world headquarters for the Saudi Binladin Group.

In the desert, coaxing beauty from the sand is the stuff of magi-cians, better known in this part of the world as landscapers and builders. The bin Ladens have made their fortune in the construc-tion trade. It was the Binladin Group that renovated the Great Mosque in Mecca at incredible expense. And it was Osama bin Laden who made his own fortune in Sudan when he rebuilt parts of Khartoum and was paid in land by the cash-starved government. He became the country's largest landowner and later cashed in his chips to fund his revolutionary vision.

Walking into the Binladin Group atrium was like walking into an abandoned palace. It was stunning and massive, with hardly a soul to be seen. We were ushered into an inner office upstairs and im-mediately offered tea.

Again, sensitivity bars us from sharing the details of our conver-sation, but suffice it to say that the bin Laden brothers immediately wanted to address the elephant in the room. They thought their brother Osama was a . . . well, a jerk. Only they didn't put it nearly so kindly. They wanted nothing to do with him. These were highly educated businessmen who dressed like anyone on Wall Street, if the occasion required, and had acquired their wealth through brilliant maneuvering.

When asked for his favorite joke, one of the brothers pulled out his cell phone and began to search for a joke he'd been e-mailed just the other day. We waited while he scrolled. And scrolled. And scrolled, apologizing profusely about taking so long to find it.

How many e-mails did he have in two days' time? Finally, failing to find the joke, he told us the best one he could remember, and we doubled over with laughter.

Can we tell this joke?

No. No, I'd rather we not.

We eventually left the meeting feeling quite jubilant. In the car Samir said that this family is a wonderful family. Most of the brothers studied in the United States and two of them have doctorates from Harvard University. They are humble; they believe in peace and in loving and helping the poor. Even Carl, the fearless traveler, attested to relief. Living in the United States and hearing nothing but terror in association with the name bin Laden has had its effect even on those who know there is only one "jerk" among the bin Ladens. It all comes down to perception, and ours had just been altered.

It would not always go so smoothly in our days ahead, but for now we were sitting pretty.

TRANSCRIPT

Ted: What is the greatest concern in your life?
Saudi driver: To work and be at peace.
Ted: What do you think of Jesus' teaching that we should love our enemies?
Saudi driver: Yes, but I'm not so religious.

"So, what now?" I asked, sliding onto the couch in Samir's office.

"Tea?" he asked. "A cola?"

"Tea, thanks," I said.

Samir walked from the room, phone plastered to his ear. Someone from Syria was on the line.

"So?" I pressed, turning to Carl. "What's the story?"

"Well . . ." Carl cleared his throat. "I've been meaning to discuss that with you."

"Sheik Yamani, right?" We had yet to interview the highly respected cleric.

"Yes. But something else has come up. They've opened the Beirut airport for flights starting tomorrow evening."

My heart fell.

"Samir says he can get us on the flight. The fighting has stopped."

"And it could start"—I snapped my fingers—"like that."

"It could. But Samir has agreed to take his youngest, Carla, who's sixteen, with us. You said if Samir thought it was safe enough to take his children back, you would consider it. Well . . . he's agreed."

"We're pressuring him. Come on, Carl, I'm serious. I don't want to go."

Samir walked in, snapped his phone closed, and spoke immediately. "Ted, they are waiting. It's all arranged. Now you must go, you understand. It will be safe, I promise you."

"Seriously," Carl said. "I don't think we have anything to worry about."

"That's what they told every reporter who's been killed since 9/11. And, no offense, but that's what you believed before you were kidnapped in Fallujah." Carl's wild ride in Iraq is a story that shook him up badly. We'll share it as we draw closer. For now I used it in an attempt to talk sense into his fast-forgetting head.

"This isn't just about Beirut," I said. "We're talking about southern Lebanon, where the Hezbollah preside over daily life."

"It's not like that, Teddy," Samir said. "My wife, Sophie, dedicates her life and resources to working with and helping the poor in the south of Lebanon, which coincidentally is also what the Hezbollah is doing there. That is why you find her very popular in the south and Hezbollah people love her very much. They all love Sophie. And thus I can say that they are my friends." He patted his chest. "I have no enemies."

"I can see that, my friend, but how rare is it for two Westerners to interview the Hezbollah leadership in southern Lebanon? It's al-most impossible, you said it yourself. Especially now with tensions through the roof."

"But, Teddy, this will make the book. Trust me, the book is be-tween Lebanon, Syria, and the West Bank. That is the land of Isa, and now a way has opened up for us to go."

"Samir can arrange for the tickets on the first flight in," Carl said. "We don't have to be on the plane, but we should let Samir do his magic and get us tickets for the flight." Grin. "Just in case."

No pressure, Ted.

Due to safety issues for ourselves and those we would meet, both Carl and I had agreed not to speak about any of our plans in phone calls back to the States. I couldn't call my wife and ask her what she thought. But before I left, she'd kissed me and told me I should do whatever I thought was right in any situation.

We've been down a few roads together, and I am typically known as the wild one. Little did she know the full extent of Carl's wild side, which at the moment was making me feel a bit silly. The green gringo among warriors. The small mouse among men of great valor and even greater purpose. A Pharisee next to the true Samaritan.

"Okay, book the tickets," I said. But my palms were sweating.

Sheik Yamani

During the last few decades of the 1900s, there were few people in the world as powerful as the minister of oil in Saudi Arabia, Ahmed Zaki Yamani. It could be said that his stranglehold now grips the West—he who controls energy controls the world.

But in Saudi Arabia itself, Ahmed Yamani's cousin, Muhammad Yamani, could be seen as even more powerful. His brother might have controlled the oil that goes into our cars, but Muhammad con-trolled the ideology that controlled the streets. As the minister of in-formation in Saudi Arabia, Muhammad Yamani was one of a handful of Muslim leaders in charge of making Islamic law.

This, then, was the kind of leader that Carl and I had set out to meet, not to understand his philosophy on all matters, but to see a snapshot of him as the man on the street might see him. Our *People* magazine–style interview. If Cairo wrote Islamic law, this was the man responsible for showing his country how to live that law.

We must make a distinction between Saudi Arabia's Mutawa, or religious police, and its clerics, because the Mutawa are a law unto themselves. Originally appointed by the king, Saud bin Aziz, in an effort to control the country through enforceable law, the Mutawa now find themselves in an awkward if powerful position. They are disliked by the general populace, who fear their rude and often brutal tactics, punishing people on the streets of more conservative cities such as Riyadh for everything from looking at a woman to not praying properly. And they are also frowned upon by the royals, who support growing Western influence in the country.

Muhammad Yamani would have had no real control over the Mutawa, but the laws that they implemented were heavily influenced by this man. Today Yamani heads the world's largest Muslim nongovernmental humanitarian organization, the Iqra Foundation, founded to fight poverty and increase education in Africa and Asia. He lives in a 28,000-square-foot palace in Jeddah and has another almost as spectacular in Riyadh. He's authored more than twenty books on Islam and sharia law.

We were ushered into a large office in downtown Jeddah, where Yamani waited for us behind a huge wooden desk. He was dressed in the same traditional white thobe worn by most royals, and he stood with the help of a cane. The sheik fills out his clothes and he smiles with a round face. The tea and biscuits came out immediately, offered by his male assistant, who also recorded our entire conversation.

"Do you mind?" I asked pulling out my tiny recorder.

"Of course. No problem."

Here, then, is our snapshot of Sheik Muhammad Yamani.

TRANSCRIPT

Ted: Where did you study?
Yamani: Cornell. I got my Ph.D. in economic geology.

Ted: What kind of car do you drive?

Yamani: A Mercedes, series 600.

Ted: Color?

Yamani: (Chuckles) Gray.

Ted: What is something that makes you laugh? Or a favorite joke perhaps.

Yamani: When I lived in the States, I went to a restaurant and ordered at the counter. My food didn't come, so I saw one table and there was a girl sitting at the table. And I said, "Is this table free?" She said, "Well, this is a free country." After I sat down, I asked her if she was free like the table.

Another time, my friend from England went to New York. He was passing in traffic and didn't see a cab that almost hit him. The taxi stopped and yelled, "What? Did you come here to die?" And my friend yelled back, "No, I came here yester-die." (He bounces with laughter.)

Ted: What is something your children do that makes you laugh?

Yamani: Well, you see the differences from generation to generation. I see the relation between my children and me, and my grandchildren with me. For example, when I enter my son's home, he stands up and greets me. When I enter the house and see my grandchildren, they don't stand but only say "Hi. Hi, Grandfather." When I saw my granddaughter, she was sitting in a chair, and I wanted to sit. But she said, "We are all family, and when the chair is free, you can have it. But now it is occupied." (Chuckles) Now she is eleven. Her name is Fatima. TV is definitely affecting their dialogue and their actions. We have to be careful.

Ted: Do you have any hobbies?

Yamani: When I was young, I played soccer and swam. And I like to watch TV, and I like to read at night, and I write articles for the newspaper.

Ted: When was the last time you cried?

Yamani: I usually don't cry. But if I see someone suffer, like if a friend has a mother or father die and I see him suffering, I feel very sad. One year ago, my friend's father was crossing a street and was hit by a car and died. The saddest day was when I lost my mother, because she was so kind to me and to others. She taught me to be kind to others. And also the death of my father ten years later.

Ted: What do you think is Americans' greatest misconception of your people?

Yamani: They look at the Saudis through the oil. They don't look behind that and see the culture and history. Communication is so important. The accident of 9/11 has made Americans think that the Arabs are out to get them. But this group of people who are terrorists does not define the people of the Arab world. We do not accept killing anyone. Bush is a miserable person for international relations. The things he has said have caused problems.

Ted: What is the common Saudi's greatest misconception of Americans?

Yamani: They look at America as cowboys who all want war. But your information is not correct about the Arab world. I think we have to put more effort in the children, because they are the future. If the American people came to the Arab world and discover the culture, they would love the Arabs. Like when I went to the U.S., I liked the people. People need to see the good in the others. Secondly, the religion has been distorted. In both America and the Arab world. All people should love each other. Let us go and teach people that there is beautiful God. Politics do not help anything. Why not talk about culture and people? Not politics. I think your book will help.

Ted: What frustrates you among your people?

Yamani: When I discover that anyone has lied to me. Lying really affects me. I'd rather hear the truth.

Ted: When asked what his most important teaching was, Jesus answered that it was to love the Lord your God with all your heart and to love your neighbor as yourself. What does this mean in relation to loving one another?

Yamani: I don't think this is the word of Jesus. It is the word of God. The same word was sent to Muhammad. It is the same teaching. The Qur'an orders us to respect Jesus and his mother, who is a noble lady. To be a Muslim, you must believe this. But people must see the good in one another in order to love each other; otherwise they cannot love each other. First you must understand each other.

4

Nicole

BEFORE DIVING BACK into our ill-advised flight into Beirut, we must share a most fascinating parable that presented itself to us in a most unusual way.

Our entire journey was centered on finding the Samaritan referenced by Jesus two thousand years ago. We would wend our way through the Middle East like a whirlwind, ending at the doorstep of those seven hundred Samaritans still alive today.

At least that was the plan, although we had yet to secure meetings with any Samaritans. Turns out they are quite hard to locate and pin down. We had some good leads at this point in our trip, and as always the phone lines were buzzing, buzzing in an attempt to confirm a meeting—something the Middle East seems to have a proclivity for avoiding.

But it's the *spirit* of the Samaritan that interests us most. The question is whether those in this land remember the great teaching and, more to the point, whether the notion of loving such unlovable neighbors might have no grounding in reality.

There may not be a tale that better illustrates our own search for the true Samaritan than the unique story of another American's firsthand encounter with intersecting faiths in the Middle East. We didn't get the chance to sit down with Nicole in person while we were in Beirut for reasons that will become obvious, but our source for this tale is impeccable. And in all truth, there are a hundred Nicoles in the Middle East today, each of them with stories as dramatic.

As part of Nicole's story, we are including several of the many e-mails she sent to her brother, Doug, while in the Middle East. This is her story.

Nicole

Beirut is a city awash in stories, an ocean of human sagas as diverse as its neighborhoods sprawled across hilly boulevards, palm-lined seafronts, and squalid refugee camps.

This is why, in the spring of 2008, few in Beirut's Shatila quarter took more than curious notice of the young woman weaving through dangerous auto traffic on a competition bicycle. The young woman's fleeting silhouette surely provoked some looks from the neighborhood's watchful citizens. Some of its more hormonal young bachelors might have indulged in longing peeks at her flowing hair, dyed blonde, or shapely limbs.

But she would have caused few *second* looks. In Beirut, unique sights are as commonplace as riveting life stories. Here, it wouldn't be unusual to spot a bikini-clad young Frenchwoman sunbathing next to a fresh bomb crater. Or a toddler being led through the park by a father fingering the shoulder strap of his AK-47.

However, a deeper look at the life of this bold young woman reveals an unforgettable story.

The heartbreaking quest that sent Nicole Wagner to Beirut began in a town nearly four thousand miles away: Burlington, Iowa. It was there, in 1987, that Iowa State University student and newlywed mother Muna Wagner first learned that she was going to give birth to a baby girl.

Muna and her husband, Daniel, had formed a wildly unlikely couple from their first date at Iowa State in the fall of the year before. Daniel, a graduate student finishing up a degree in education, was a pale-complexioned Midwesterner with a shy, awkward manner. Muna was a just-arrived, foreign scholar of clearly Arab origins whose darker skin matched her volatile moods and highly verbal intelligence.

Fresh from a mysterious Middle Eastern city she would not name, Muna had clearly been as anxious to rid herself of her Islamic past as she was her foreign citizenship. This exotic beauty swept into Daniel's life like a spice-laden whirlwind. He had found her lithe figure and brown eyes and skin intoxicating. She, on the other hand, had been drawn to his humility, his rigorous work ethic, and his obvious integrity.

Daniel had proposed marriage two days after their second date. Apologizing for the suddenness of his proposal, he argued that true love was a force to be reckoned with and had to be acknowledged as soon as it presented itself. And, he confessed, he was afraid of losing such a beautiful woman to the countless prospects savvier than himself. Their relationship at this early stage was a passionate one.

To his surprise, Muna gladly accepted his proposal and willingly surrendered to the wedding traditions that his Iowan Methodist family immediately plunged into. Her own background, Muna repeated sadly when asked by some of Daniel's nosier relatives, was a painful subject best left on the other side of the world. No one pushed the issue. Overjoyed that their geeky young Danny had landed such a winsome and willful beauty, his family readily agreed to leave the subject alone.

The wedding was arranged in only a few short weeks. Two nights before it took place, Muna took Daniel aside and whispered the truth into his ear. She was expecting.

On the second of June 1987, Muna gave birth to a baby girl in the master bedroom of a modest frame home on Burlington's northeast side.

In retrospect, Daniel and Muna's marriage never truly survived the postpartum depression and sexual drought that followed Nicole's arrival. But, challenged by the job of raising a tireless baby daughter, neither spouse addressed the problem for several years.

Daniel spent long hours at the high school where he worked as an administrator, away from both his wife and his new daughter, Nicole. But, struggling with depression, Muna spent hours alone in a secretive life that made little room for a needy child. The state of affairs did not improve when, two years after Nicole's birth, her brother Doug was born.

Nicole would come to picture her childhood as the life of a loner, sharing a home with two distant parents. It was hardly a surprise, therefore, when cycling—her means of transportation to and from grade school—emerged as the guiding passion of her youth. Riding her ten-speed on ever longer routes from one destination to another, Nicole swiftly developed capacious lungs and muscular legs. When she entered the local Burlington Criterium race and found herself handily winning her age group, the victor's medal went above her bedroom mirror and became her beacon to a happier future.

Her friends and neighbors remember Nicole as a fixture on a bicycle in and around Burlington. Almost every day, weather permitting, she took extended rides on the roads along the nearby Mississippi River. Often she returned home via wandering routes across eastern Iowa's hardwood forests and rolling farmlands. The rush of wind in her face and the burning in her legs became second nature. "I'd rather ride ten miles than spend ten minutes in any mall," she would say to her friends.

By the time she entered high school, Nicole Wagner was not only a lanky and beautiful young woman but also a cyclist gifted enough to travel beyond Iowa in search of competition. The thrill of watching their daughter excel on a national level, along with handling the logistics of transporting her to far-flung races, became a welcome distraction in her parents' cooling marriage.

At age seventeen, Nicole finished third among women in the celebrated seven-day-long RAGBRAI, the *Des Moines Register*'s Annual Great Bike Ride Across Iowa, and began to attract serious attention as an athlete. Just weeks before her high school graduation, Indiana University offered her a full athletic scholarship. Then came a startling piece of news: The UCI, the governing body of world cycling, had just ranked her seventh in the world for her age group. It was enough to earn her the most thrilling honor of all: an invitation to race for a spot on the United States Olympic cycling team.

Daniel was too busy with work to attend, so Nicole, her mother, and her brother, Doug, traveled together to Redlands, California, for the event.

The night before her primary road race, Nicole overheard a heated cell phone exchange between her mother and her father back in Burlington. Nicole inquired anxiously if her mother was all right. She received little more than a teary shake of the head in reply.

"I'm fine," Muna finally whispered.

The next morning, Nicole rode like a woman possessed. She finished fourth in her time trial and became the second-youngest cyclist ever invited to the Olympic Training Center in Colorado Springs. She was being groomed for the 2008 Games.

The dream lasted exactly nine and three-quarter hours—just long enough for Nicole, her mother, and Doug to return home.

The first thing they noticed as they walked up to the house was that Daniel's old Dodge was missing from the driveway. Her face white with worry, Muna rushed inside and found confirmation of her fears: Daniel was gone.

He'd moved out completely, every sign of him swept clean except for two notes on the kitchen table, one addressed to Nicole, one to her brother. Hers simply read:

> *I'm so sorry, my dear. It was the only way. I pray someday you'll come to understand. You'll never know how proud I am of you. Deepest love, Dad.*

Card in hand, she wandered through the house looking for her mother. She found her kneeling beside the bed in the master suite, weeping openly and sweeping up a pile of faded letters.

"What are those, Mom?" Nicole asked as gently as she knew how.

Muna only nodded her head and gathered the letters to her bosom as swiftly as her sobs would allow.

Nicole, wracked by curiosity, peered at one envelope. She recalled seeing only a fragment of an address. A city line.

"Beirut, Lebanon, 961."

It was later discovered that Daniel Wagner had moved into a nearby hotel, refusing for some reason to tell them its location. He was dead set on the divorce, however. The paperwork sailed through, unopposed by Muna. He fought for, and received, ample visitation rights and did his best to remain a force in his children's lives.

Although crushed by this turn of events, Muna seemed to understand his reasons, even if no one else did. Nicole spent hours trying to piece together the true reasons behind her parents' divorce, to no avail. She suspected that her father had caught her mother in a betrayal of some kind, though probably not adultery. However frosty the marriage might have become, Nicole was sure her mother had no inclination to find a lover behind her father's back.

Those letters, however, hinted at something far more mysterious and somehow even more painful. Nicole pleaded with her mother over the months that followed to tell her about the letters. She deserved to know, she argued. After all, it was *her* family that had just splintered apart. But Muna refused. Revealing the truth seemed a prospect too remote to even consider.

Three months later, just as the strange living arrangements had settled into an awkward new routine, a police officer appeared at the doorway. He was flanked by a soft-looking man in a clerical collar.

Daniel Wagner had suffered mortal injuries in an automobile accident, just north of town. A single-car accident. Cause unknown.

The weeks that followed would disappear whole from Nicole's life, as cleanly and completely as though cut out and removed by some kind of cruel saw. The only thing she would later remember is riding her bicycle for hours, slow and aimlessly now, with a mournful disregard for her own safety.

A fierce, condemning rage toward her mother rose from the ashes of her father's death. She began to suspect that her mother was responsible for his death, as sure as if she'd pulled a trigger. Or more precisely, those secret letters, and whatever hid behind them, had done the deed. Their return address might as well have read "Smith & Wesson."

Finally, late one night after hours of cajoling, Muna gave in and told her the story behind the mysterious letters.

"I never loved your father," Muna told her in a halting whisper. "I was too young and confused and vulnerable to know it at the time. I respected him, and depended on him, and I came to have high regard for him. But I did not love him. And there's something worse than that. In order to explain it properly, I have to go back to the beginning."

Muna had been born in a Lebanese refugee camp, the daughter

of Palestinians who were once farmers in the vicinity of Nablus, Israel. The baby of her family, she had grown up with stern but loving parents and three boisterous brothers. Like so many others, they had been displaced from their land during the fighting that followed the creation of Israel in 1948.

The conditions of her childhood had been unbelievably bleak and squalid, she explained. But Muna had shown a gift: a defiant eloquence. From the earliest, her family had groomed her to someday leave the camp and attend a foreign university. A number of generous scholarships awaited any refugee child who displayed unusual intellect and talent for schoolwork.

She was almost grown up, preparing to leave to study at Iowa State University in the second semester, when death arrived at her camp. The year was 1982. Weeks before, the Israel Defense Forces had invaded southern Lebanon and besieged Beirut for three long weeks.

On that morning, tanks appeared around the camp's perimeter, their cannons turned inward. Men in unfamiliar uniforms popped up on the roofs, aiming rifles down at her and her family. Late that afternoon, another group of soldiers arrived in noisy pickup trucks and ambled into the camp itself.

These were Phalangists. Christians.

"I was hiding with my mother inside our house," Muna said, "when I heard the shooting begin. Then the screaming started. The howls and moans did not stop for two days. We hid in our bathroom and lay there, praying and holding each other, for the longest forty-eight hours of my life. Every second was filled with agony and terror.

"On the third morning two militiamen kicked in our bathroom door, and they would have killed us except for their superior, who walked in and stopped them. He looked me up and down, and I knew immediately that he was interested. He asked me how old I was.

" 'Eighteen,' I answered. 'And I have a life to lead. I am going to college in a few months, now that I have at last gotten a scholarship. Furthermore, your men have no reason to harm my family. They are innocent of any violent or illegal act. Back in our homeland, we loved our Jewish neighbors. And we revere Jesus Christ as a gift from Allah.'

"He nodded and turned to his men. 'We have no reason to harm this family. You, my dear,' he said, 'would you kindly accompany me?'

"My mother started with a whimper, then caught herself as I met her terrified gaze. The commander gave her a reassuring look. He took me by the arm and led me outside. The dead were lying in the gutters like rainwater. I heard a loud rumble, turned, and saw a tractor rolling down the street with its blade down and shoving the corpses forward, like mud after a storm. The man saw my face.

" 'I can't stop these things that are going on here. But I can stop it for your family, if you'll just agree to come with me. You're a very pretty girl, and unusually persuasive, and I'd like to spend some time with you. Let me take you away from here.' "

Muna sighed and shut her eyes against the memory's power. Nicole asked her what she'd done.

"I said yes. He was quite handsome and young: thirty. His men drove me to a nice apartment in a distant part of the city. I never saw my family again. Nor did I ever know if he kept his promise toward them. I was alone in this place, and when he showed up the next day, he apologized for the fact that I'd been locked in. He said it was for my own protection. Then he . . ." Muna faltered.

Nicole placed a hand softly on her arm. "That's all right, Momma. I can imagine."

"It wasn't what you think. He did not force me. I wanted so much to be in charge of the situation, to take the initiative in ensuring my family's safety, that I willingly gave myself to him."

"But you were a hostage!"

Muna made an uncertain face. "Things became confusing. He was very kind to me, Nicole. Something real happened between us. He was gentle and genuinely caring. Eventually he told me he loved me. His wife had died the year before, and he was lonely. Gradually I became convinced that I loved him too. And today I can't tell you that I didn't."

"How did you leave him?"

She shook her head. "The more our feelings grew, the more impossible we realized the whole situation was. There was no way he could ever present me to his family or his peers. We could never marry. After almost four years, I finally left him in a hurry, without telling him. There was a special reason for that, which I don't need to get into right now.

"He could have held it against me, gotten his revenge, or grabbed me and taken me back. But instead we talked on the phone and he offered to give me money and renew my scholarship to university here in the States. I told you, he was a kind man. We decided that I would go on with my life and he would go on with his.

"Leaving him was the hardest thing I've ever done, but I made a clean break. I came to Iowa on the first flight I could get and entered school. It was unbelievably disorienting and confusing. Especially when I realized"—she lowered her head and her voice—"that my period was six days late."

Nicole stared at her mother. "You mean . . . ?"

"This is what I've been leading up to tell you. Darling, Daniel Wagner wasn't your biological father. I quickly agreed to marry your father to cover my own shame."

Not a word was exchanged for more than a minute.

"Did Dad know this?"

"No. He learned when he found those letters, the weekend we were away. They were from Beirut. From the man I'd truly loved all these years. Love letters written through the years begging me to return to him. He regretted sending me away and wanted me to live with him again. Of course I couldn't accept; I'd vowed never to return to Lebanon, and I meant it."

"That's what drove Daddy away?"

Muna only looked at the ground and wept.

Two months later, still confused by the discovery that her biological father was alive and living in Lebanon, Nicole determined to give herself some space. She packed up her mother's car and moved a thousand miles west to the Colorado Springs Olympic Training Center. She enrolled in college, secured a waitressing job, and settled into a routine of grueling mountain cycling at the young age of twenty.

Life began to take on a semblance of normality.

But that all changed once again with a single cell phone call. It was her brother, Doug, in tears.

Mother had suffered a brain aneurysm. Doug had found her passed out in the kitchen and immediately called for help. She was en route to the hospital at that very moment, still unconscious.

Nicole turned her bike around and sprinted downhill, desperate to get to the airport. Red lights, slower cars, obstructions—they all flowed around Nicole like water.

Muna Wagner passed away in her sleep at Burlington's Great River Medical Center the following morning, at 2:43 A.M. At that moment her daughter, Nicole, was an hour away, flying toward her at thirty-six thousand feet.

The rest of Muna's secrets went with her to the grave. Twenty-four hours after her mother's death, Nicole found the love letters from Beirut and pored over them for more information. She had to know more. Who was her father? What did he do for a living? What did he look like? He had signed his name only as "R—" and given only "Beirut, Lebanon, 961" as a return address.

Without a mother or a father to fill the void in her life, Nicole's need to know about the man in the letters grew into an obsession over the following few weeks. She and Doug were essentially alone now, cared for by an extended family, but with less enthusiasm since Daniel's death.

So it was that Nicole, for better or worse, made some bold decisions. She sold their childhood home. She enrolled her brother in a local junior college.

Then she wrote a letter to the United States Olympic Committee, officially declining the invitation to be considered as a competitor for the upcoming Games. She had experienced recent family tragedy, she explained. And she had business to attend to.

Nicole Wagner was a young woman on a quest. The only thing in life that mattered to her now was finding the other survivors of Muna's tragic story: her family and, most of all, the kind lover who had saved her mother and given Nicole life.

E-MAIL FROM NICOLE

Dear Doug,

I hope you get this on the e-mail account we set up. Are you doing all right? I miss you so much! I hardly know where to start telling you about Beirut. Talk about a different world! I hope I can halfway do it justice.

First of all, it was such a thrill to just pull my bike out of the over-size check-in, yank it out of the box and put it together, right there in the terminal, slap on my backpack, and just ride off the sidewalk. All my other stuff I'd sent to my flat near the camp ahead of me. I memorized every turn from the map ten times over, but it was still the most mind-blowing thing I've ever done.

The first few minutes of riding, I saw very little, since I was concentrating mostly on avoiding all the BMWs and Mercedes headed straight for me. But gradually I got my head straight and was able to look around and drink things in a bit.

First of all, I never realized how beautiful Beirut is in parts. We landed right next to the ocean, which is all lined with palm trees. It's an incredible place to ride, because it seems to change completely with every new block. One stretch will look like Paris, with coffee shops and restaurants and very expensive shops, the next will look like a war zone where I have to get off and walk through rubble, and the next will look like an Arab bazaar from Morocco.

Still, nothing prepared me for the refugee camp, Shatila. I have to say, I smelled the garbage a quarter mile before reaching it. There's piles of trash lined up along the street. Then the architecture changed pretty drastically. It's like somebody took these big cubes of rickety plaster or stucco, then piled them on top of each other without any support, several layers high. I learned later that's exactly what they do; because the camps have nowhere to expand, the only way to give newlyweds their own house is to slap a pre-fab apartment right on top of the family home and let it go four, five stories high. The result looks like you could tip it over with a hard shove. Dirty, sagging walls that look like somebody soaked them with mud and mold. And since nothing's pre-wired, all the electrical and television lines are just strung everywhere, at five different levels above your head, twisted and broken and even dragging down to the ground.

But you forget about that once you enter, because it's the people who blow you away after that. They mostly stand around, with pretty much nothing to do all day but talk and smoke and read the Arab papers. Men standing on the corners, women in the doorways, kids trying to make games out of anything they can find, playing soccer with melons or balled-up socks.

I found out my second day at the clinic about the prostitution trade. "Auntie" is the name of a single woman who controls the whole camp and who can earn a young girl twice her father's daily wage for a couple hours of "work." She even takes payment on credit; you pay your bill at the end of the month along with your electricity and car payment. I looked at the doctor who told me and stared at him. I wanted to run out and stop it right then, hit somebody in the face. Go find this "Auntie" person and kill her. I mean, we're talking about girls being sold for six, seven bucks. And for them, it's like they won the lottery. Much quicker than begging all day on the streets for a few dimes.

I'm here for another purpose, of course, and I'm going to find out all I can. But maybe, while I'm here, I can help these girls. No one stands up for them. Everyone wants to get along. The clinic doctors shrug their shoulders and promise to give them shots and all the contraceptive help they can. But otherwise, they tell me, the trade actually feeds families.

I look around and see the misery, smell the despair, and think of Momma. I can't believe this is her heritage, where she's from. These are her people. So they're my people, too. Somehow, given how long Momma hid everything from us, it doesn't seem real.

I guess I'd better go, Doug. I don't think I've recovered from jet lag yet. Riding my bike helps, though. It's the only thing that gets me through—literally and figuratively.

Nicole

To be continued . . .

5

The Lion That Bites

BEIRUT

OUR MIDDLE EAST AIRLINES jet touched down with a screech of tires, bounced once, then settled safely to the runway. Okay, so far, so good. Carl was staring out the window, lost in memories, no doubt. On my other side, Samir was humming softly, shoes still off. I seemed to be the only one itching to climb out of my skin.

Carl's marriage proposal to the beautiful Greek woman he was courting, Chris, and his decision to move to Beirut came in the same year. It was 1985, two years after a fledgling Hezbollah was accused of blowing up the U.S. Embassy and Marine barracks in Beirut, which had killed more than three hundred American servicemen and foreign service workers. Additionally, American hostages were being held in Baalbek, again, reportedly, by the Hezbollah, though Hezbollah has denied involvement in the bombings and the kidnappings.

To the marriage proposal, Chris said yes. To the prospect of moving to Beirut, absolutely no.

Seven years later, in July 1992, Carl, Chris, and their two baby daughters (eighteen and four months old at the time) landed on the bomb-cratered runways of Beirut International Airport for the first time, ready to "love Arabs." Evidently Carl's time in a Saudi prison had neither quenched his fire nor gifted him with common sense.

That first landing in Beirut should have given them both a clue of things to come. No sooner had the plane come to a standstill than the stewardess began to yell frantically in Arabic. Puzzled by all the pointing out the windows, Carl looked out to see flames engulfing the right wing. Soldiers waving machine guns greeted the shocked, jet-lagged family from Colorado who rushed off the plane. They spoke no Arabic, had no accommodations waiting for them, no transportation to whisk them to safety, and very little good sense by most Westerners' accounting.

What they did have were two babies, two suitcases, and a young, naive love for Arabs. Welcome to the world according to Carl Medearis.

In the twelve years that followed, Carl's comings and goings from Beirut were of no less drama. He was imprisoned twice in Beirut for saying the wrong thing at the wrong time on this mission of love to the Arabs. He had no interest in making Christians of Muslims in a part of the world where Christians are as likely to kill Muslims as Muslims are to kill Christians, but his emphasis on the teachings of Jesus was frequently misunderstood as threatening.

Finally CIA agents appeared on his doorstep dressed in dark suits. They explained that they'd received death threats against "Carl Medearis of Colorado" and demanded that he accompany them to the U.S. embassy immediately. There he was given two weeks to leave the country.

Five months later he was back in Beirut, this time with three children in tow. And he would live in Beirut today if his name had not mysteriously appeared on a blacklist that prohibited him from acquiring the right papers for any extended stay.

No, now Carl resorts to first flights in after the Hezbollah has staged a coup, of sorts. And I was naive enough to join him. Sometimes I wonder whether Carl takes some kind of twisted pleasure in seeing those with less valor than he sweat. God knows I've done the same in the jungles of Indonesia when Americans came to visit.

"Here we are," Carl said, unbuckling. "Safe and sound."

There is one distinct advantage to being on the first plane into a war zone: no crowds. The new airport was almost deserted. Immigration brought no long delays, only raised eyebrows. And once we were outside, there was no traffic. In fact, the streets were empty. Of cars, that is.

Tanks, on the other hand, were stationed along the main drag at every major intersection.

I am a writer cursed with powers of observation and even greater powers of imagination, and by this point a hundred or so scenarios were now so real to me that our driver became the kidnapper, whisking us away to a compound where we would spend the next ten years until the United States finally broke down and sent Rambo to free us. The tanks along the street had their guns pointed directly at us, firing already. The impact would come with a ball of heat and . . .

"Don't you think, Ted?"

"Huh?" I snapped out of my reflection and turned to Carl.

"We still don't have the meeting with the leader of the Hezbollah in the south confirmed and probably won't until we are in their cars with their drivers. It's a security issue for them. So tomorrow we can meet with Sheik Mohammed Fadlallah here in Beirut."

"As long as it's safe."

"Safe? Everything is safe, buddy." He chuckled, enjoying seeing me sweat, I was convinced of it. "Although Sheik Fadlallah has been known to attract a bit of drama now and then."

"Drama?" My eyebrow arched. "What kind of drama?"

"Five attempts on his life over the past twenty years. Once by the CIA, twice by Saddam Hussein, twice by Israel. The buildings he occupies tend to get blown up. But I think we're safe now."

"When was the last attempt on his life?"

"Two years ago when Israel leveled his apartment."

"But he wasn't in it?"

"He wasn't, but eighty people were killed. We'll drive by it—it's still a pile of rubble."

By this time I was either finding some fresh courage or sinking into self-preserving denial. A small part of me felt a certain kind of masochism starting to set in. If you can't beat the feeling, join it, right? Or so I told myself. Ah, the liberation that comes with the final and gracious acceptance that you are going to die and there is nothing you can do about it.

We arrived at Samir's downtown penthouse flat, where his wife, Sophie, awaited our arrival. As Carl had promised earlier, there were two tanks guarding the building. Good guys, supposedly, and I felt comforted by those piles of green metal, never mind that they looked like leftovers from World War II.

The guards let us by and we climbed into the elevator with Samir and rose eleven stories to relative safety.

Inside we were enthusiastically greeted by Sophie, who exceeds even Samir in her fervent embrace of life. Sophie always speaks highly of Hezbollah because she says they love the poor. She gets upset when the West calls them terrorists.

We stepped out on a balcony that ran around the entire building, overflowing with greenery and statues, a virtual garden paradise from which to gaze upon Beirut's skyline. Below us, the two tanks held their stations. To the right, a large Hariri complex, the opposition to the Hezbollah in the government—thus the need for the tanks.

Sophie is the kind of woman who will stand for the truth in the face of any danger. When she goes to Saudi Arabia, she can be seen walking down the street bared of the black abaya. If the Mutawa confront her for improper dress, she has been known to confront them in return.

She has earned the respect of bitterly opposed parties wherever she goes, willing to tread where few dare. Her fearlessness is enough to make most cower.

We looked at the quiet skyline that night, joined by Rob, a Dutch humanitarian worker who collaborates closely with Sophie on a project to rebuild bombed-out homes in the south. Rob pulled out his cell phone and showed us five minutes of footage he'd taken the other night on his own balcony. Flashes of machine-gun fire and massive explosions rattled the tiny speaker.

"This was all around your house?"

"And here too!" Sophie interjected. "Nobody could go outside. Nobody. But I did, you know? I stood there"—she pointed to the railing—"and screamed at the men shooting 'Be afraid of God and stop fighting and killing each other!'"

Samir winks at me. It's no secret that he treads the political mine-field with far more care than she. But Sophie is Sophie, and she's earned a right to her opinion.

Hearing her calmed me. She loves all people, including Hezbollah, one of those whom many in the United Sates would count among their enemies for her association with Hezbollah alone. Yet this enemy appeared to be the kind I could love, as directed by the greatest of all commandments.

Carl and I weren't in the Middle East to unwrap politics or religion; we were there to find the proverbial Samaritans among our perceived enemies. We wanted to know if the land in which Jesus gave his teaching (the Middle East) was doing any better with that teaching than the dismal job displayed by those who claimed to follow it back home.

But it's impossible to engage anyone in the Middle East without a passionate discussion of politics, which invariably comes to raised voices. This is particularly true in Lebanon, the region's only democracy where there are openly opposing parties. Politics is much more a part of their social fabric than it is in the West.

"With Sophie, you know where you stand," Samir said, kissing his wife on her forehead. She waved him off.

"You must understand," Samir said, "in Lebanon there is a great struggle between the sitting government, controlled by Saad Hariri, and the opposition, which includes a coalition of Hezbollah and a majority of Christians."

"Christians?" This sounded impossible to me. "Hezbollah has joined with Christians?"

"There are many Christian factions, but yes, some of them side with the Hezbollah. The struggle isn't as much Christian against Muslim. It's about party power, like Democrats and Republicans. At this time the Western-supported majority controls 55 percent of the government. The opposition to Western and Israeli occupation controls 45 percent. So we have a conflict. Some here support the Palestinian cause; some do not."

"It's crazy, but Americans just can't get their minds around Lebanon," Carl said. "They want it all nice and neat, good versus evil—Christians being the good, of course."

Samir sat back and crossed his legs. "Do you know, Teddy, where the first suicide bombing in the Middle East was?"

"Let me guess—it was in Lebanon."

"Yes. Resistance to Israeli occupation was run by a group of political parties. Among them was a Christian woman who blew herself up in an Israeli barricade. The atrocities committed by Christians in the Middle East over the last forty years are no less than those committed by Muslims. But here it's as much about politics as anything else."

The revelation stunned me. I wasn't there to talk religion, but I had to follow up. "Christians, as in those who believe that Jesus was the Son of God?"

"Yes, Christians. To call yourself a Christian in the world today can be deeply misunderstood. As can be calling yourself a Muslim. I am a Muslim, and I prefer to speak of love. If we can love one another, then the world will find God, as Isa himself insisted."

The thoughts swirled in my head. How little I, a world traveler, really know.

"Like the Christians here, the Hezbollah has used many disturbing tactics, but—"

Sophie interrupted, begging to differ.

"But it's true, Sophie," Samir insisted. "No one is without blame here! But the Hezbollah is seen by all in Lebanon, including most who oppose them, as a party of liberation. They are like your own revolutionaries, resisting the English control of the colonies, yes? Until this past week, they have never, not once, turned their guns on any Lebanese, only on Israel, seen as the occupiers by most. Al-Qaeda is very different, rejected by Hezbollah. Hamas . . . Well, Hamas is a different story altogether."

Carl chuckled and slapped my knee. "Welcome to Beirut, buddy."

I left well enough alone. If all went according to an ever-changing plan, we would meet with the Hamas in the West Bank in about a week.

I watched Samir and couldn't help thinking that we had found a true Samaritan. Like the Samaritan in the parable, Samir's language was love. And like the Samaritans two thousand years ago, Samir, as a Muslim, would be considered a heretic by many.

Later that night Carl and I stood alone on that same balcony, looking south. The impenetrable border with Israel lay roughly seventy-five miles directly south. Damascus awaited us to the east, the same distance away. On open American freeways it would take us only an hour of driving to reach either destination as the crow flies. An Israeli F-16 could make the trip in a few minutes. From that balcony we felt we could reach out and touch the world.

"So here we are in Beirut, only a stone's throw from where the Samaritans lived during the time of Christ," I said. "But the only way there is to go all the way around."

Carl pointed east as he spoke. "Beirut to Damascus, Syria, by car. Rob will take us, and Samir will come. It's too dangerous without Samir." He traced the horizon south. "Damascus to Amman, Jordan. Just you and me. Then across the border to the West Bank, if they'll let us. Then into Jerusalem. Then north to the Samaritans." He lowered his hand.

"Then home," I said.

"Then home. After we finish what we came to do."

"Any luck with the Samaritans?"

"It's being worked on."

The Samaritans

To understand the significance of the parable of the Samaritan, one must look back into history for a moment. It's hard to fully measure the verbal quicksand Jesus stepped into when he chose to cast a Samaritan as the hero of his famous parable. Not only was the enmity between "Jerusalem Jews" and Samaritans centuries old even then, but in fact it was as bitter as any divide today.

To those in Jesus' audience, Samaritans were nothing more than a gang of mixed-breed, fratricidal religious heretics. By the time of Christ, the schism between Jews and Samaritans had grown into one of the most entrenched and mystifying political and religious feuds ever to afflict the Middle East. Which is saying a great deal, for the Middle East is hardly a stranger to feuds.

To a Jew of Christ's day, no insult was worse or more likely to provoke an instant fistfight than to simply mutter the word *Samaritan*. Crossing each other at the occasional highway intersection, Jews and Samaritans were as likely to start throwing rocks at each other, or even weapons, to avoid each other's path. Truly, the Jews' hatred for their northern neighbors was far more than just disgust or derision.

Sound familiar? It is like a story taken from today's headlines.

Despite this fact, Jesus seemed to know something more. Across the span of his life, he betrayed a soft spot for these wretched outsiders. He brought them up on several occasions when he was teaching. He intentionally passed through Samaritan towns instead of crossing the Jordan to avoid them, as most Jews did. One of his most insightful and compassionate personal encounters was with a Samaritan, the woman at the well.

Like many of the worst feuds, this one's genesis is so obscure and so little known that finding its absolute beginning becomes a daunting search.

If you follow the Samaritan account of history, you would need to travel as far back as 1200 B.C., to the time of Joshua. Shortly following Joshua's death, Eli the high priest left Moses' desert tabernacle on Mount Gerizim and built a second one under his rule among the hills of Shiloh. This, in the eyes of many, created an illegitimate priesthood, a false place of worship, and set the stage for the later northern/southern split within Israel. Eventually the northern kingdom would repudiate the Jerusalem temple in no uncertain terms, instead locating the seat of God's presence high atop Mount Gerizim. They would be accused of practicing idolatry in the capital, Samaria, just south of the current border between Israel and Lebanon.

But the feud began in earnest around 722 B.C., when an Assyrian ruler named Sargon II swept through the meager defenses of Israel's northern kingdom and conquered Samaria. Rather than push south into Judah, which had stayed militarily strong, he was satisfied to carry away thousands from the northern kingdom and resettle them amid other far-flung provinces of his empire—part of his cruel practice of destroying enemies by shattering their sense of belonging and heritage.

Those taken to Assyria became lamented as the Ten Lost Tribes, one of history's most mysterious disappearing acts.

Hundreds of years later, during the closing days of the Persian exile, Ezra and Nehemiah returned home, only to find it occupied by a group of apparent squatters who called themselves Jews—and who indeed took great offense at being thought of otherwise.

Whether these people deserved the title depends upon which group you believe. The Samaritans claimed to be descended from a contingent Sargon had left behind, a remnant of ethnically intact Jewry.

But more traditional sources advance a different story. The Talmud, the Bible passage 2 Kings, and the renowned historian Josephus alike claim that the evil Assyrian ruler Sargon sent back a diverse and piecemeal bunch of pagans to repopulate the land. Second Kings 17 indicates that these newcomers expressed interest in worshiping Yahweh only after a plague of wild lions killed many in their group.

Realizing that they knew nothing of the local deity, these heathen squatters pleaded for help to the Assyrian king. He promptly complied by sending back an exiled Jewish priest to instruct them in the Jewish creeds. Eventually, though, these foreigners were believed to have mixed his teaching with their own religions to form a witches' brew of half-baked, heretical beliefs.

One equivalent might be the hijacking of Islam by Islamic fundamentalists or the absconding of Christianity by Crusaders. Heretics who use religion to further their own political cause.

The result made for an awkward reunion upon the return of the Israelites from exile under Ezra and Nehemiah many years later. The Samaritans initially welcomed the Israelites home like long-lost brethren, even offering to help them rebuild the temple. However, finding little in common with the strange-looking and foreign-speaking group, Ezra rejected the offer in contemptuous terms. The rebuff incensed the Samaritans, who promptly turned into determined opponents, sending complaining letters to King Cyrus and launching a campaign of intimidation and interference.

The Samaritans became nothing less than freedom fighters against a much larger group of occupiers who sought to disband them.

Despite the opposition, Jerusalem and the temple were successfully rebuilt. The two groups settled into enduring enmity. The Samaritans worshiped in the temple on Mount Gerizim and claimed to be the only legitimate representation of Judaism, and the Jews worshiped in the newly built temple in Jerusalem.

The final break came in 167 B.C. when the Seleucid king Antiochus Epiphanes ruled the land. Striving to Hellenize his whole kingdom and standardize all forms of worship, Antiochus proclaimed himself the incarnation of Zeus and condemned to death anyone refusing to worship him. Sensing a danger of genocide, the Samaritans petitioned him to spare them at any cost.

Their request was granted and their people saved, but at a high price. The Samaritans would become highly Hellenized. Worse still, the insulting request would become the last straw, forcing a final, hostile breach between the Jews and the Samaritans.

It would also mark the lowest point in each of their respective histories. Antiochus erected an altar to Zeus in the Jerusalem temple and sacrificed a pig there, an act known to history as the "abomination of desolation." He also forced the worshipers at Mount Gerizim to dedicate their temple to Zeus. One of his successors destroyed the structure entirely in 128 B.C.

Under the Romans, Samaritan culture experienced a resurgence. Their temple was rebuilt, and an ambitious high priest established a liturgy, complete with the Samaritans' own version of the Torah. By Jesus' time, the Samaritans had matured into a large and established culture occupying a sizable chunk of Palestine's northern hills between Judea and Galilee. The chilly standoff with their southern relatives had hardened over time into a stable, if implacable, animosity.

Jews cursed Samaritans in their synagogues. They barred them from being witnesses in their courts. They denied them the opportunity to convert to Judaism and stated that they were excluded from any kind of afterlife.

Geographically and physically, both sides went to considerable lengths to avoid contact with each other. Because of the Samaritans' frequent hostility, and because Jews believed they could become contaminated by passing through Samaritan territory, Jews traveling from Judea to Galilee would cross over the Jordan and avoid Samaria entirely.

In effect, the Samaritans of Jesus' day were treated as a spiritual brand of lepers, to be avoided at all costs and vocally condemned by any respectable Jew. They were openly counted as enemies, hated for their fallacious religious beliefs. They were hardly considered human. Idolaters worthy of death.

Shortly before Jesus gave his famous teaching regarding the Samaritans, two of his most revered disciples, James and John, had suggested to him that he call down fire from heaven to destroy the Samaritans. It was into this context that Jesus issued the statement that, among others as audacious and contrarian, would soon get him killed.

The parallels between the Samaritans of Jesus' day and feuding enemies in our own can hardly be misplaced in the light of this history. You could change the dates and names and be speaking of the conflict in the Middle East today.

Whether you are Muslim and consider Jesus the greatest of all prophets, or whether you are a Christian and consider him the Son of God, Jesus' claim that the heretic in his story was the one following the greatest commandment to love your neighbor is immediately offensive.

Perhaps that's why so few follow that teaching, even to this day.

Late that first night in Beirut I called and talked to my wife at length for the first time since leaving the United States. She was in Austin, moving us into a new house, and her problems had to do with delayed furniture deliveries—a matter of considerable and normally understandable frustration for her.

But in my current state of mind the only frustration I felt was that she couldn't possibly feel the frustrations that I was grappling with. I didn't even try to explain them.

As I lay in bed talking to her on Sophie's iPhone, I inserted myself into her world for a half an hour, thankful for the escape. I love you, Lee Ann. I love and miss you like I never have.

TRANSCRIPT

Ted: What is the greatest concern in your life?

Palestinian cab driver: To make a good living. I am fortunate to have this job, but many cannot make the money they need to eat. I want to live at peace in Beirut, my home, and raise my family.

Ted: What do you think of Jesus' teaching that we should love our enemies?

Palestinian cab driver: Nobody will listen to this. They talk, but it's too late for that.

Sheik Mohammed Hussein Fadlallah

Beirut by day. An incredibly diverse city with a Starbucks and a Kentucky Fried Chicken on one street and a bombed-out building two streets over. What surprised me most was just how normal everything appeared. Cars honked as they clogged the streets, pedestrians strode down the boardwalk dressed in everything from miniskirts to hijabs.

Two thoughts crowded my mind. One, the Mutawa of Saudi Arabia, from where we'd just come, would wear out their striking canes in a few hours in this cosmopolitan paradise. Two, didn't these fools realize that there were tanks in the streets?

"You see, this is Beirut!" Samir said, spreading his hands. "You have to love it. Fighting in the streets one day, and the next"—he snapped his fingers—"people everywhere. They are used to it. Life must go on."

Carl laughed. "That's about it."

But all signs of Chili's restaurants and Internet cafes soon disappeared as we made our way south, toward the Shatila Palestinian refugee camp, a ghetto of sorts that had been established for Palestinian refugees who'd been displaced from Israel during the 1948 war, sixty years ago. It was there that we first encountered the story of Nicole, which we have already begun sharing in segments throughout this book. Looking into the haunting eyes of Palestinians still trapped in the camp after three generations sent my imagination scurrying after their story.

I asked our driver, Mohammed, why the Lebanese government didn't just make the Palestinian refugees citizens like they did everyone else born in Beirut. He shrugged. "Refugees make a better story for the world."

They live in absolute squalor, and they proudly display large banners with the face of their savior, Hassan Nasrallah, the leader of the Hezbollah. It is Hezbollah that brings free blankets in the winters. It's Hezbollah that brings toys for the children and food for their parents. While American bombers leave white vapor ribbons high overhead on their way to kill more children, Hezbollah hands out candy to these children.

At least that's the impression on the streets, where young minds observe and form lasting opinions.

A smile came to Samir's face as we drove away. "Teddy, write this. After the Israeli invasion in 2006, Sophie and I did a huge humanitarian relief project for displaced people. Late one night a man from Hezbollah told me I needed to come immediately. So I went and it was one of Hassan Nasrallah's top men. He told me he'd heard that my wife, Sophie, was passing out very dangerous items in the refugee camp. What was this? I couldn't believe it. Two days later they came to my house and showed me the T-shirt with the damaging message. The shirt said 'Push Up.' It was a shirt promoting exercise, you know. But to the Arab, the *P* is like a *B* and they thought it was a shirt promoting President Bush: 'Bush Up.' When I explained, we all had a good laugh. But it could have gone very badly."

We drove by whole city blocks that were now holes in the ground next to intact five- and six-story apartments—leftovers from the war between Israel and the Hezbollah in the summer of 2006 in which Israel bombed many targets in Beirut. Rebuilding takes time; they hadn't gotten to these yet.

"Pull over, pull over," Carl said.

The driver honked and cut across two lanes. It hardly mattered; no one uses lanes in Beirut.

"Follow me."

Carl led me into a vacant apartment and up four flights of stairs, out onto a landing from where we had a view of a full city block.

"I was in this apartment, visiting a friend, when a massive explosion blew out the windows. We ducked, then ran to the balcony to see what had happened. See that apartment?"

He pointed to a pile of rubble that had evidently once been an apartment. "It was boiling smoke from a direct hit from an Israeli war plane peeling away above us. But what really scared me were the two Jeeps full of Hezbollah fighters that came piling out from the garage below us. We were up here, eating lunch, totally oblivious to the fact that the Hezbollah used this very building as a staging area. I've always wondered if the Israelis meant to take out this building and got that one by mistake."

"Close call," I said.

Carl laughed. "Close call."

We arrived at a quiet neighborhood ten minutes later, focused on our interview with Sheik Fadlallah. It was the first interview he'd granted in several years, and the security around the building was significant. We parked a good fifty yards from the building, were relieved of our cameras and recorders, then were ushered through metal detectors before being led to a small office.

Quiet had replaced the jovial atmosphere that typically followed both Carl and Samir. The air seemed thick.

"You do realize what's happening, don't you?" Carl asked, crossing his legs. "The interviews going forward, starting with this one, are unprecedented. Nobody gets in here. Not ABC, not NBC, not CBS, no one."

"Why us?"

"Because it's us. We're with Samir." Carl laughed.

The sheik's assistant closed the door behind himself and shook our hands warmly. "They are preparing the security. Welcome. Welcome, my friends. First I would like to say some things."

"Could we record you?" Carl asked. "They took our recorder."

The assistant hesitated, then left the room. "One moment." He returned five minutes later with the small white Sanyo recorder and handed it to me. "Clean."

I took that as a sign I could record, so I turned it on.

The assistant launched into a speech that seemed utterly genuine, though well rehearsed, and was softly spoken, if delivered in a bit of a rush.

TRANSCRIPT

Assistant: Fadlallah is completely independent. No government party can impose on him. Hezbollah was growing in 1982, but there wasn't a prominent figure in the organization. At that time, media started giving a title to the spiritual leader of Hezbollah.

The title was false because we are not connected to Hezbollah, although he did have an effect on Hezbollah. Fadlallah's effect was more spiritual than physical. This title came from the West.

After around twelve years, Fadlallah started to show the world that as a Muslim authority he was not physically connected to Hezbollah. Fadlallah is independent. He has many followers, though. He is very well known. Mohammad Sadr is thought to be one of the most influential Shiite leaders at that time. Fadlallah and he were friends. Now Mohammad is dead. He was killed by Saddam Hussein.

Mr. Fadlallah's books are about dialogue and social aspects of Islam. He has written over one hundred books. He has written four books of poetry. Through his poetry, you might understand his character. He is the most aggressive in positive aspirations of the Qur'an. For example, he believes a woman is free and independent. No one, not even her father or husband, can force her to do something. Also, he uses science. He is very intelligent. He is very liberal concerning women and science. He has modern teachings.

Still, they all want to kill him. In 1981 Saddam Hussein told his people in Beirut to attack his house for political reasons. One of the sheik's bodyguards was killed.

Then the American CIA tried to assassinate him through some local Lebanese people on March 8, 1985. A car bomb with four hundred pounds of explosives killed eighty people and wounded two hundred. The operation was financed through the ambassador of Saudi Arabia, but it was coordinated by the CIA. The U.S. Congress knew nothing. The reporter Woodward has reported on this. The CIA director Casey admitted to this when he was dying.

Then in the mid-eighties Saddam bombed his house. The rocket almost hit his own room.

Then in 1987 an Israeli spy entered a mosque with weapons.

And finally two years ago, in 2006, Israel completely demolished his house in an attempt to kill him.

Fadlallah agrees on what Islam says. In practical thinking, in America if something wrong is done to you, do you react? Do you condemn the sin or the human being? Do you punish those who killed someone? Does Christianity agree that the whole world stay without law? Did Jesus allow the thieves to control the temple?

The phone rang and the assistant answered it, listened for a moment, then set it back down in its cradle. "They are ready."

We were ushered into a long room for tea. The sheik was already seated at the end, like a king in long, flowing robes, waiting to meet his guests. An entire camera crew with full lighting was in position and would record every word—nothing could be taken out of context. It was the first interview they'd granted in several years, and they were taking it very seriously.

Sheik Fadlallah is an elderly man with a wizened face and kind, droopy eyes. A long white beard reaches down to his chest.

He pushed himself slowly to his feet and took our hands with a feeble grip. I don't know what I was expecting—anything but this meek mouse of man who looked every bit the poet and nothing like the kind of fellow who could a harm a flea.

But then it is the power of this man's pen that makes him so dangerous. We had come to the Middle East to talk to ideologues like Sheik Fadlallah. If anyone influences the hearts of millions, it's this seventy-three-year-old man who originally came from Iraq.

We call him Sheik Fadlallah, but to those he serves, he is the Ayatollah Fadlallah, and not without cause. He is one of two people in the entire Arab world who speaks the mind of the Shiite Muslim. The second would be the Ayatollah Sistani of Iraq, a man of equal import.

The title *ayatollah* literally means "sign of God." Both Sistani in Iraq and Fadlallah hold the more distinguished title of grand ayatollah, given to a select few recognized internationally for their expertise on Islam and sharia law.

Fadlallah is best known in the West as the spiritual voice of Hezbollah, although he would be quick to point out that he is *not* Hezbollah, because Hezbollah is political and he is not partisan but lives for dialogue and reconciliation. But he can be considered the voice of Hezbollah in the sense that he represents the spirit of Hezbollah at its foundation, which came out of the early eighties as a movement for his people. Indeed, the term Hezbollah was first used in 1984 as Fadlallah was rising in influence.

No matter how you unravel Sheik Fadlallah's tangled history, one fact remains: This aged man who smiled at me with drooping eyes was unequivocally one of the most influential ideologues in the Muslim world today.

I was eager to hear his thoughts.
As always, unfiltered.

TRANSCRIPT

Ted: May I record?

Ayatollah Fadlallah: Of course.

Ted: I hear you are a poet.

Ayatollah Fadlallah: Yes. We believe that writing poetry is an expression of the inner being, so your fiction writing is nice. When truth and imagination are mixed together, it gives a nice flavor.

Ted: I'd like to ask some rather nontypical questions to help us know you.

Ayatollah Fadlallah: I think dialogue is the only way to reach all people. And I would like to present that a nation of people is not just a bloc. Some people in the Middle East have a negative view of the West, and it's the other way around too. The negative view is caused because the people here confuse the government of America with the people of America. And the Americans do the same thing. I don't think there is any stupid question, so you can ask anything.

Ted: What kind of car to you drive?

Ayatollah Fadlallah: (Chuckles and looks at his entourage, who chuckle with him) My car is a gray Mercedes, but I don't drive any longer. I would kill myself!

Ted: What makes you laugh?

Ayatollah Fadlallah: First of all, I smile for any feeling that seems to agree with my psychological state. I laugh at jokes. I also laugh when the full moon shines its light. Also I smile at the water that comes from the mountains. I have a verse of poetry that says, "I'm the one who creates his own poetry and I feel pleasure in the depth of my service." I don't believe life is all sadness. But there is both joy and sadness in the world.

Ted: Do you have a family?

Ayatollah Fadlallah: I am married and have five children, all grown now. My son Jalal is a very important Shiite leader in Lebanon.

Ted: Do your grandchildren make you laugh?

Ayatollah Fadlallah: When I stay with my grandchildren, they just make me happy. Or when my grandchildren act funny. I believe that when you are with the children, the most important thing is to turn yourself into a child.

Ted: Jesus said, "Unless you become like a child, you cannot enter the kingdom of heaven."

Ayatollah Fadlallah: Muhammad said, "If you have a boy, try to talk and think like he talks and thinks." I used to carry my grandchildren on my back. Once I was praying, and we kneel down when we pray. So the grandchildren came and sat on my back. I didn't finish praying; I let them stay and I didn't yell at them. They told me I am a good camel and they were good riders. (Chuckles. His entourage chuckles with him.)

Ted: Besides poetry, what other hobbies do you have?

Ayatollah Fadlallah: All my hobbies have to do with writing. It is said that I have the largest personal library in the entire Arab world. I also like to deal with social and political issues and have founded many foundations and mosques. This is my life. I also have a dialogue with children. I don't believe in religion most. I used to talk about man's love to his fellow men. I believe that we ought to love him. I believe we should live with humanitarians.

Ted: Do you like sports?

Ayatollah Fadlallah: I like sports, but my health doesn't allow me to practice any sports. Lebanon has a soccer team. We are pretty good. Sports are good for the body.

Ted: What makes you cry?

Ayatollah Fadlallah: I usually cry before the hands of God because I love God. I cry out of love. I feel that the love of God is the greatest love because it's unconditional love. I love God out of his greatness. There is a prayer that says, "I love you not because of what you give me, but out of the greatness of yourself. I love the beauty of your nature. And you are beautiful and you love me."

Ted: When was the last time you cried besides in prayer?

Ayatollah Fadlallah: You are asking very interesting questions, not the common kind. (Holds out his hand to his personal assistant, who looks as if he might want to object. Takes a deep breath.) Someone I knew was ill and he died, so I suffered a lot. It was a few years ago. I always feel sad when innocent people are victims of the arrogant West or the extremists around here. I am always sad for the Palestinians or even the Jews who suffer. I'm not talking about politics but about humanity. I believe that politics should be just. We call for peace in the world on justice.

Ted: What is your hope for the Christian children in America?

Ayatollah Fadlallah: I sympathize with children all over the world. If I oppose the policies of America, it doesn't mean I oppose the American people. I would love to be a friend of the American people and all other nations. There is a verse that says, "If you have any problems with a person, you have to solve it so that it turns an enemy into a friend." Islam tells us to be friends of the whole world.

Ted: What would you say specifically to the mothers and fathers, to those in America who have lost sons and daughters in Iraq?

Ayatollah Fadlallah: I would tell them with all my love and condolences that you have lost your children in the wrong place. There is no reason or right for the Americans to occupy Iraq. The terrorists of bin Laden have killed thousands of Americans, but the Americans have killed tens of thousands of Arabs. In the 1940s the Arabs believed that America wanted to help their nations and they were peaceful. But that has changed. If an American asks, "Why do you hate us?" we would say, "Why should we love you with all your policies?" We love the American people but not the Administration.

Ted: Jesus teaches us to love our enemies. Do you believe we should love our enemies? As followers of Jesus and Muhammad, should you love Bush even though you hate his policies?

Ayatollah Fadlallah: (Without a beat) When someone commits a sin, he is the one responsible for his actions. So he's the one who has hidden his humanity.

Ted: Would you advise me to pray for Bush, as an American?

Ayatollah Fadlallah: We pray for all those who are misguided and who persecute others. We ask people to change their ways.

Ted: Jesus' greatest commandment is that we should love our neighbors as we love ourselves. What are your thoughts on this teaching?

Ayatollah Fadlallah: Islam tells people to have mercy and be kind. Islam tells people to have dialogue with the Jews and Christians. They should never have aggression on any people. Only in self-defense. There is a verse that says God wants you to be pious. The Qur'an says the closest to

Muslims are the Christians because they are humble and spiritual. There
should be peace between Muslims, Christians, and Jews.

Ted: Do you love Christians and Jews, putting policies aside?

Ayatollah Fadlallah: I open up to Christians and Jews, but not on Israeli
Jews and not on occupying Christians. The Zionists don't have the right to
occupy Palestine. It's not just.

Assistant: Now the sheik must rest. We are finished?

Ten minutes later we were back on the road, driving in silence. As
much is communicated by what isn't said as by what is. Late into the
night we would discuss both. But here our purpose is simply to report what was said and what wasn't, not to offer any opinions or con-
clusions from the words of the powerful ideologues we interviewed.

"So, tomorrow the Hezbollah?" I asked after a long silence.

"No," Samir said. "It's not yet confirmed. I think the next day."

"Still not yet?"

"These are not easy things, Teddy. You want to go where no man
is going and I can't just pull a string. Do you have any idea how
many in your own government would like this leader we are trying
to meet dead?" He blew out some air. "But it will happen, I am con-
fident."

"Just a slight correction," I pointed out. "This was Carl's idea, not
mine."

Carl laughed. Carl always laughs. The scary part is that his laugh
is genuine. He really does find levity in my attempt to place any
blame for what might or could happen on him.

But by now I was growing bold myself, if only a tiny bit, and I
smiled with him.

"Tomorrow, Baalbek," Carl said. "Hezbollah headquarters."

But first we must return to Nicole. I had spent more time with
my source earlier and jotted down copious notes. An eye-opening
story was beginning to emerge from the deep, and I was eager to
dive back in.

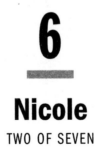

Nicole

E-MAIL FROM NICOLE

Dear Doug,

I was at the camp clinic helping bandage an actual gunshot wound (received in a short machine-gun skirmish that I actually slept through last night!) when one of the workers handed me your letter. Imagine that, a real letter rather than an e-mail. And it made it! Though he said delivery was a fifty/fifty deal.

Just the sight of your messy handwriting and bad spelling on the envelope was so cool. I realized how horribly I miss you, little brother. I sat there, in this hellish place right out of a nightmare, and almost broke into tears thinking about you starting college all by yourself halfway around the world. I had to take a break just to try and swallow this load of guilt and second-guess whether I was nuts to have come out here on this mad search at all.

I've been here three weeks today and am just now starting to feel halfway adjusted. Out of necessity, I've built up this whole set of coping skills to help me get through being in this place. The best of all will come as no surprise to you: It's my bike. But it's a lot more than recreation for me here, or even exercise or competition. It's my freedom. Without spending tons of my money for cabs or a private vehicle, it's my only way of breaking out of the camp and trying to make headway on the real reason I'm here. I bought a cheap GPS unit off of some hawker on this fancy boardwalk called the Corniche, so after I've gone as far as I want, I just check my location and work my way back.

Better yet, I've started to meet people and find out things about Shatila's history. I felt like such a fool asking people about anything that happened around 1982. I just assumed that, it being Beirut, killings like what she described just sort of happened all the time. But what Mom told us about turned out to be one of the most shocking massacres in all of Middle East history, I'm told.

It sent a shiver down my spine, repeating Mom's secret history, only to find out it wasn't secret at all but actually a world event that claimed maybe thousands of innocent people and is known in the history books as the Shatila Massacre.

I got my best account of what happened from the neatest, most interesting man named Walid. He's kind of the community know-it-all, because he runs a hookah bar. I met him a few days ago and told him everything. I have to admit, the place was a bit creepy for me, mostly men. I'm actually going there after work today with an American girlfriend named Sandra. She's been there before, and she knows how to hang there without getting too many come-ons from the single men.

I'm rambling. Okay, a hookah is basically a big wooden and glass bong. I tried a puff. The smoke is quite smooth and fruity. It's a social thing. You rent this contraption called a nargileh pipe and pay for a dose of marinated tobacco, and everybody gets their own mouthpiece. It takes a long time, so you get a chance to talk as you mellow out.

The owner, Walid, sees everything, because his bar sits right at the eastern edge of the camp. He sits right out on the farthest table and just smiles at everybody going by, nursing one drink and enjoying the view.

Anyway, Walid has a reputation for knowing everything and everyone who's worth knowing. So I made a point of saying hi to him one morning on my bike. The next day I stopped and talked to him. He knew things about the events of 1982 that nobody else did. I told him my whole story, who I was looking for, and right away he thought of someone I should meet. Somebody well connected, he said. He's a very devout Muslim with a deep hatred for the Druze, one of the Muslim sects in Lebanon known for its heresy and brutality, according to Walid.

But Walid sounds promising. I'm also slowly meeting some of the camp mothers. I've been volunteering extra hours at this place called the

Palestinian Youth Center. It's desperately understaffed and underequipped, of course. There are about six computers for several hundred kids. But I play with them, even teach some of them about cycling. The mothers don't speak much English, or I would have made much more progress. But one of them does, and she translates for the others.

I told one of them the other day that I was related to a family in the camp. They laughed, reminding me that I was an American. I realize now that I have to be careful, learn what I can before speaking too quickly. It hit me, my translator could honestly be my cousin. How would I know? How could I possibly find out? I'll figure it out, one way or another.

Gotta go. Sandra is waiting her turn at the computer.

Kisses, Nicole

BY NATURE an outgoing and engaging young woman, Nicole Wagner wasted no time learning the patterns of daily life in a Lebanese refugee camp. Her official duties, those for which she had specifically volunteered, consisted of a single four-hour shift as a medical orderly in the refugee camp's clinic. After that work was finished, however, her day was her own, and Nicole hardly wasted a minute of that time in pursuit of her quest.

One of the more popular hangouts for men proved to be a broad, low-slung building along a busy street on the camp's eastern edge. There they could be seen sitting for hours, reclining in comfortable chairs, sucking on the ends of long, black tubes.

"Hookah bar," she was told when making her initial queries about the building's function. She had to look up the term to learn that hookah bars are a fixture of daily life throughout the Middle East. Essentially a coffee and tobacco bar, the lounges promote social harmony by allowing patrons to smoke *shisha,* or flavored tobacco, from central nargileh pipes, or hookahs, placed at each table. Those who run such establishments invariably become some of the most connected patrons of their communities.

Which was why Nicole quickly made the acquaintance of Walid Khaleem, age fifty-three, who had operated the Bekáa House hookah bar just outside Shatila for nearly thirty years. The man was a walking encyclopedia of the comings and goings in that part of the city.

He was also a very religious Muslim, who faithfully prayed five times each day and dedicated himself to the five pillars of Islam.

As it turned out, more than idle curiosity had once occupied Walid's hookah bar. There was no secret that the Palestinian refugee camp was actually a beehive of covert activity for numerous factions, including the Hezbollah, who'd befriended the refugees long ago. The camp even hosted (albeit only on rare occasions) meetings of Israeli Mossad agents seeking to initiate discreet communications with Lebanese factions.

As such, Shatila had once been far more than a neglected blight on the chic outer skin of modern Beirut. Up until three years earlier, it had also been one of the most scrutinized places in the country. To understand how and why, one only need take a peek at the bar's history.

Most of the city's underground traffic blended in perfectly with the normal human currents in and out of Shatila. But a trained eye could detect the slight anomalies. There was the overloaded food truck. The slightly overdressed visitor. The visit from a well-known leader.

Walid, the owner of Bekáa House, was well entrenched as a local legend of sorts. He was the rare kind of man you might initially write off as just a neighborhood personality, until you climbed higher in the halls of power and influence. There you would discover a renowned and trusted figure who was respected for his neutrality.

Asked point-blank, Walid would claim only an allegiance to the greater welfare of Lebanon. Within those broad ground rules, he did not discriminate among Islamic and Christian, Western and Eastern, Shiite and Sunni, Armenian and Catholic and Greek Orthodox. He greeted Hamas and Mossad with equal deference and discretion, which made him a rare bird indeed. The only exception to his general benevolence was his implacable hatred for the Druze.

Because the area was rarely frequented by the wealthy and well connected, it was the perfect spot for officials to meet in utter secrecy. Bekáa House contains hidden alcoves and meeting rooms behind beaded doorways, places where emissaries of the nearly countless Lebanese factions could haggle through the intricacies of piecing together coalition governments without the prying eyes of media, hangers-on, foreign snoops, families, and mistresses. Some of these were disguised as actual walls, opened only by the most knowledgeable tug of a velvet rope or wall ornament. There, secret talks could be held indefinitely, lubricated by copious amounts of strong coffee and, of course, hookah smoke.

There can be no doubt, Walid is a fascinating character on the stage of Lebanese politics, and by extension world politics, considering the influence of this small country. But unbeknownst to Nicole, the smiling, portly man to whom she poured out her heart two weeks after arriving in the Middle East wasn't without his demons.

Walid's greatest challenge came in 2005 during upheavals known as the Cedar Revolution. The assassination of former prime minister Rafik Hariri had triggered mass demonstrations across Lebanon, toppling the country's pro-Syrian government and triggering the withdrawal of occupying Syrian troops. World leaders made sweeping comparisons to the celebrated Prague Spring of 1968, when Czechoslovakian reformers had defied Moscow, or to Ukraine's Orange or Georgia's Rose revolutions.

It was Lebanon's great moment of liberation, and it was also Walid's moment. During those heady days, the bar became a de facto headquarters of the entire movement. Planning meetings for million-member protest marches and new governments stretched long into the night. Walid had truly arrived as an agent of influence. In fact, many whispered that when it was all over he would be offered a cabinet position in the government.

It never happened.

When the new Siniora government was eventually formed, one of its leaders—a man whom Walid came to hate like no other—was quoted describing Walid as "the man who cleaned our tables" and a mere tobacco slinger with no stature. The chairs aligned themselves without a place for him.

In truth, no one received a seat at Lebanon's political table unless some concession or tip of the hat was owed to his personal faction. And Walid had no personal faction; that was his trademark. He was the man whom everyone liked but to whom no one owed enough to share power with him. His own famous neutrality had done him in.

For the first time in his life, Walid became a vengeful man.

He started with the only area in which people truly *did* owe him: the free hookah he had been dispensing for years. It turned out that Walid might have dispensed plenty of freebies, but he'd been keeping records as well. Soon factional leaders found themselves served with overdue bills dating back decades for tens of thousands of dollars in tobacco and food charges. When the bills went unpaid, Walid took action. He filed claims in small claims courts, no matter how modest. He hired walkers to picket outside his enemies' homes and offices, wearing placards whose slogans embarrassed them by name. In the case of the man who had disparaged him, he filed police charges for theft and pressed the charges to his utmost.

When the stubborn resisted, he took out ads in the newspapers, detailing the dates and times of meetings not only politically sensitive but also life threatening. He published the dates of trysts leaders had conducted in the Bekáa House with their mistresses and lovers, whom he also named. He even threatened, in several cases, to serve the CIA, the Mossad, and the Syrian Embassy with bills of their own. The elite got the point.

According to rumors, some highly placed power broker even dispatched a group of Phalangist thugs to go "talk some sense" into Walid. The three young men were found two days later lying in a Harbor District junk pile, unconscious and near death, most of their bones broken. Word had it that Walid had enlisted the protection of a local militia to provide the Bekáa House with protection—something he had never needed to do before.

Within weeks, all of Beirut society knew that the once self-effacing Walid had become a man with a grievance and that his grievances were better off addressed. Sitting at his bar, Walid received phone call after phone call about the chaos he'd created. He listened and laughed at last, his first occasions for smiling since the whole affair had begun.

No, Walid would never again be thought of as a mere lounge owner. He was a lounge owner who could bring down governments if you crossed him.

He was still living down the aftermath of his revenge campaign when Nicole first came careening down his street. The sight of her immediately sparked both his suspicion and pure curiosity.

Delicate matters were also underway during that very period, and for the first time, the Bekáa House was not playing a role. Knowing this made Walid livid, because in the back of his mind he had always hoped for some kind of reconciliation, a second coming of sorts back into the ranks of the connected.

Once again, he was being naive. His name had been forever erased from the old map, just as his life would be if he violated the customs of discretion again.

Hezbollah was quietly moving to take over power from the weak Lebanese government, and those in office were powerless to stop the juggernaut. Many of the Cedar Revolution's gains were in danger of being rolled back in one swift move. The most delicate of diplomatic touches was required to avert disaster, and the Bekáa House would have been the perfect venue. Only it was now a political no-man's-land.

The truth was, Walid still had some scores to settle. He was far from finished exacting revenge from those who had shamed him. And those very people were blacklisting him from any future influence.

On the very morning of some tense negotiations between backdoor representatives of the Lebanese government and Hezbollah, Walid saw a head of long hair fly past the Bekáa House's front windows.

When he finally met and spoke at length with the young American, he was shocked at the questions she was asking.

Nicole noted his reaction as she sat across from him in the corner of the hookah bar, and she knew immediately that she had hit a vein. But she also knew that she couldn't make demands to know everything he knew; this wasn't the Middle Eastern way. She had to step carefully, accepting her role as the outsider here.

What she couldn't know was that the questions reached all the way into the highest, murkiest, and most dangerous pinnacles of Beirut's power circles, ending with an unnamed leader who had taken away Nicole's mother back in 1982. The very same man who had made disparaging remarks about Walid, shattering all of his political aspirations in the process.

Walid grew quiet, covering his shock with a simple smile. Truly, his own need for revenge might find satisfaction in Nicole's quest.

He would make a phone call on her behalf, as much for his own sake as to help her.

That first meeting between Walid and Nicole ended suddenly. The proprietor's eyes shot over Nicole's shoulder and in the space of single beat changed. Nicole would never forget the look of bitterness that replaced his amusement at her quest. One moment his eyes sparkled above a gentle smile; the next they glared past her, black and ugly.

She turned and saw that he was staring at a good-looking young man dressed in cotton slacks and a dirty white shirt who'd walked into the bar.

Walid muttered a curse. "Akram. What the hell is—" He caught himself. His voice was low, but it slashed with as much edge as if it had been a sword.

Nicole faced him again, at a loss from the fear that suddenly gripped her. In a few seconds she saw, heard, even felt the deep rifts that had torn Lebanon to shreds during its protracted civil war from 1975 to 1990.

Walid remembered his guest and forced some calm, but he was powerless to hide the hatred in his voice.

"The Druze should know they are not welcome here," he said, as if this offered enough explanation.

"Druze?" She knew about the Muslim sect but wasn't aware how deep the divide was between the devout Muslims and the Druze.

Walid diverted his eyes from hers and locked them on the young man behind her. "These are heretics who do not believe what good Muslims believe. They do not accept the final authority of Muhammad the prophet, and they do not pray."

"But they are Muslims?"

"Some would say. I do not. They do not respect all of the laws of Islam. No, they are evil."

"But they believe in one God? Muhammad, Jesus, Moses, all the prophets?"

"Yes, but they are filled with heresy. During the war, they ruthlessly butchered whole villages."

Nicole thought about asking how this was different from Muslims who'd done the same, or from Christians, like those who'd raped and murdered so many in the refugee camp during the

Shatila Massacre when her mother was there. But she knew it would be presumptuous. And what Walid said next ended the possibility of any such discussion.

"The Druze slit the throats of my two brothers in the war. Then they killed their wives and three of their children." He made a spitting motion to show disgust. "These are brutal people, worse than any terrorist who has attacked your country. I will never accept the Druze. They come to the camp to recruit fighters."

"They proselytize?"

"No. For this sect you must be born a Druze. Thank God. Now you must excuse me."

Nicole looked back at the door, but the young Druze fighter was gone.

To be continued . . .

7

Ancient Sacrifice

BAALBEK

THE DRIVE TO BAALBEK took about two hours, winding out of Beirut eastward, through the Bekáa Valley, into this ancient destination that many say would be labeled the eighth wonder of the world were it not so remote and so dangerous to visit.

Trucks spewed blue smoke as they chugged over the passes leading east; rusted cars zoomed by us on thin wheels without hubcaps. We came to our first checkpoint and I instinctively hauled out the camera.

"No, no!" Mohammed, our Palestinian driver, snapped. "You cannot!"

Carl immediately reached over and shoved his expensive camera down. "You don't want to do that, buddy."

"No pictures?"

"They'll think we're Israeli spies or something. No pictures of any military vehicles."

"What, they don't know that Google satellites are snapping pictures from above now? Besides"—I nodded at an ancient tank with a machine gunner mounted on top—"we're not exactly looking at groundbreaking technology."

"Trust me. Don't let them see the camera. At the very least, they will take it."

We came to a long bridge that spanned a deep valley. Problem was, the bridge, which looked to be almost new, was missing a huge section in the middle. Carl explained: "The Israelis bombed it two years ago during the 2006 war. It had just been rebuilt from the last time they bombed it."

Construction cranes were busy rebuilding now, but the task looked daunting to me. We were forced to wind our way down into the valley, cross a checkpoint, then climb back out.

The small town of Baalbek looked like anything but what I'd imagined. The mountaintop destination was known for two things: the ancient ruins of numerous temples built on top of each other and the Hezbollah. But I saw signs of neither.

Instead I saw a very poor town, lined with cars parked bumper to bumper on dusty streets. Every car appeared to be badly in need of repair. It seemed unlikely to me that any of these rust buckets would actually run.

We were stopped at one crowded corner as several cars backed up so that another could get out. The operation took five minutes, and no one seemed to mind the long delay. The driver of the car wishing to be liberated from his prison made of cars might have been better off walking, I thought. He'd held up dozens of cars, each for five minutes—that was a couple of man-hours wasted for one driver to work his way out of his parking spot.

But then that's Western thinking.

Carl nudged me and pointed out the window. "See that corner down there? I was here about ten years ago with some friends, solving the world's problems, when suddenly a mob of about . . . I don't know, twenty or thirty started screaming that they were going to kill us."

"Kill you? Serious?"

"They didn't even know what we were doing, just some angry few who obviously felt threatened by Westerners here. Never happened again, just that one time."

Let's hope it stays that way, I thought.

Every society has its heroes, and the Middle East is no exception.

Their faces are plastered on buildings and hung from lampposts. Here it's not Brad Pitt or Angelina Jolie; it's the shaper of this society, Hassan Nasrallah, or other clerics who have pointed the way before, often martyred and now honored. The people, not the government, idolize them and display their pictures. This is their *People* magazine.

These are the superstars of the Middle East. Muftis and sheiks and ideologues. This is why Carl and I sought to speak to them above all others on our quest.

We managed to navigate our way through the town and came immediately to massive pillars that rose against the skyline like sentinels guarding terrible secrets beyond. The bustle of the streets gave way to a quiet wilderness sanctuary, and within a single turn we found ourselves facing the famous ruins of Baalbek, which means "the place of Baal."

Ten minutes later, Carl and I climbed the fifty broad marble steps with a guide named Charbil, who spoke perfect English, and stepped past the pillars towering twenty meters into an expansive scene that took my breath away. The ruins looked to run half a mile in, with towering granite pillars perfectly formed, carved temple walls, steps leading nowhere. I had been instantly transported thousands of years back and stood in the cradle of history.

"Wow."

Carl nodded. "Yeah, wow. I've been here twenty or thirty times and every time it's still wow."

I'd been to Greek ruins before, to the Parthenon, famed worldwide for its majestic pillars, but this . . . These ruins shamed any I'd ever laid eyes on before. We were the only visitors that day.

"People know about this?" Of course they did, I knew that.

"They do, but not many are willing to risk life and limb to get here."

Thank you for the reminder, Carl.

We stepped in, climbed to the tallest platform in the ruins, and stood on some rocks overlooking the entire region. To our right, a long row of columns reached into the sky, survivors of the wars and earthquakes that have shaken the pass since they were built thousands of years ago.

The small town we'd jig-jagged our way through lay below us in silence now. And behind the town rose a tall hill topped by a military installation, now occupied by the Lebanese army.

"See that building up there?" Carl pointed to a small shack on the hill. "That's where the Hezbollah supposedly kept the American Terry Anderson captive for so long. This is where it all started for them."

What is amazing about the archaeology in Baalbek is the unique tale it tells of changing religion. Behind us were the remains of the Phoenician temple to Baal, the god to whom ancient worshipers sacrificed animals and children. On top and around these excavated ruins from which Baalbek takes its name stands the two-thousand-year-old columns from the Jupiter temple, built by the Romans. Among these ruins lies what remains of a Byzantine (Christian) church, and finally, the ruins of the walls of a Muslim citadel and mosque.

Nearby is Mount Carmel, where the prophet Elijah went head to head with the four hundred prophets of Baal and had them all slaughtered.

In Egypt we'd found the tale of two citadels, one Muslim, one Christian. But here in Baalbek we'd found four temples, one built upon the other as a monument to humanity's ongoing search for God.

The temple to Baal had been swallowed by the temple to Jupiter, which in turn had fallen to the temple to the Christian God, only to be replaced in time by a Muslim citadel. Nowhere else on earth can one find such a thickly layered slice of religious history.

So . . . what on God's green earth was so important about these brown hills so far out of the world's mind?

The Place of Baal

The tale of Baalbek is so ancient that only a few these days bother to tell it properly, to start all the way from a beginning. It is tangled around the deepest roots of human history. Ask many of the world's most informed experts on the recorded legends and the archeological record that help make up our understanding of history, and here is the story they will more than likely unpack for you.

It all began many thousands of years ago, long before the advent of Christ. Cursed and adrift in the world, Cain, the banished son of Adam and Eve, had wandered west of Eden in search of a safe and fertile place in which to live out his exile.

According to tradition, Cain eventually arrived at a large, grassy outcropping ringed by snowy peaks, commanding a fair valley aglow with promise. Knee-deep swirls of sweet grass stretched as far as he could see. A lively breeze lifted his grim mood, wrapping him in aromas of mulberry and cedar. His weary eyes were soothed by the sight of splendor.

But something deeper about the spot, beyond its majestic landscape, took an even stronger hold of the weary explorer. Cain sensed a hidden power in this place. A faint, enticing throb seemed to beckon him with inwardly whispered promises. He suddenly became convinced that if he graced this perch with a proper shelter, it would offer him the good life: power, peace, and prosperity, along with the refuge he had sought for so many lonely miles.

This prospect sent Cain into a fit of creative madness. In short order he single-handedly built a wall and a house, a haven that would prove impregnable against attacks from his family's other offspring, who detested him. He named the shelter Enoch, after the boy whom he had fathered years earlier and who awaited him some eight days' journey back.

Cain moved into the small dwelling, then brought back his wife and boy. There they lived for many years. In the year of his father Adam's death, the stone roof collapsed and killed Cain. He was buried nearby, in a grave overlooking the vast valley he had loved for so long.

In the ensuing centuries (periods that modern historians would label late prehistory and the Bronze Age), Cain's majestic landing beckoned to other pilgrims and wanderers. Each one seemed driven by a personal search for the good life—power, peace, and prosperity. One by one, caravans of shamans, witches, and holy men arrived at the site, drawn by its burgeoning reputation as a center of supernatural power.

A thick, stone altar was erected at its most imposing spot. Hardly a day passed without some sort of living thing being sacrificed there to some deity or other, whether a choice bit of harvest, a small animal, or even a young child. Always, along with the constant reek of blood, there would be shouting, mumbling, and chanting—invoking some piece of the good life that the pilgrim had been promised by his god in return.

Harvests and weather came and went, but one morning, 2,400 years before Christ's birth, a rainstorm arose that did not end after the usual few hours. For day after day, its downpour continued, until even the deep valley below appeared to sink beneath a pale sheen of floodwater.

Panicked sacrifices were soon being made without ceasing, pleading for an end to the deluge. But the rain did not relent. The day came, shocking and unbelievable, when the water's surface reached even the altar's own height.

The flood, recorded in the Old Testament as Noah's flood, would eventually engulf all of the land. When the waters gradually retreated, it appeared Baalbek would remain yet another discarded pile of stones, soberly testifying to passersby about the folly of human ambition.

However, Baalbek's silent beacon was far from extinguished. Four generations later, its light drew the attention of the legendary hunter-king Nimrod, great-grandson of Noah, who came to believe that rebuilding the citadel would make him equal with God and bring him a good life of power, peace, and prosperity. To reach his goal, he brought to the task a race of newcomers whose very appearance would have made most inhabitants of earth faint with fear.

These exceedingly tall and powerful men were known far and wide under a variety of names, ominous terms such as *giants, gigantes,* and *Titans.* They were of an ancestry merely hinted at in the most obscure and disputed of records.

Nimrod rebuilt the citadel, laboring with a savagery and power unseen in the world, carving pillars from the underlying stone larger and heavier than any hewn from the earth either before or since. How the workers managed to heave these staggering monoliths into position remains a mystery. Nor is it known what they were promised in exchange for their Herculean achievement.

Yet to this day the pillars stand in defiance to any who would doubt, and are known far and wide as the Great Platform. It embodies one of the world's least-known and most enduring mysteries, an enigma that makes the importance of Stonehenge or the Nazca lines pale by comparison. Quite simply, it contains the three largest building blocks ever used in a man-made structure. Even the strongest modern cranes would barely come close to lifting any of them.

Around 2000 B.C., the great seafaring Phoenician culture emerged and came to dominate the area. Its people were of Semitic origin known as the Canaanites. Drawn to the place by its reputation for power, peace, and prosperity, the Phoenician kings not only established it as a bustling trading center between Damascus and the Mediterranean but also built a temple to Baal, god of the sun, whose blessing was sought to keep the golden sun constant in its path across the sky and in its blessing of the earth.

Driven by the farmer's perennial dependence upon the weather, people came from far and wide to burn their produce, their livestock, and sometimes their own children on the altar, desperate to ensure the success of a coming harvest.

During this period, a mysterious link arose between the worshipers at Baalbek and those of sun gods in the great empire of Egypt to the south. A delegation of priests arrived from that distant land bearing a great statue of their deity Isis-Osiris, promising peace and prosperity to all those who would give it their adoration. The locals welcomed the group, and the icon was planted in a prominent spot and worshiped, but using local Assyrian, rather than Egyptian, rites.

This new influence reinforced Baalbek's stature as a hub of sun worship against the growing influence of a newly arrived race from the south, a band of monotheists calling themselves the people of Israel. Not only had they taken the land to the south as their own nation, but also they fiercely opposed the cult of Baal. They sought the good life through the commandments of a Creator-God, Yahweh, who fiercely reviled the pagan cult.

It was upon a nearby mountain peak called Mount Carmel, during the ninth century B.C., that the cult of Baal suffered its greatest defeat at the hands of the God of Israel. The prophet Elijah, weary of contending with the sun god for the loyalty of the Israelites, challenged the priests of Baal to a face-off on the peak. Both factions would prepare sacrifices, and the deity who consumed his own by fire would be declared the God of Israel.

The priests of Baal went first. For an entire day they implored their god to show himself. Eventually resorting to slicing open their own limbs, they failed utterly. Nothing happened.

Then, in a spectacular display that would have been clearly visible from nearby Baalbek, Elijah drenched his sacrifice in water three times, prayed, and stepped back as a great column of fire descended from the skies. Elijah then killed four hundred prophets of Baal. To the faithful, the victory at Mount Carmel sealed the issue of Israel's devotion. However, it did not end the worship of Baal throughout the region.

In 336 B.C., Alexander the Great rode through Baalbek on his way to conquer Damascus and claimed the temples as his own. The Greeks immediately began to reshape Baalbek. They renamed it Heliopolis, the City of the Sun, after the great complex of the same name in Egypt. They expanded the temple courts and paid homage to its oracle, who reminded them of their revered Oracle of Delphi. Their newly enlarged sanctuaries were now dedicated to Greek gods, who promised a good life of power, peace, and prosperity through the proper adoration of Zeus, Aphrodite, and Hermes.

The worship of Baal, however, never stopped, either in its outer courts or throughout the surrounding region.

Following the death of Alexander, Phoenicia was ruled successively by the Ptolemaic kings of Egypt and the Seleucid kings of Syria, until the Romans' arrival under a general named Pompey in 63 B.C. Like the Greeks before them, the Romans wasted no time in recognizing the temple's spiritual potential. The emperor Septimius Severus and his successors made Baalbek a place of solemn imperial importance, but now in the worship of the Roman pantheon— according to them, the only true way to power, prosperity, and peace.

In all, the period of Roman construction would last for nearly three centuries: from the first century B.C. until Philip the Arab's final, hexagonal forecourt during the third century A.D. Atop the foundation of the Great Platform, Roman artisans constructed three magnificent temples: one to Jupiter, Bacchus, and Venus, set amid an imposing series of courts, terraces, and staircases. The towering temples rivaled the Acropolis in height, held aloft by dozens of massive, sixty-foot-high stone columns.

The resulting grandiosity would be known throughout the empire as the Temple of the Sun. During this era, Heliopolis' extravagant homage to Jupiter, the greatest religious building in the whole empire, actually became the object of an annual pilgrimage. Emperor Thracus made the journey to consult with the oracle on matters of royal concern.

The temples became notorious for orgies and ritual prostitution, both voluntary and forced. According to the oracle and ancient tradition, Jupiter made a promise to the oracle's followers: In return for their devotion, including surrender of their sexual virtue, he would provide the good life of power, peace, and prosperity through abundant harvests, most notably of the wine grape. According to historian Eusebius of Caesarea, "men and women vie with one another to honor their shameless gods; husbands and fathers let their wives and daughters publicly prostitute themselves" in the process of giving Jupiter his due.

In 15 B.C., Heliopolis was declared a *colonia* and home to a Roman legion. Centuries of succeeding emperors would prove their devotion by adding yet another feature to the majestic site. They eventually built Heliopolis into a sprawling complex that rivaled Rome in splendor; its soaring temples linked by acres of esplanades, grand staircases, and courts of approach. Together, the lavish structures made up the largest sanctuary in the Western world, and would remain as such for centuries.

In the fourth century A.D., the old gods of Rome were supplanted by a new means of achieving the good life: through allegiance to Jesus Christ, risen son of Yahweh, the monotheistic God from, of all places, nearby Israel. Incensed by the wild debauchery of his Roman predecessors, the newly converted Emperor Constantine sought to please his new Christian God by putting an end to the rites being performed there. Convinced that he would be rewarded with God's power, peace, and prosperity for his efforts, he built a soaring basilica atop the most flagrant sites. His successor Emperor Theodosius built another, actually within the court of its temple to Jupiter. For three more centuries, the Christian God prevailed as the only deity legally worshiped amid the ancient altars of Jupiter, Zeus, Isis, and Baal.

But even the might of the Romans could not withstand the gradual onslaught of time and the emergence of a brand-new pathway to the good life. In 637 A.D., shortly after wiping out a superior

Byzantine army at the famous Battle of Yarmouk just to the south of Baalbek, the troops of Abu Ubaidah ibn al-Jarrah, Islam's first great conqueror, swept through Baalbek and made it their own.

Anxious to please their God and ensure for themselves his promise of that same good life in heaven, they renamed the site Al-Qala and recycled the complex into an imposing structure thereafter known as the Great Mosque of Baalbek. Where once the cross had dominated the area from an imposing transept, now a soaring minaret called the faithful to ritual prayer.

However, being in Muslim hands meant the locals had to choose among a whole new subset of combating factions. Al-Qala quickly found itself in the grasp of various caliphs, generals, and dynasties. Syria claimed Al-Qala for years, then the renowned Saladin did the same. A Byzantine emperor, as well as several Crusades, tried to wrest it from Muslim hands. They failed.

In 1517, Baalbek passed, along with the rest of Lebanon, into the Ottoman Empire and de facto domination by a local Shiite tribe. Baalbek became, for a time, a wild and forgotten place, consigned by the vagaries of history to being just another bygone pathway in a secondary, relegated nation.

But this story is too powerful to remain mired in the past.

Today one might be tempted to consider the place a relic, if not a magnificent one. Baalbek has been named a UNESCO World Heritage Site, one of the world's richest archaeological treasures. The temple of Bacchus retains its full glory, framed by forty-two columns nearly sixty feet in height. Its grand courts of approach and intact colonnade form such an eerily preserved picture of antiquity that today it plays host to the renowned Baalbek International Festival, the Middle East's largest and oldest celebration of the arts.

Yet none of these matters makes up Baalbek's ongoing, modern story—the living and breathing tale.

In 1982, the aftermath of an Israeli invasion gave rise to a new force, a new creed, atop Cain's ancient perch.

That force is known worldwide as Hezbollah. The Iranian-backed militia's skirmishes with Israel have defined the region's modern borders more directly than has any treaty or governing body. Hezbollah fighters called Baalbek simply "home base," their headquarters. During the tumultuous years of the 1980s, Hezbollah reportedly smuggled Western hostages such as Terry Anderson, Thomas Sutherland, and Father Lawrence Jenco among Baalbek safe houses (though they deny it to this day). Two years ago, in 2006, Israel actually landed helicopters on the streets of Baalbek, striking the local hospital in their search for Hezbollah leaders and engaging in fierce combat that took dozens of lives. But still, Hezbollah thrives.

A new overseer has emerged in the holy city called Baalbek.

And what is Hezbollah's driving compulsion? A fierce conviction that by expelling Israel from Lebanon it will win the good life for its people—power, peace, and prosperity for the descendants of the ancient Canaanites, who in turn could be counted among the sons and daughters of another wanderer. His name was Cain.

It seems we have come full circle.

TRANSCRIPT

Ted: What is the greatest concern in your life?

Lebanese teacher: To do God's work. To help the children here find freedom.

Ted: What do you think of Jesus' teaching that we should love our enemies?

Lebanese teacher: Yes? Jesus, like Muhammad, was a great prophet. We are an oppressed people and the aggressor should be pushed back.

The Bedouin Prince

We left Baalbek as we had found it, a monolith in human history that is not likely to fade into the dust anytime soon.

Among the most mysterious and alluring purveyors of ideology in the Middle East must be the famed Bedouin princes, who command the respect and loyalty of so many desert dwellers and who grace the frames of so many Western movies. The West has a fascination with the tribes plodding over desert dunes on their camels and living nomadic lives in tents.

In search of the true Samaritan, we knew we had to arrange a meeting with a prince among the Bedouin. Did they remember the great teaching that had divided history two thousand years ago? And were they to be counted among America's enemies?

It took us an hour to reach the small Bedouin camp where Carl had pulled strings to arrange a meeting for us with a Bedouin prince.

"We were once in Sidon, passing out cloths to some Gypsies, when we noticed someone pouring gasoline on our van," Carl said as we passed shacks with tin roofs that replaced the tents of old in this region of Lebanon. Black-covered women ducked out of sight the moment they saw us.

"Gas?" I said. "What did they expect to do, burn you out?"

"Pretty much. We were trying to get them to stop when someone ran up with a box of matches, trying to light one. We piled in and took off before they could light us on fire."

"Do you always attract so much trouble?"

Carl looked out the window and laughed. His laugh was starting to grow on me. It actually made sense. In this part of the world you can laugh at yourself, leave, or blow yourself up. Clearly this group was leaning toward the latter.

We arrived at the prince's "palace," a simple home with concrete floors and a plain parlor, where he received us. His wife offered us tea, which we gladly accepted, and the prince prepared a hookah for us to smoke together. The fruit-soaked tobacco is a mainstay in Lebanon, sampled by all, much like coffee in the West. Tea and hookah.

Here, then, is the prince in his own words.

TRANSCRIPT

Ted: Please, Prince, tell us a little bit about your place among the Bedouin.

Prince: There are about two thousand people in this village that I am responsible for. Total between Lebanon, Syria, and Jordan, there are thirteen thousand in our tribe. After my father's death, they met and decided I would be prince. In this area there are thirteen Bedouin tribes in the Bekáa Valley. Most of the Bedouins now are living in homes, not tents. In tents you are free and it is easier to travel. But in a house, it lasts longer.

Ted: When you think of Americans, what is your thought of them?

Prince: The media is a big problem. They show us as if we were monsters. But people that get to know us like us.

Ted: What is something about your culture that would surprise Americans?

Prince: We live like all people. We have cars and TVs. We have satellite.

Ted: What are your children's favorite TV shows? And what is your favorite?

Prince: Cartoons. They watch about two hours a day. As for me, I like movies from America. I like action movies. I like *Die Hard* and *Braveheart,* and *Gladiator* is my favorite. I like comedies too. I like Jim Carrey, I like *Dumb and Dumber.* In our local station, we have Arabic stations so the people who don't speak English can understand. I like *The Godfather,* too.

Ted: Do the younger people listen to the music?

Prince: They listen to the Bedouin music. They don't understand the English music and they don't like it. They prefer the traditional music. They like to play soccer and like to run. Some ride bikes and swim.

Ted: How do they make money?

Prince: Some are truck drivers. Some work in the fields. And some work in farms and ranches. The women work in the fields.

Ted: What is a good Bedouin joke?

Prince: (Grinning broadly) The sheik in the mosque on Friday told them to go and kiss his wife and make her happy. Then one man went up afterwards and said I am not married yet. The sheik said to kiss your own hand because you are not married. (He laughs, but Carl and I must appear perplexed.) I think it is funnier in Arabic.

Ted: How about another?

Prince: Here is another joke. A man wanted to sacrifice a sheep, so he went to the mosque. He took his sword and went inside. And he said, "Who loves God?" Nobody answered, then someone said, "I love God." So he went and killed the sheep and gave it to the man. The man went back to his house with the sheep and went inside with the blood on his sword. He asked, "Who loves God?" And the sheik said, "I love God." And the man said, "No, you are a liar." Because he thought he would have to kill the man outside if someone said they loved God.

Ted: When was the last time you cried?

Prince: There is a family that has six children who don't have a father. It makes me cry. But the last time I cried was last week about the situation in Lebanon and the hundred guys who died for nothing. The last time I cried in this village was when my father died three years ago.

Ted: What makes the Bedouin different from the other Arabs?

Prince: Our tradition. We have special traditions. We have our own law. We are also under the law of Lebanon. If we have a big crime, then the government deals with it. If we can fix it within this village, we will take care of it with our law.

Ted: Jesus' greatest commandment was that we love our neighbors as we love ourselves. What is your opinion of this teaching?

Prince: Our tribe likes all people, not the governments. They hate Bush. We have no problem with the people, though.

Ted: Jesus and Muhammad both taught to love our enemies. What does this mean to you?

Prince: But first you have to have peace with your enemy to love them. For example, the Jews are our big enemies.

Ted: Yet Jesus says to love those who persecute you.

Prince: You should love the man but not his actions. If he changes his way with Arabs, then I will love him. But I don't hate him as a person.

We left the Bedouin camp torn. It seemed to us at the time that finding the true spirit of the Samaritan would be no easier in the land from which the great teaching came to us than in the land founded upon it. Perhaps, in killing Christ two thousand years ago, his enemies had also tried to silence this teaching.

"So tomorrow, Hezbollah?" I asked Carl.

He whipped out his phone and placed a call to Samir, who was back in Beirut making arrangements. He exchanged some cryptic dialogue, then snapped his phone shut.

"We're on."

"When?"

"Tomorrow afternoon."

8

Nicole

Hey, Doug,

Greetings from Shatila Camp, Beirut. I have news! It's taken weeks, but Walid, the hookah bar owner I told you about, really did have someone useful for me to meet. He had me come up to the bar late last night to meet him. Walid walked me in to this special, curtained-off sitting area, and there sat this man in religious clothes. His name was Father Stephen, a Christian priest. Not Catholic. Maronite. It's a special, Lebanese kind of branch.

Right away, I could tell he was nervous. Nervous to be there, nervous to meet me, nervous about what I had to say. I told him my story, and as soon as I got around to our personal connection with Shatila, and the man behind Momma's letters, he got real quiet and his eyes went dark. I can't describe it any other way.

I was almost through when I pulled out Momma's oldest photo, the ID from Iowa State she always kept. I handed it to him and his face went white. Then tears came to his eyes. My heart was pounding.

He wouldn't say much, but he did say that once, during the most stressful period of his life, he'd known Mother. And despite the most trying and unlikeliest of circumstances, they had fallen in love. She was under the control *of another man, someone very powerful and also very much in love with her. And she was torn between the two of them.*

He told me that she made the hardest choice of her life. He said it saved him from certain death. By then, as you can imagine, I was ready to climb onto this man's head and claw out the rest of his story. But he suddenly had an urgent appointment he'd forgotten about. He stood up to leave. He had already drawn back the curtain to go, when he turned, walked back, and leaned over where I sat.

"Perhaps I give you a name. Naum Sareel. Walid will know how to contact him. Call him and ask him what his son was doing at the time of the massacre here. Tell him Father Stephen asks him to share this with you."

Then he was gone.

Today I'll call this man whose name he gave me and see if I can learn anything more. Meanwhile, I'm just praying he works up the courage to tell me more. Walid was quite disappointed to learn that Father Stephen had chickened out, although he didn't seem all that surprised. He promised to try and put us together again.

That's it, dear brother. I hope all is going well for you. I've actually started praying here, believe it or not, and I pray for your safety and happiness every day. I know that sounds weird coming from me, but trust me, Beirut is the kind of place that makes you want to pray.

Kisses, Nicole

DURING THE WEEKS that followed her first meeting with Walid Khaleem, Nicole Wagner was completely unaware of the dozens of phone calls and private inquiries crisscrossing Beirut as a result of her investigation. Walid had left her with a pledge of support, an offer that had sounded like nothing but great news to Nicole. Then he had asked her to be patient.

Awaiting further word from him, she buried herself in her medical duties. She also volunteered her free time at the Palestinian Youth Center, where she befriended many of the young refugee daughters being sold into prostitution along the camp boundaries. One of them, a beautiful girl named Fahima, made an especially strong connection with Nicole. Blessed with a gorgeous singing voice, the young girl desperately needed support and an opportunity to develop her gift. It was her only ticket away from a life of prostitution and abuse.

As the days unfolded, Nicole vowed to help Fahima in any way she could. It was her way of paying something back to the lost birth family she seemed incapable of locating.

One day Walid flagged Nicole down on her daily bicycle pass beside the Bekáa House. He had arranged for her to meet someone who might help her in her search for truth. A Maronite Christian priest, Walid explained, but despite his being a clergyman, he was a man with a fascinating story to tell.

Although Nicole learned only a small part of the priest's story during that first meeting, the full story behind Father Stephen Dachome would later emerge as a linchpin in her quest.

It began in April 1986, more than three years after Muna Wagner was taken from her Shatila home during the massacres of September 1982. The place was Beirut's pleasant Gemmayze district, a stronghold of Lebanon's Maronite Christian community.

On that date, Father Stephen of Saint Thomas Church was stepping out of his church side door when it happened—in typical Beirut style. A Mercedes sedan raced up alongside him and screeched to a halt at the curb, where all four of its doors were thrown open. Suddenly, Father Stephen was facing the business end of four submachine guns. The air filled with barked orders to jump in the car.

Stunned and terrified, he complied. Within seconds he was sitting between two men in the backseat, feeling a black hood being pulled over his head.

When it was yanked away nearly an hour later, it was to the weak light of a single electric lamp, in a bare, painted room.

"Stay still," a male voice growled, "or I will have to tie you up. See my face and I will kill you. Understood?"

"Yes."

"Is your brother George Dachome?"

Father Stephen hesitated for only a second, considering his words. Was there any good reason to play the hero in this situation? Surely this question was a mere formality. Father Stephen never hid the fact that his brother was a well-known member of the Lebanese Parliament.

"Certainly. I would have told you that out on the sidewalk without the need to commit a crime by kidnapping me."

The kidnapper chuckled. Then he was gone.

For Father Stephen, the ordeal held no particular trauma beyond the simple tedium of captivity for days on end. He was locked in a windowless bedroom somewhere in the city. There were many such stashes throughout Beirut, homes of assorted sympathizers and militia members who could go to work, come home, and feed their children without ever acknowledging that they had a hostage locked up elsewhere in the house.

No, what brought Father Stephen into a full-fledged encounter with human frailty was not the twists of Lebanese politics or the hardships of being held hostage.

It was the woman. The one who watched over him.

Her presence had started as just a hand, a soft and pale one, extending plates of food three times a day through a barely cracked door. Over time, the caution had dissipated and her face had shone through, luminous and inviting. Her voice, once clipped and reserved, became infused over time with human warmth, then humor.

Soon, mere questions about food preference and basic human needs began to lengthen, to stray from their original subject.

Gradually, he realized that the two of them were alone in the house. It struck him as a bizarre allowance for a Muslim, for surely he was being held by Muslims. He guessed that he was not being held by a particularly fundamentalist branch. His best guess was that they were modern, even indifferent Muslims at best.

It became clear that the woman was lonely. Housebound and isolated.

Bored without his normal mental stimuli, Father Stephen began to spend hours thinking about her, replaying endless, invented conversations with her in his mind.

Father Stephen had remained single, not because his church demanded celibacy, but because he had not yet found the right woman during his years of seminary and wasted and directionless living. So he began intentionally prolonging conversations with this woman, seeking her out. He extracted more and more words from her, using all of a clergyman's considerable counseling and conversational skills.

She gave her name as Sophie.

Then one day the floodgates opened. Literally, you might say. The door to his room flew open all the way and she walked in. She wanted to talk.

She was not the kidnapper's wife, she explained in a torrent of speech. She had been a college-bound Muslim girl living in the refugee camps when, during the massacre, one of the commanders had whisked her out and brought her here. She had been frightened, terrified by the sight of so much death, and easily manipulated. He had seduced her. She had fallen in love with him. Apparently he had returned the favor. He promised to give her her freedom back someday. But several years had passed.

Now she had no words to describe her status: hostage, love slave, lover, other woman . . .

The first part of her revelations sent Father Stephen's mind reeling. He had assumed, until now, that he'd been kidnapped by Muslims, but her admissions suggested otherwise. He had been abducted by fellow Maronite Christians—by the Phalangist militia blamed for the Sabra and Shatila massacres. He and his church tended to support a different side, the more pro-Western Maronites loyal to a brigade known as The Tigers.

Sophie (if that was her real name) had no idea why her captor/lover had taken him, only that it concerned some power struggle within the Lebanese Parliament.

Soon the two were sharing their most intimate hopes and fears. Her boldness grew stronger, and to Father Stephen she became more beautiful by the day as the thrill of such forbidden disclosures began to envelop them like incense.

So far, he had never even touched her. He wasn't sure what even the slightest graze of the skin would have provoked. He began to wonder how long his resolve would last.

Fortunately, events did not force him to wait that long. Early one weekday morning on day 112 of his captivity, there came an emphatic knock on his door. It flew open. She rushed in, ready to leave. Weeping.

"Listen, Stephen. They're talking about killing you this afternoon. The Phalangists have fallen out with the Israelis. There's nowhere else for them to turn, and they're ready to start reprisals. You must come with me if you want to live."

She led him swiftly through rooms he had never seen and outside to a waiting car, which she started and pulled away with a chirp of new tires. Weaving wildly through the streets of Beirut, she explained her tears. Her real name was Muna. The relationship with her powerful lover had reached its end, she had finally realized. Both of them had admitted that there was nowhere to go. He was not going to marry a young Muslim and compromise his position in society and his wealth, no matter how much he might love her.

Her decision to free Father Stephen was also a choice to leave that day and never come back. Her lover would have been compelled to punish her when he discovered that she'd helped Father Stephen escape.

She let him out at the doorsteps to his church and drove off despite his objections. Just that quickly, Father Stephen was a free man. And for a brief period, he was a newspaper hero.

But unknown to everyone else, he felt more imprisoned than ever. Muna had vanished. Naturally, neither he nor her captor breathed a word of her.

One morning less than a week after his release, there came a knock on the outer church door. A visitor in a veil of shadow. He squinted.

It was her! Muna! He stood drinking her in with his eyes for a moment before moving a muscle. She rushed past him and closed the door. She had come to say good-bye, she said in barely more than a whisper.

She did care for him, she explained. But she was a Muslim woman and could not convert to Christianity. Conversion would have made her an attractive target for murder in the eyes of any fundamentalist Muslim. Stephen was a Christian cleric.

Furthermore, she could not stay in Beirut. She dared not return to Shatila and search for her family for fear of endangering them further. Already, she knew, her boldness in leaving a Phalangist leader might have exposed them to reprisals.

But she had talked to her lover, who still cared about her, and he had agreed to renew her previous scholarship to a university in the United States, where she would be starting classes in mere days. She was leaving the country immediately, leaving it forever.

With nothing further to say, they bid each other a tearful and affectionate good-bye. Father Stephen pulled back from their kiss knowing that he could, if he loved her enough, resign his position and follow her.

But in that moment he also realized that he truly loved the trappings of his position: the comfort, the respect, the material ease. In that sinking moment, he admitted the truth to himself.

He was not a courageous man. He was not, truth be told, even a particularly righteous one. He accepted that, because it was the only thing faith had ever told him that he knew he could believe completely.

So, cursing himself and weeping for her at the same time, he watched her step into a taxi from the front step of Saint Thomas Church and speed away into the streets of Greater Beirut.

The moment her cab turned the corner, something physically wrenched within his chest and he knew he had made the biggest mistake of his life. He would never love anyone with that same purity and strength ever again. He would never find a woman with her winsome combination of vulnerability and strength.

Father Stephen resumed his normal life, but he found himself a sadder, more haunted person than before, ever watchful of his surroundings, easily pierced by expressions of love.

One morning years later, he received a phone call from one of his family's more interesting acquaintances, the infamous hookah bar owner Walid Khaleem. His voice sounded strained with unusual intensity.

Walid had someone quite unusual and fascinating for him to meet. No, not a romantic possibility, although the young woman was quite beautiful.

And that is how Father Stephen met Nicole Wagner, the only person more afflicted by his secrets than himself. She told him of her quest at the Bekáa House, and he knew the truth at once.

The man she sought was also the man who had held him captive. The man who had kept Muna as his mistress. A man who deserved much of the blame for the Shatila Massacre. A man who still lived at the highest and most precarious levels of Lebanese politics.

This man was Nicole's father and he was a monster.

If Nicole persisted in her search, she might well earn herself her own screech of the brakes and gun muzzle in her face. But she also threatened to expose this leader's secret involvement in the

Massacre. A secret no one in Lebanon would ever forgive. A secret Walid was dying to expose. And one that Father Stephen had longed to expose for years, never daring for fear of exposing himself.

Nicole now gave him, as she had given Walid, the perfect cover for a perfect revenge.

To be continued . . .

9

Tea with Hezbollah
SOUTHERN LEBANON

THERE SEEMED TO BE a common theme emerging from those we spoke to on our quest for the true Samaritan spirit, two thousand years after the parable of the Good Samaritan was first delivered. Neither Carl nor I had any intention of putting words in anyone's mouth or of leading them down a path that served any secret agenda. We were predisposed to believe that the teaching of Jesus so revered by Muslims would be seized upon by clerics in the Middle East even more so than by Christians in the West.

What we were finding thus far, however, was the general notion that the teaching to love your enemies, or to love your neighbors as you love yourself, came with as many qualifications in the Middle East as back in the West. The radical teaching that contributed to Jesus' death sentence so long ago was still too radical, it seemed.

In the West everyone speaks about love, love, we all gotta love, but when it comes down to showing the kind of love that got the prophet killed, few seem much interested. I'm not a pacifist, and if someone came into my house to blow my wife's head off, I would likely blow his off first.

But then again, that's part of what makes the parable of the Samaritan so radical. Remember, Jesus' story claimed that the heretic worthy of death (fire from heaven, James and John suggested) was the only one following the great commandment by going way out of his way to tend to the wounds of his greatest enemy.

Perhaps we in the West have it all wrong. And so far Carl and I weren't finding clerics in the Middle East eager to set us straight. There was always a caveat when it came to enemies. They don't seem to count as neighbors.

But we were only halfway through our journey, and the most demanding of our interviews lay ahead.

We entered the town of Sidon, halfway to the southern border. Carl wanted me to see an old Crusader fort, and Samir was eager to show me the houses his foundation has rebuilt using millions of dollars donated by Saudis. Both the houses (many of which were beautifully constructed to reflect old Lebanese architecture) and the fort were absolutely fascinating. Or so they tell me.

My mind was farther south, where the Hezbollah made their southern headquarters. Where Israeli warplanes obliterated entire villages. From where thousands of sophisticated rockets were fired in retaliation in this never-ending cycle of violence.

Everywhere I looked, I saw people going about their business, seemingly oblivious to the fact that they'd built their houses in a target zone. But then violence is nothing new in this part of the world. During the life of Christ, the Romans conquered, using the sword and crucifixions to enforce their will. After Christ's death, a new religion called Christianity spread north to Sidon and Tyre. In the late 600s another new religion called Islam conquered the region. But Christianity made a strong comeback in the 1200s, when Crusaders pushed back the Muslims and built citadels like the one we visited on the coast of Lebanon.

Now Muslims and Christians side together against an Israeli occupation in Lebanon. It's never ending. At the time of this writing, peace reigns as the country tries to decide what to do about the demands of Hezbollah in Parliament. By the time this book is published, the whole country might be at war again. That's just how it is.

The Gospels tell us that Jesus ventured as far north as Tyre, our own destination this day. It was there that he met a Phoenician woman and extended a message of peace and forgiveness. But today, forgiveness isn't part of international politics.

This is what occupied my mind as we worked our way south, closer with each passing mile to the epicenter of this thing called Hezbollah. Spoken with trembling lips on television. Written into a hundred speeches as the devil incarnate.

A brief word on the history of Hezbollah from a mile above the complications that confuse all politics in the Middle East: Hezbollah's "Party of God" emerged in the early 1980s after Israel successfully invaded and occupied a third of Lebanon. It was a time of sweeping change for the country, particularly for the Shiites in the south, who'd borne the brunt of the violence. A U.S. peacekeeping force had taken up station in support of Israel, and the PLO wasn't resisting. To make matters worse, Christian Phalangists had entered the Palestinian refugee camp in Beirut—Shatila—and slaughtered hundreds of innocent refugees, as referenced in our story about Nicole.

In the view of many, the country was now being ruled by outsiders—the Israelis, the Americans, and the PLO—leaving the common, poor, Shiite population exposed and expendable. Enter the Party of God. Hezbollah. A desperate group of freedom fighters supported by Iran, willing to do anything to push the foreigners out of their country.

In the early days they used kidnapping and bombing to dissuade their enemies and quickly became identified as terrorists. As their influence grew, they distanced themselves from any violence against civilians or against their own countrymen, preferring to be seen instead as a valid political force in the Middle East. Over time they gathered support among numerous political factions in Lebanon. And in a few days, Carl and I would learn that as a result of their most recent power play, which had caused us so much concern, Hezbollah and its allies would control half the votes in the Parliament.

No Arab in the region would equate Hezbollah with Al-Qaeda or Hamas. For starters, Hezbollah now publicly condemns suicide bombers and more desperate methods that inflict terror upon civilians for a greater purpose. The U.S. State Department sees Hezbollah (which has a history of terrorism) differently, but in the

Middle East, the organization is now largely regarded as a sophisticated group of freedom fighters eager only to dislodge the occupiers from Lebanon. In fact, in Lebanon the Hezbollah, led by Hassan Nasrallah at the time of this writing, carries a badge of heroism. When the Israelis invaded Lebanon in 2006, Hezbollah took credit for having pushed the much larger and more sophisticated army back out of their country. They are the first force in the Middle East to have successfully repelled the Israeli forces, and for that feat alone they have gained much respect among friend and foe alike.

Both Al-Qaeda and Hamas, on the other hand, embrace terrorism against civilians as a means to their objectives. The complications and true associations between all of these groups are not clearly understood by the West, however, and it would be absurd for either Carl or I to pretend we know more than we've been told by either side. Even then, talk is cheap, as they say, and history renders many words moot.

Besides, our purpose here isn't to identify the nature or scope of any enemy or perceived enemy, but to sit at the table with them and discuss that crazy thing called love.

We passed a white UN tank with an open hatch occupied by a machine gunner. "Wasn't far from here that Bonnie was killed," Carl said. "Did I tell you about her?"

"That was here?" I asked, taken aback.

"Yep. Sidon."

Bonnie was a nurse in her early thirties who worked in a humanitarian mission with her husband, Gary. One morning she went to the local clinic, where she administered medicine, mostly to Palestinian women, and opened the door. She was alone when a gunman shot her in the head at point-blank range.

Hearing the tragic news, Gary rushed to the clinic. The police on the scene tackled him as he tore for the bloodied body. He lay on the floor ten feet from his dead wife, screaming in agony.

It was then that his choice mushroomed in his mind, like an audible voice from heaven itself. Either he could hate or he could surrender and love. Against all natural tendency, he did the latter. Immediately peace flooded his whole being.

The story was picked up by the BBC and CNN, and at the memorial two days later, more than seven hundred people crowded in and around a building that was designed for one hundred and fifty. There, in front of the world, Gary calmly and with stunning sincerity spoke his message of hope for the peace of Lebanon. And there, for all of the cameras to see, he forgave the gunman, who to this day has never been apprehended.

Perhaps this was the love that Jesus talked about so long ago.

"Now just remember, be yourself," Carl said as we pulled up to a coffee shop off the beaten track. I immediately noted that all eyes were on us. In Beirut, even in Baalbek, Westerners came and went. But down here they were rare enough to garner curious gazes from passersby. What Westerner would be so dumb as to venture so far south? The people here had experienced more violence and tragedy in their lifetimes than most can dream about, yet one thing that still brought them to attention was the presence of a few Westerners.

"I thought our meeting was two o'clock, farther south," I said, swallowing my thoughts.

"This isn't the big guy, no. We talked about meeting some Hezbollah fighters, right? They've agreed to meet us here."

"Fighters. As in the kind of maniacs that kidnap Westerners and shoot their AK-47s into the air when they don't have a target at hand?"

Carl chuckled. "Yes, those kind of fighters."

By this point in the trip, I'd acclimated. Sort of. But after living in the West for the past twenty years, the constant barrage of influence had worked roots of fear deeply into my nerves, and I just couldn't shake them free. The whole trip was like that. Just when I thought I was finally starting to settle in, another obstacle would present itself.

Today the Hezbollah. Tomorrow the road to Damascus. The next day, Hamas.

Dear Lord, who would rescue me from the fear and death of this world? Little did I know that they would get progressively worse.

The two Lebanese Hezbollah fighters who sat in the corner wearing the telltale yellow color of their party broke into wide grins when they grasped our hands. These were Sharif, a fighter who takes up arms when he is called upon, and a friend of his, Hassan, who spoke nearly perfect English. (Both names have been changed for their safety.)

I set my trusty Sanyo recorder on the desk as the proprietor brought in tea. So this was it, then. I was having tea with the Hezbollah, and my stomach was in knots, just as I'd imagined it would be.

But the smiles eased my fears. As did Carl's booming laughter after an exchange in Arabic. They were probably making fun of me, the lily-white American who was trembling like a leaf.

Yeah, well, first off, I'm Canadian, not American. Second, I'd been tricked into coming to Beirut, hadn't I? And at the moment I was keenly aware that not all had always gone well for Westerners in this part of the world. I had every reason to be slightly nervous. Right?

We settled in, sipping at the hot tea, and then Sharif, the more seasoned of the two fighters, stared into me with soul-searching eyes and came right to the point. "Do you wish to ask some questions?"

"May I record your answers?" I asked.

"Please. Please, I insist."

TRANSCRIPT

Ted: Can you tell us about yourself? What you do?

Hezbollah fighter: Yes. I am now forty-three years old. I have a wife and two children, ages twenty and nineteen. I am a business administrator and this is how I earn my living.

Ted: How long have you been with the Hezbollah?

Hezbollah fighter: For a very long time. Since the first invasion.

Ted: What do you do for Hezbollah?

Hezbollah fighter: I do what is required to help the people. I sometimes speak for the organization. Everything. Most of the time I do my normal business, but when war comes, then I will fight.

Ted: So . . . you've fought in these wars recently? You pick up a gun and fight?

Hezbollah fighter: Of course. But I only use a gun when it is required to defend my homeland. I am a peaceful man most of the time, but then I will pick up a gun to defend my home and children.

Ted: Have you ever killed someone?

Hezbollah fighter: Yes.

Ted: When was the last time you cried?

Hezbollah fighter: A week ago, when I went on TV and said that whoever shoots at us [in Lebanon], we would shoot back. And this is the toughest decision I have ever made. This is what made me cry. Nasrallah knows that my decision was very tough because he knows that we will now be seen as evil persons with weapons.

Ted: What is the greatest misconception Americans have of your people?

Hezbollah fighter: There are many. Mainly, the government of the U.S. know that we are not terrorists, but they give the wrong message to the people. The Americans treat us with a very heavy political background. They don't look at us as people. We actually would find a lot in common. The proof that we are alike is that we are sitting together now talking. I meet many foreigners who are not political leaders. When I sit with them, I see we are very much alike. Also Americans tend to link Hamas, Hezbollah, terrorists, fundamentalists, and Al-Qaeda all together. It is because they know very little or nothing about Islam.

Ted: What is the misconception your people have of Americans?

Hezbollah fighter: Many don't differentiate between the American people and the government. If you ask me about the Jews, I would say I don't have a problem with them, but I have a problem with the Zionists.

Ted: What kind of toothpaste do you use?

Hezbollah fighter: Crest. Because it tastes good. (Grins)

Ted: What is your favorite music?

Hezbollah fighter: It's a religious, Arabic music that is like poetry.

Ted: What is your favorite joke?

Hezbollah fighter: I have learned that many of our jokes, you wouldn't laugh about. We just find things funny that aren't necessarily funny to you.

Ted: Do you use the Internet?

Hezbollah fighter: Yes, it is spreading in the south.

Ted: (Addressing the friend, who looks to be in his early twenties) And what about you? Can you tell us a little about yourself?

The friend: I study computer and communication at AUB [American University of Beirut]. I have two years left. I live in the south, but when there is school, I'm staying in Beirut. Because of the difficulties, there is no school now.

Ted: And you are Hezbollah?

The friend: My town is actually a stronghold for Hezbollah. The people there are very pro Hezbollah. There are about fifteen thousand in my town. Hezbollah means more, recently, especially after the last two weeks. It is protection for our country and for me. It represents safety and protection. It is not religious. I'm not very religious, although I'm Muslim. It is protection against discrimination from all kinds. Hezbollah has also given us financial relief like building schools.

Hezbollah fighter: Two days before the war ended, there were thousands of families that were trapped. Their homes were destroyed. Nasrallah stated on TV that Hezbollah would pay for these families to rent a house and buy some furniture. When the war ended two days later, $12,000 was given to each family with the Hezbollah's money. There were about seventeen thousand families. This is Hezbollah.

Ted: (To the friend) When was the last time you cried?

The friend: A week and a half ago. I had a social problem with someone. Not a girlfriend. Usually in the south, crying is a good thing. Here you might cry if a martyr dies. It is not crying out of fear but because of pain.

Ted: What is the greatest misunderstanding that Lebanese or Muslims in the Middle East have of the United States?

The friend: Many people say they are infidels and whoever is not a Muslim is an infidel. But this isn't true. Another [misconception] is that we think Americans have everything and are happy because of what we see in Hollywood movies, which are mostly lies.

Ted: What kind of clothes do you wear and what kind of shoes do you wear?

The friend: I wear jeans and Nike shoes.

Ted: What kind of cars are most popular here?

The friend: Mercedes, BMWs, and Toyotas.

Hezbollah Sheik Nabil Qaouk

We left the coffee shop with firm handshakes and much more discussion. In another place and another time, not all might have been so congenial, but at that time and place, I felt no animosity from this feared fighter.

We drove farther south, into the deepest folds of Hezbollah-controlled lands. "In my younger days I used to come down here to debate imams in the mosques," Carl said. "They called them 'dialogues,' in which we'd discuss Jesus, because I was seen as something of an expert on Jesus. It was crazy, thinking back on it. Two or three of them would say their piece, then I would stand and say mine while hundreds listened."

"You mean like preaching?"

"No, nothing like that. I was just talking about his life. But not everyone rejoiced. The CIA claimed the threats to my life were linked in part to my activities in the south. I was talking to a blind man once—his name was Hussein, I remember that. Another man came up, pulled a gun out of his belt, and held it to my head."

"Good night! How often does this happen to you?"

"I just stood there while he yelled and screamed. But I was watching his trigger finger, 'cause it was tight. Seriously, I thought that was it. Eventually it was Hussein, the blind man, who talked him down. Maybe that's why I remember his name so clearly. He saved my life."

One more story to calm my nerves.

The hour for our meeting with the leader of the south, Sheik Nabil Qaouk, had finally arrived. South Lebanon is the epicenter of all Hezbollah defense today. Two years earlier, munitions had pounded homes and caves and office buildings for weeks as the Israel Defense Forces sought to rout the resistance to their north once and for all. But it was not to be. Hezbollah was too strong in the south.

We would now sit down with the top man responsible for the south, second only to Nasrallah himself in the Hezbollah hierarchy.

Getting to such lofty leadership is a chore, even in the protected south, where large banners with pictures of Hezbollah martyrs are hung from nearly every building. We first met a trusted source, close to the sheik, at a restaurant where we shared some food. Then a change of cars. I was separated from Carl and was driven by a man who spoke no English. We wound through narrow, crowded streets in an old Toyota sedan. Naturally, all of our electronics were carefully inspected.

Another change of cars.

Now I sat in an old BMW. I remember looking into the eyes of dozens as we passed, trying to climb inside their minds. What would it be like to live here, in a strip of land torn by war for decades while the rest of the world had its eyes on the stock market, or the Iraq war, or the next presidential candidate?

We arrived at an office complex in the middle of a busy street, climbed out with hundreds of eyes on us, and slipped into a lobby, where Carl waited.

"Good?"

"Good," I said.

An elevator took us up three floors and we were ushered into a long room with cushioned chairs, clearly prepared for our meeting. At the far end were both a Lebanese flag and the yellow Hezbollah flag.

We were seated and offered tea. Always tea.

Sheik Nabil Qaouk stepped into the room wearing a broad smile. He quickly kissed the other guests, then turned to take my hand. Kisses are for those to whom it is customary, but so as not to offend those from the West, a friendly handshake will do.

I was immediately struck by the twinkle in the sheik's eyes. His beard was black, tinted by gray, and he wore a white headdress with brown robes. He seemed grateful we had come, greeted Carl with a traditional kiss, and invited us to sit.

Now the number-two man in Hezbollah, in his own words:

TRANSCRIPT

Ted: Thank you for your time, sheik.

Sheik Nabil: Today is the busiest day, but when I heard about your purpose, I set everything aside to give you the whole day because I believe this type of dialogue is worshiping and pleasing God. This is a way to peace. We think that the three religions complement each other. We have to believe what Abraham, Moses, and Jesus taught as Muslims. We believe that Jesus and the nephew of Muhammad will come and unite all humanity. And all people will come together and pray one prayer.

Ted: I would like to ask you some questions that will help us know you a little better. Is that okay?

Sheik Nabil: Please.

Ted: What kind of car do you drive?

Sheik Nabil: (Chuckles) A Mercedes.

Ted: What color?

Sheik Nabil: Black. But you won't see my car from the sky, because I park under tarps. Many times I have nearly been killed by assassins and bombs targeting me.

Ted: Where do you live?

Sheik Nabil: I move many times so that my enemies can't find me. This isn't appropriate to discuss, you understand?

Ted: Of course. And your family?

Sheik Nabil: I have a wife and four children. My son Mokdadi is preparing an educational movie about children. I have a daughter who is in college in Iran. My third child, Abass, is nine years old and loves karate and soccer. He is also in Iran. And my youngest daughter is three.

Ted: When was the last time you cried?

Sheik Nabil: Every time I pray to God I cry. Recently I cried when I heard that a husband was killed with a cluster bomb. Now his wife and children are suffering. I met with them and showed them sympathy. The youngest child was crying. He was only three years old. He cried so much that everyone started crying with him. The thing that makes me cry the most is when I see children crying and suffering.

I cried during the massacre in Kana. Those children that were killed in Kana, the rocket didn't hit them directly; it hit ten meters away from them. It was one of the advanced bombs that weighs ten thousand pounds. It penetrated the earth. The building collapsed and they were buried alive under the soil. We heard the children crying, but nobody could save them. There were sixteen young children, thirty altogether. When we buried them, their bodies were completely blue because they suffocated. One of the mothers touched the hand of her daughter underneath the rubble and she didn't let go until her daughter died. My dream and hope during the war was that I would see children playing again after the war in 2006. The most beautiful scenery to me is seeing children playing after the war.

Ted: What makes you laugh?

Sheik Nabil: I like your questions. Very good. (Clears his throat, smiling) My son was playing in our house and broke his arm. I called him and asked him if he was angry. He said, "No, everyone is giving me gifts and food and drinks. And I don't have to go to school." (Everyone in the room laughs.)

I also have a daughter who is three. She entered my office and closed the door. I was outside and she locked it. She started crying because she didn't know how to open the door. We tried explaining how to open the door. I said, "Give me the keys and I'll give you all the dollars in my office." She forgot the keys and went to look for the dollars. She said she wanted Kleenex to wipe her tears. I said, "Give me the keys," but she said, "Bring me the Kleenex and I'll give you the keys." Then she wanted watermelon. This whole time she was locked inside this room. Then she remembered that she was locked in, so she started crying. Finally we got her out. She said, "Give me the dollars. You said you would give me them if I gave you the keys."

Ted: What is your favorite joke?

Sheik Nabil: People think I am very strict, but I am soft-hearted and I laugh a lot. One recent joke that made me laugh: A very bad man died and he went up, so he was judged. He was told that he would go to hell and he did. "Where is my place?" he asked. "Any place in hell is yours," they said. He opened the first room and it was all fire. He opened the second door and found more fire. Every room was full of fire. He opened another room and he found people sitting in chairs. He saw one open chair and said this was the best place in all hell. After some time, the king of fire opened the door and said, "Come here come here! Put on the fire."

(Everyone laughs. I did too, though I didn't get it.)

Sheik Nabil: Now may I say something? I love peace. It pleases God. The problems in humanity keep God far from us. If we all knew that God knows and observes us, then our actions would be good. Faith is not mathematic; it is from the heart. For faith to be true, the mind and heart have to go together. If you are strong and award mercy, this is faith. If you are weak and speak kindly, we don't really know who you are. But when you are powerful and speak with humility, then you have faith. Hezbollah is strong in military weapons, but our strength is our obedience to God. We are humanitarian and we have faith.

We promised the Lebanese people that we would never use our weapons inside of Lebanon for political reasons. But at the same time, we will fight in defense. For three years, we insisted for peace and there was no political or military reaction. Nasrallah said, "Don't react." But a week ago, he said if someone shoots at you, defend yourself.

Everything that happened in Beirut was out of defense. When we knew that the other party wanted a religious conflict like a religious war, we decided we needed to end it in a few hours. The objective of controlling Beirut was to stop the religious war. We took over, then gave the control to the army. The battle was over in two hours. We withdrew, but we were shocked when we heard two Hezbollah were captured by the Druze in Allai. They had to face the consequence of this. In three hours, we took twelve villages.

We defend ourselves. We don't impose any religion on anyone. We don't want Christians to become Muslims. When Hezbollah took over the south, there was no stealing or rape or anything. What is the reason? It is because Hezbollah listen to and obey all the teachings of the prophets that we believe in. We believe in everything that Jesus and Muhammad have taught us. We believe in it and act in it.

Ted: What are the greatest misunderstandings between our countries?

Sheik Nabil: The U.S. is a combination of many nations. There are some parts that understand us, so I don't want to give a general picture of all America. There are many there who don't believe in war. There are millions who believe in the justice of the Palestinian cause. There are many that believe they should not be involved in other countries. We should not judge America as a whole.

In the media there is not enough shown on how much Palestinians and Lebanon suffer from Israel. For example, the massacre in 1996 was hardly publicized. I did not see any serious objections from America. I did not see sorrow or sympathy. I never heard anyone say they condemn what happened. This a pure humanitarian case. We were definitely disappointed with America at that time. If Jesus was there, would Jesus stay silent? If Moses was there, would he stay silent? Till now, America forbids condemning Israel for this massacre. I want the American people to understand our humanity.

God wants us to love each other and to be close to each other, Christians, Muslims, and Jews. We are not against the American people, but the American government is with the opponent that occupies our land.

In 1993, in the village of Abu Hassan, a village was hit and hundreds of people were killed. A man was making a documentary about how many were killed. On accident he filmed a cat that was hurt. After the war, he received eighteen faxes requesting to adopt this cat, take it to London, repair it and take it back. Nobody asked about our children. It was horrible.

Every time I see children playing, I think of this one girl who was hit by a rocket. Now she is completely paralyzed. She cannot eat, drink, or speak. When you see her, you cannot help but cry.

Ted: Jesus' greatest teaching was that we love our neighbors as we love ourselves. How do you recommend we love each other as he taught?

Sheik Nabil: Love has many stages. The highest level is when you cannot decide whether to love or not to love because there is no room for hatred. The love of your neighbors comes naturally in response to obeying Jesus and God. Loving the neighbor is proof that your heart is full of love. When we say neighbors, we mean all of humanity. All people are brothers because we all come from God.

If you believe in one God, you become equal with all Muslims. We believe there are many ways to God but there is one God. Praying is one way. Helping people is another way. Pleasing the heart of a sad person is a way to God. Serving people is a way. Only God can know what is in our hearts. It's not that you pray more, you become better. Some things might be more important than prayer. You cannot do things for yourselves or for show. You have to act from your faith. I know many Christians who are devoted to service and are very good people. We respect and love those people.

Ted: If you had one thing to say to all Jews and Christians, what would it be?

Nabil: Please, know the truth. If you know the truth, then you will know who is holding the truth. Don't follow the person who claims to know the truth, because there is no person who has that truth. Find the truth yourself and it will set you free. For example, don't only follow the U.S. Administration, because they are not always right. You have to know what is the truth, then decide what is the truth.

Ted: If you fire a rocket at your neighbor, how is that loving them?

Sheik Nabil: But we don't fire rockets at our neighbors first. Only in defense, as much as the Americans do to stop those who provoked the attack on 9/11. This is justice.

Ted: In your worldview, do you have to be a Muslim to go to heaven?

Nabil: God forgives everyone unless you say that there is another God. The mercy of God is much greater than we think. So that answer is no; you don't have to be Muslim. God tells us to visit and protect Christians and Jews. We must love them. Our faith is not full if we are full but our neighbors are hungry.

Late that night Samir, Carl, and I sat on the balcony overlooking the two tanks and quiet streets below us. Heavy thoughts crowded our minds. We had no desire to plumb political difficulties in the region, but in the Middle East, politics is an addiction shared by every man, woman, and child.

We were after the ideologues' perspectives on a narrow subject, which was turning out to be misunderstood by most in the region. In fact, Sheik Nabil was the first who seemed to truly embrace the parable of the Samaritan as a crucial teaching. His perspectives are quite different from those of many clerics, much closer to the Western Christian way of thinking than I would have ever guessed.

The fact that many would call him a terrorist created an oxymoron that had us sitting in silence for a long time. What the heck were we supposed to do with this?

Nothing, we decided. Let the words speak for themselves. Sheik Nabil loathed the taking of innocent life. He had nothing kind to say about terrorism and distanced himself from the likes of Al-Qaeda. He was a man of words; the fact that his banners showed an AK-47 raised high seems irreconcilable to many, but his words speak as loudly.

I very nearly slept like a baby that night. But just as I was drifting off, I began to think of our trip to Damascus early the next morning.

Syria.

Dear God, why on earth had I agreed to this?

10

Nicole

FOUR OF SEVEN

Doug,

I have news—both about my work at Shatila Camp and my search for the truth. I don't know quite which is the more exciting to me, right now.

See, I've made friends with about a dozen of the little girls being used "in the trade," as they put it so nonchalantly down here. It would just break your heart. In many ways, they're still little girls, who improvise dolls out of stockings and old flour bags and ask me what Britney Spears and Miley Cyrus are like, as if I know them. They say such girly things, then turn around and are sold for the value of a fast-food meal by their own families.

Fahima has won my heart. She has the most beautiful singing voice I've ever heard in someone that age. I don't understand her lyrics, but they tell me she's written everything she sings, which is in itself amazing. And get this—she doesn't even know what a musical instrument is. She's heard them on the radio but has no clue what produces their sound or how they're played. She just sits there and sings a cappella in the most haunting falsetto you'd ever want to hear.

I say all this because all of these girls need an outlet, something at which they can excel in order to get out of this place. There are grants and scholarships awaiting any one of these refugees who show unusual aptitude or intelligence.

So I had this idea. You know how you've been saying your old laptop isn't cutting it anymore and you're just dying for a new one? Why not send it to me? Just pack it up super tight and ship it over to me. And make sure it still has all that music software still on it. I'll give it to the Youth Center, earmark it specifically for music training. For Fahima. It could really help her realize what a gift she has.

The thing is, don't send it to me here at the camp. I've been warned not to have anything conspicuous or valuable shipped to me here. It may not reach me. I'll figure out some postal box at the downtown post office and go get it. That'll be safest.

Now on to a more critical matter. My search for some sign of Momma's family here at Shatila has taken a crazy turn. I already told you about the priest who just up and left after I told him my story. Well, I called the man he told me to. Naum.

Turned out he was a very old Jewish man, one of the few dozen left here in Beirut. And when I did what the priest had suggested, asked him about what his son was doing at the time of the massacre, there was this long pause. I thought either the line had gone dead or the man belonging to that creaky voice had just keeled over at the phone.

Then he came back on and there was caution in his voice. He wanted to know who I was, asking such things. It almost seemed like he suspected me of being some kind of impostor, somebody sent to expose one who had to stay hidden.

Then he started talking about things that made no sense. His son had not masterminded the camp massacre, he insisted. He had monitored the situation, sure. His son was a spy, but no killer, he knew better than anyone. He was Saul's father. Who better to know the heart of a boy, even when he has become a man? His son had not done this thing, but the man who did was a monster and needed exposing if only to finally prove Saul's innocence.

Then he stopped. He said Walid had invited all three of us—Father Stephen, me, and him—to hookah the following night. He would fill in the rest. The name I was looking for. The man who had accused his son of killing thousands and had been the real mastermind.

I'm terribly nervous, Doug. It all sounds so dangerous, this talk of mass

murder and . . . I don't know. It's just crazy. But this is it. I have a feeling that
I'm going to finally learn the whole truth about Mother and my true father
tomorrow night.

> *Pray for me, Doug. Even if you don't know how, pray for me. I'm nervous.*
> *Nicole*

NICOLE WAGNER'S QUEST to learn the truth about her dead mother's Lebanese past was now poised on the knife's edge of a major breakthrough. In her weeks at Shatila she'd met Walid, the Muslim man who knew everyone. Walid had led her to Father Stephen, the Christian priest who'd loved her mother. And now Father Stephen had led her to an older Jewish man named Naum Sareel. A Muslim, a Christian, and a Jew, all mysteriously linked to her own father.

Such was the nature of the Middle East. And Nicole, an unwitting American, was in the middle of it all.

The story of how Naum Sareel became linked with Nicole began in 1982, more than twenty-five years earlier. Only weeks before Nicole's mother, Muna, was taken from her home during the Shatila Massacre, a bomb fell from the sky and exploded in the heart of the city. The blast largely destroyed one of the Middle East's most famous religious structures—the Maghen Abraham Synagogue, the heart and soul of Lebanon's ancient Jewish population.

The synagogue was being guarded (allegedly for its own protection) by soldiers of the PLO, the Palestine Liberation Organization. The PLO of Yasser Arafat and the 1972 Munich Olympics.

And the bomb that destroyed the Jewish landmark? It allegedly tumbled off the underbelly of an American F-16, flown and launched by a Jewish pilot of the Israel Defense Forces.

This almost unbelievable incongruity—a Jewish landmark guarded by PLO guerillas and destroyed by the Israelis—is just one example of the mind-numbing ironies that fill Middle Eastern history. When it first happened, however, the bombing was not foremost on the mind of Beirut's Jews. At the instant of impact, most of them were more afraid of stray artillery shells and crossfire on the ground than of being absurdly targeted from the air by their own people.

Twenty-five years later, however, the fate of the synagogue was assuredly on the mind of at least one Beirut Jew: Naum Sareel, now ninety-one years of age and a survivor of that day.

He stepped from his tiny apartment in the old Jewish quarter of Wadi abou Jamil for his morning walk. The first sight that greeted his eye upon turning the corner, as it had for two and a half decades, was the still-unrepaired hulk of the vacant synagogue itself. It still appeared just as it did five minutes after the explosion, when Naum had peered out of his home and beheld the unthinkable.

The wizened old man now tottering toward the downtown Beirut bus stop could have been, by outward appearances, the beloved old grandfather of most of the other Lebanese walking around him. Yet beyond the brown skin and Middle Eastern features, Naum Sareel was far from being an average Arab-descended citizen of Beirut.

He was a Lebanese, and a proud one, but he was also one of the last forty Jews left alive in the city. And he was the eldest of an already aged group.

Naum allowed himself one long, sad glance at the synagogue in which he had worshiped his whole life. It was the place where he had celebrated bar mitzvahs for not only himself but also his sons, Ben and Saul, now grown and moved away. Where he had married Golda, may she rest in peace. Where too many of his memories lay buried to try and move anyplace else.

His people had lived in Beirut for more than two thousand years. Even the restoration of Israel could not budge him now, as he had proved quite stubbornly. He was a Lebanese who happened to be of Jewish descent. He was a fixture in his neighborhood, a name known to many in the business and charitable communities.

Still, despite the loneliness and isolation of his life, Naum rigorously kept to a challenging daily routine. He arose around dawn every day, made an effort to pull on his one frayed suit and slip into his old leather shoes. Then he walked this very path down to the heart of Centre Ville, the vibrant core of downtown Beirut. Here he boarded a bus for a far more blighted part of town—the Shatila district. Here was now his place of greatest danger, the part of town where anti-Jewish sentiment raged the strongest.

After reaching his final destination, the Bekáa House hookah bar, he would always nod at his old friend Walid, forcing his very best smile. As always, Walid waved him over to his usual table, the very best. It was already laid out, as always, with a slice of *mankoushe*, the Lebanese breakfast pizza, and a slice of cold toast. The nargileh pipe for one was already loaded and ready.

The natural question is, why would a Jewish man travel so far into dangerous territory every day? For Naum, the answer was simple. He was stubbornly fulfilling a promise to his son. And if nothing else, Naum was an exceedingly stubborn man.

The memory overwhelmed him even now. The face of his own son right here, in this very chair before him, back during the 1982 invasion, the sound of that beloved voice failing to rise over the sound of tanks growling past . . .

He tried to shut it out, but his mind replayed his son's words.

"Papa, this time you've got to come with me. You can't live here anymore."

"What, you're telling me what to do now? My own son is ordering his father around?"

A heavy sigh. "Of course not, Papa. But give me credit. I know things. Look, I shouldn't say this, but I'm now part of Mossad. You know what—"

"Of course I know! Israeli secret police. You think I don't read the papers? You think I sit around ignorant of the world around me? I'm too old to move to Israel. What am I going to do—go down to Israel and start some new life? I'm sixty-six years old. I have roots here. You want to be a part of my life, stay here in Lebanon, your country."

"A Jew belongs in his homeland. You have two sons in Israel, and we miss you."

"I miss you too. I wish you'd never left."

"It's where we belong. And it's where you belong too, Papa."

"Don't talk to me that way, Saul. Don't tell me I don't belong in my own country."

There was an awful pause. Naum remembered it well. Then the question.

"Is this your final answer, Papa?"

He had thought for a second. Then, for some reason, resenting the finality of this situation, he felt a surge of rage rise beneath him. How dare he, or Israel, put him in such a quandary!

"Yes, it's my final answer. Why should I abandon my country and all it's given me for a government that comes over here to invade my land, slaughter its innocent refugees, and drop bombs on our synagogues? You think I feel some kind of kinship with *that*?"

His son just sat there and stared at him. He did not try to interrupt or even visibly react.

"Fine, Papa," he said at last in a heartbroken tone of voice. "But just know, I can't protect you here. Try to come back to this bar. Walid is a good man. I've asked him to show you special consideration as a personal favor to me and my country. And should I ever return, this is where you can find me. Otherwise . . ."

"Then I will," he said. "I will wait for you to come to your senses every day here, in this bar."

Naum would never go to Israel, for reasons even he didn't fully understand. It felt as though his emotions had taken on a life of their own, a path wholly separate from his innermost wishes. But he would keep his promise, every day as circumstances permitted.

So it was one morning, many years later, when Walid sat down at Naum's table. "You know that your son is never going to meet you here," he said in a quiet, kind voice.

"You don't know that, my friend. He might, someday. Mossad always has some business to do here. How can you predict the future between Lebanon and Israel?"

"Naum, you've been neglecting your arithmetic. You're ninety-one years old. Do you realize how old your son is? He's almost sixty. I hear he's now one of the Mossad's highest leaders, nearing retirement age. Do you think Israel will send such a figure, in some future conflict, right into the heart of Shatila?"

Naum gave the shrug of a man with no argument. "You've come here to torment me with this?"

"No. Actually, I may have a solution. I have a young American woman who may just provide you with the means to clear your son's name in this country. You might even get the pretext you need to see your son again. I know how much you long to do that. To do it, you will have to break her heart. Shatter her illusions. But . . . this is Beirut. And this young woman has some growing up to do."

"Walid, you speak in riddles. What possible connection could there be?"

"I will answer you with a question. Who in Beirut has been the biggest thorn in the side of Mossad and Israel's government for the last twenty years?"

"There are many. Which one?"

"The one responsible for the Shatila Massacre, in the camp behind us," Walid said.

"Ahhh, that Phalangist Christian," Naum replied.

"Yes. Israel's blamed him for years. And he's blamed them right back, hasn't he? He practically ruined Ariel Sharon's career. And he specifically implicated your son as the on-site leader of the killing."

"So, what does that have to do with the American?"

"This American girl can hand you the Phalangist's head on a platter. She has incriminating information that would exonerate your son by placing blame where it is deserved, on the Christian man who was responsible for the massacre. She has letters, written in his hand, in which he admits taking the lead in the killing madness back then. These letters also incriminate him in having kidnapped and seduced a young refugee woman during the '82 massacres. He, the lion of the Maronite Christians. This would literally destroy him. And you can be the one to give it to the world. For that, your son would return to Beirut."

"And why does this concern the American?"

"Because"—Walid glanced around—"I believe the monster we both know so well may be . . . related to her."

A light slowly came on in Naum's eyes.

"In this I would gladly help. But why would the young woman want to give me these letters?"

"She is searching for her father. She doesn't know. She will call you today. Show your outrage. Then tell her I've arranged for a meeting tomorrow night, here at the bar. Tell her to come. We will help her see the truth. And then she will show us the letters."

To be continued . . .

11

Road to Damascus

SYRIA

DRIVING TO DAMASCUS from Beirut brings to mind Saint Paul's journey to Damascus two thousand years ago. He was likely on horseback, and we were piloting two hundred horses packed under the Jeep's hood, but the threat of danger wasn't so dissimilar.

The border crossing went smoothly. In fact, the only thing that stood out were the children begging for money. They had the art down, pleading with soulful eyes that brought to mind the inner child in all of us. Despite being told not to give in, I finally handed the most persistent among them a fistful of coins. Four other children pounced on him, demanding to share in his loot. Before my eyes, they changed into far more seasoned souls, screaming at each other with such bitterness that I immediately regretted giving them any money.

But then you can hardly blame children who've grown up watching their fathers throw far more than angry words at each other. I imagined one of these kids pointing up to the sky. "What's that, Papa?"

"Those are the American bombers going to kill your brother."

Right or wrong, this is the world through the eyes of a child in the Middle East.

Once we were inside Syria, the country turned bland. My imagination kept me busy, wondering what manner of bad guys might be building nuclear missiles behind the hills we passed. We saw poverty, terrible poverty. Unlivable shacks belonging to the fabled Bedouin nomads. Desert. More desert.

"Looks like Iraq," Carl said.

"Delightful."

"I have one word for Iraq. Fallujah."

"Something tells me you intend to ease our fears with a story of hope."

"Road tales."

Carl told his story in a calm voice, but it raised the hair on the back of my neck.

On May 1, 2003, the day President Bush stood aboard the USS *Abraham Lincoln* and announced that the major part of the war in Iraq had ended, Carl and six friends were driving back home to Lebanon along the long and lonely road headed west out of Baghdad. Theirs had been a humanitarian mission, delivering three semi-truckloads of paper, pencils, crayons, rulers, erasers, and other supplies to schools south of Baghdad. They had been wonderfully well received in Iraq, and the trip was a huge success with virtually no problems.

But this being the Middle East, constants are nonexistent.

Carl rode in the passenger seat of the lead Range Rover, doing a good seventy miles per hour on a long, isolated stretch, when a car loaded with five men pulled up alongside. Two men leaned out with machine guns and began screaming.

The driver of Carl's Rover, Sameer Petro, started to weave. "They're telling us to pull over!"

"No. Keep going."

But the Toyota sped up and cut them off, forcing them to the side of the road.

"I don't like this," Sameer Petro said.

"Doesn't look good, does it?"

Four men rushed back and two piled into the back of each Range Rover. A rifle butt jabbed into the base of Carl's head, and he instinctively raised his hands.

"Drive! Go, go!"

The Toyota sped off and Sameer Petro pulled back onto the road, urging calm. The men were anything but. They kept looking back, making sure the road was clear.

"Faster! Go! Follow!"

By this point, Carl was leaking buckets of sweat. Images of executions on YouTube played through his mind. He needed little imagination; this was really happening. They were being kidnapped at gunpoint.

"This is not good," Carl said again.

Sameer Petro stared back with wide eyes. "No."

They were ordered off the main artery and down a long, dusty road. Only when they were satisfactorily clear of the highway did their abductors bring the situation to a head. The lead Toyota slid to a stop in a cloud of dust.

"Stop! Pull over, stop!"

Sameer Petro did as ordered.

They were hauled out of their two Rovers and shoved to their knees on the desert sand. "Tell us where all your money is or we will kill you here."

This was a moment of relief, actually. It was robbery. No videotape of an execution, after all. Probably.

All seven quickly complied with the demand for money, emptying their pockets. All except one, who decided he needed that last $700 hidden in the trunk.

But these particular bad guys weren't easily fooled. They searched through everything, dumping luggage in the dust, yelling and shouting at the seven on the ground.

Naturally, their intent was to terrify, and as they were armed with AK-47s and one pistol, their task was an easy one. It occurred to Carl that robbing a group of internationals and leaving them alive to tell would be foolish. And these guys didn't appear to be foolish. He kept his face to the sand and begged God for mercy.

Then one of the four kidnappers found the $700 and all hell broke loose.

"Why have you lied? What else did you not tell us? Why are you here? We are going to kill you and then we'll take everything." This while shoving their guns into the cheeks and necks of the cowering group.

Carl never confirmed it, but I'm thinking a few of them wet their pants. Sameer Petro wasn't among them. Assuming they would die anyway, he stood and offered to help out.

"Shut up!" The crazed thug whipped up his gun and fired. A crack rang through the desert as the bullet snapped past Sameer Petro's right cheek. Sameer Petro dropped back to his knees. Perhaps now he wet his shorts.

Having successfully relieved the internationals of their valuables, the four abductors began arguing among themselves as to the fate of the seven men on the ground. Should they be killed? Left to die? Or just left alone? The debate raged for a full thirty minutes, gifting Carl with far more time than he needed to fully consider his own death. Trembling, he wept silently for his wife, Chris. For his three children. It was okay, dying was okay, but not yet. Please, just not yet, not in this godforsaken desert.

After heated discussion, the thug with the pistol shouted down the one who'd shot at Sameer Petro. "Don't move for an hour or we'll kill you." With this one last threat straight out of the movies, they piled into the Toyota and sped toward the highway.

The desert fell silent. It took a few minutes for the stunned group to collect themselves and accept their good fortune. Waiting an hour as directed didn't agree with any of them, so they climbed back into their Range Rovers, cautiously crept back to the highway, then, seeing no sign of the Toyota, sped back down the road.

They now had no money, little gas, and a twelve-hour road trip ahead of them. The first town came quickly and they pulled over, desperate for help. No one had yet heard of this nest of resistance called Fallujah back then.

The line at the town's only gas station was hours long, so they sought out the owner. For all they knew, he was a cousin to the abductors—everybody seems to be cousins with everybody in the desert. But they had no money and no other alternative, so they told their story.

Immediately the owner gathered a crowd, started slapping the top of his head (a sign of shame), and jumped into Carl's Range Rover. He pulled both cars to the front of the line and filled them up, uttering many loud and sincere apologies for this tragedy.

"These thugs are not Iraqis!" he cried. "Not Muslims. They are dogs. Only dogs would treat a foreigner in our country this way!"

The crowd then offered some food and sent them on their way with blessings and kisses.

"You see?" Carl said as we sped toward Damascus. "You could say it ended up being a blessing. It all worked out for good."

This was spoken by the man who'd heard a voice telling him he'd grow up to love Arabs. As for me, I would rather forgo such blessings.

Damascus sits in the desert, one massive dust bowl crowded to the seams and beyond with people. Our first destination was the same as Saint Paul's so long ago: Straight Street. Immobilized by blindness, he was led to the house of a man named Judas. It was there, several days later, that Paul began his obsession to advocate the controversial teachings of Jesus—teachings that would eventually get him killed, a fate shared by nearly all the early leaders of The Way, as it was called back in the day. Teachings that urged people to love their enemies were no more popular then than they are now.

Unlike Saint Paul, Carl and I weren't compromised by blindness. No, today it was traffic that threatened to sidetrack us. After driving around in circles for half an hour looking for the smallest gap in the lines of parked cars, we finally gave up and asked Rob and Samir to drop us off. We would make the trek on our own and meet them at the far end.

Straight Street

We could have been anywhere in the Middle East. The beeping of mopeds and screeching of brakes drifted over the chatter of a thick street crowd. Whiffs from strong cigarettes, sweet spices, and cardamom-infused coffee were everywhere.

It could have been Cairo, Beirut, even Baghdad—any large Arab metropolis. But this was Damascus, the oldest continuously inhabited city in the world and one of the most fascinating ones I'd never considered visiting.

And this was Straight Street, or "a street called Straight," as the book of Acts puts it. It looked like just another overstuffed pedestrian district. But that appearance was deceiving. This road was packed tight with bits of history not just Christian but Muslim as well.

Anxious to immerse myself, I started off with Carl. The street was eighty feet wide and not quite a mile long, and on both sides it was lined with covered porticos and shops. We quickly discovered that the street doesn't quite deserve its name. "The street called Straight is straighter than a corkscrew," Mark Twain said more than a century ago in *The Innocents Abroad,* "but not as straight as a rainbow. St. Luke is careful not to commit himself; he does not say it is the street which is straight, but 'the street which is called Straight.' It is the only facetious remark in the Bible, I believe."

On our right there rose a cluster of impressive homes with dramatic balconies and handcrafted woodwork, except they were deserted and obviously decaying. This was once the Jewish Quarter, and these were the homes of Jewish leaders who fled during the 1967 Six-Day War between Israel and—among other Arab nations—Syria itself.

Pondering their fate, I remembered with a shiver that Paul himself walked down this very street, his ears still echoing with the sound of the voice that would pursue him for the rest of his life.

About a quarter mile from the western entrance of Madhat Pasha Street, in a stretch covered with a large metal dome, stood a small mosque with a balcony in the form of a pulpit, which serves as a minaret. It is here that the Christian tradition locates the house of Judas, the place where Saul remained for three days without eating or drinking. It is considered likely that Paul was also baptized here by Ananias.

About halfway along Straight Street's length, we passed under a majestic Roman arch and into a whole new experience. Here the road underwent a dramatic transformation from broad thoroughfare to a narrower, crowded street market. This marketplace ushered us into the Hamidiyeh Souk, a half-darkened labyrinth of neon-lit shops and alleyways crowded with endless rows of stalls and shoppers and itinerant salesmen offering everything from sugary sweets to stuffed eagles.

Brightly colored spices and damask silk and jewelry greeted our gaze at every turn. The sensory contrast from the bright, modern road heady with gas fumes to this dim, exotic shopping area was overwhelming.

But we didn't come here for a marketplace, no matter how interesting. We were after the story of the coming and going of religion beyond this marketplace.

Suddenly, the shade stopped, the shops fell away, and we faced a vast courtyard, an imposing wall, a towering colonnade, and a minaret taller than I had ever seen. The revered Umayyad Mosque is one of the Islamic world's most striking and famous places of worship. Built thirteen hundred years ago on the top of millennia-old sacred sites, the mosque is considered one of the holiest in all of Islam.

A delicate, minor-key tune drifted down from high above. This was no Muslim call to prayer but a carefully preserved Byzantine Christian tune. Ironically, the minaret from which it emanated (the mosque is the only one in the world to have three minarets in total) is called the Minaret of Jesus, because Muslim tradition claims this is where he will appear on the Day of Judgment. Even more ironically, this mosque is built upon a site that was once graced with a temple to Baal.

A man with an official-looking badge beckoned us inside the mosque, explaining in broken English that we need not be Muslim to worship here. As long as we believed in God, we were welcome. Taken aback, even oddly moved by the revelation, we removed our shoes and stepped inside the vast, towering prayer hall.

A carpeted floor stretched almost without obstruction from wall to distant wall. Slowly, we approached the huge room's centerpiece: a glittering, domed shrine bearing ornate windows of a deep, almost emerald green.

This enclosure is said to contain the buried head of John the Baptist. The number and scope of worshipers crowding around took us off guard. Prior to this trip, I had no idea the head of John the Baptist was in Damascus, and I hadn't expected it to be so revered by so many religions.

We peered inside, but the head itself could not be seen, only an enticing display of vases and tapestries and a painting of the saint.

How could such a relic have found its way all the way here, in the middle of a Syrian mosque? The explanations are as numerous as the other locations claiming the same distinction. At last check, John's head is concurrently claimed by the San Silvestro In Capite basilica in Rome ("In Capite" refers to the decapitated head) and Amiens Cathedral in France, Antioch, and in the possession of the inescapable Knights Templar. The rest of his body, or assorted pieces of it, are claimed by religious institutions too far-flung and numerous to mention.

As to its arrival here, one rumor has it that Herod sent the head to Damascus so the Romans could be sure of his execution. Another legend says that when the previous Christian church dedicated to John was demolished, his head was found underneath, complete with skin and hair. Another story merely claims that when the Arabs took over the church site from the Byzantines, John the Baptist's blood bubbled upward, revealing the head's location.

The only helpful clue as to the relic's authenticity is a late-coming one. In 2001 Pope John Paul II paid the first visit ever by a pontiff to a mosque, and he chose this shrine upon which to bestow the honor. One would imagine that with countless biblical scholars and secret archives at his disposal, the Holy Father would have avoided a relic considered less than reputable.

With history swirling through our minds, we left the place of reverence. We passed by the tomb of Saladin, the great Muslim general and archfoe of the Crusaders, in a garden tomb. The mosque also contains, in a corner crowded by robed pilgrims, the head of Hussein, grandchild of the prophet Muhammad.

We finally found our way back to Straight Street, but one final curiosity awaited us. Nearby stands a small stone church called the Chapel of Saint Paul, the place where Paul was lowered from a window over the Kisan Gate that once marked the southeastern boundary of Damascus. From there, Paul hurried down the road toward Jerusalem and the ministry that awaited him there.

We turned off this fascinating boulevard of ancient history and immediately returned to the din and bustle of a modern Arab city, where our car picked us up. A meeting with the mufti of Damascus awaited us.

But the past was not so quick to leave us. It's simply amazing that this one spot in the middle of Damascus holds so much evidence of the coming and going of religion—and by extension the abject failure of religion to fulfill its promise to bring heaven to earth and vice versa.

Institutions have arisen here and relics are worshiped to this day. But where is the sacred teaching of the Samaritan that once divided the world?

Mufti Abdul Fattah Al Bizem

The lofty title of mufti is rarely handed out, and only to one man in a single governed region such as Damascus. A mufti must be someone well-grounded in Islamic law and granted the authority to issue formal rulings on matters concerning that law. Considering how closely knit government and religion are in most of the Middle East, this is a powerful position indeed.

When you hear the term *fatwa* in the news, as in "So-and-so has issued a fatwa," more than likely that So-and-so is a mufti, such as the mufti of Damascus.

Being granted such a status in the Bashar Assad government within Syria is not only exceedingly meaningful, but it can be likened to sitting in a den of lions. In fact, the name Assad in Arabic means "lion."

Syria has been known for its brutality to its own for many years. It's still much like Iraq under the heel of Saddam Hussein. If you say something against the wrong party, you might quickly disappear. In 1983 Hafez Assad, the father of the current president, killed twenty thousand of his own people in Hama to crush a small group of antigovernment reformists holed up in the town. Overnight, the town of Hama was pounded into the sands of history.

Eighteen million people live in the largely desert country. Roughly 16 million are Muslim, another 1.5 million are Orthodox Christian, an estimated two thousand souls are Protestant, and in the neighborhood of eighty are Jewish.

Vast sums are spent on weapons and the military—one reason for the abject poverty that prevails throughout the country. Most of the weapons secured by the Hezbollah, whom we'd just visited, flow through Syria. No missionaries are allowed in the country for any reason.

Damascus, the capital in which we found the street called

Straight, bursts at the seams with more than five million people, or nearly a third of the country's population.

And we were on our way to meet with the one mufti who oversees this vast, ancient city and significantly influences the interpretation of Islamic law throughout the entire region.

We were ushered into a plain-looking building downtown and climbed a flight of stairs to the mufti's office. His assistant clasped our hands and greeted us with a warm smile. The tea was being brought in before we could sit.

Tea, always tea.

Mufti Abdul Fattah Al Bizem walked in, dressed in flowing black robes with a round white headdress topped in a dark red. His English was surprisingly good and his manners were, as with all Middle Easterners, impeccable.

We settled in for what felt more like a fireside chat than an audience for a fatwa. This is what the mufti of Damascus had to tell us.

TRANSCRIPT

Ted: Thank you for your time. Can you tell us a little bit about yourself?

Mufti Al Bizem: I was born in 1940. I am married and have five children. I have visited many universities—Yale, Harvard, and University of Boston—to build bridges. I went to New York and noticed it was very similar to England. What kind of Christians are you?

Carl: The spiritual kind who worship God.

Mufti Al Bizem: (Nodding) The muftis of the Islamic world and all the scientists and engineers of the world have an obligation to understand one another and work on international love. As Muslims, we believe in all three religions: Islam, Christianity, and Judaism. In the Qur'an, Muhammad told us that believers are anyone who believe in God. As I respect Muhammad, I also respect and believe in Jesus. I believe in the Gospel and the Qur'an, before humanity interfered. If we go back to the origin and the messages of the religions, behind our interference, we all meet at the same religion, because it was sent by one God and all our God of the three major religions.

It orders us to pray and believe in one God. To forgive each other and cooperate—exactly the opposite of what is happening today. In the U.S.,

I found very many similarities. People were kind and showed respect. I felt like I was living in Damascus. If the nations united, then we can conquer the intentions of the bad people. I'm very sorry that the U.S. government has made the American people angry.

Two years ago, I had dinner here with a man from the American cultural association. I asked him why he was visiting me. And he said he had come to see if our institute was graduating kidnappers and terrorists. But this is nonsense. With communication, there is no conflict. We have to know and honor humanity. Is what we see in Iraq just? People here hate the word *democracy* because it is not democracy. We must meet continuously so that we know each other and cooperate for the humanity. Not, as Bush has said, that God has ordered him to go to Iraq and kill people.

Zionism controls the media and economics. Zionism is also very dangerous for America, not only us. Judaism is good. It is a religion. Zionism is not good. Every day we pray that God would bless all people, not only the Chosen People. I cannot be useful to you unless you obey God and treat people well.

Ted: I'm surprised you travel so much.

Mufti Al Bizem: In New York a lady came to me and asked me what religious dress I was wearing. I said I am a mufti. And she asked what a mufti is. So I started explaining. Then she said that is very nice.

Ted: What makes you laugh?

Mufti Al Bizem: I will live with my children as friends. We speak as brothers. The confidence between us builds trust. We share a lot about their family problems. They go to meetings with me. They graduated from this institute and are working on their master's. My father and I were the same way. He said he didn't want any money for religious work. We serve God without money.

Ted: How about a joke? Do you have a favorite joke?

Mufti Al Bizem: All my friends say that I am funny. Muhammad told us that if you smile, you are doing a good thing. We consider that a smile makes us closer to God. God made Muhammad softhearted. I always tell my children it is nice to smile.

Now the story. My son was sleeping with his wife, and my granddaughter entered to her father's room and wanted to sleep between them. Then her older sister came. And then there were four of them in the bed. But my son told them to go to their rooms. But his young daughter said she wanted to sleep with them. He told her she had to go. But she said she would tell her grandfather—this is me—that she was kicked out of bed. (Chuckles) And she's only four years old. When she visits me, I joke with her and pray with her.

Ted: Do you have hobbies?

Mufti Al Bizem: I was always a leader in the basketball team. Two years ago, I visited my friend at his farm, and he has a basketball court, so our children were playing. Then I took the ball and shot and made a swish. I practiced in high school in the 1960s. My hobby was also flying small airplanes. The kite airplanes. I also am a swimmer. I think it is important to be healthy and in good shape. When people meet me, they think they are meeting with a serious man, but then after talking for a while, they realize that I am a soft person. I think it is important to reach the heart to affect people.

Ted: When was the last time you cried?

Mufti Al Bizem: The humanity has risen so much in technology, but emotions have gone so down. Now we live by survival of the fittest. Instead of the conflict of civilization, we should have dialogue. Injustice makes me sad. The noble messages from God that have been distorted makes me unhappy.

Carl: Do you believe a Christian should become a Muslim to go to heaven?

Mufti Al Bizem: Every believer, if he believes in his prophet and the holy book without any change, and lives within the teachings, we think he will go to heaven. It is important that they believe in Muhammad and the Qur'an. I believe Islam started with Adam, and that is believing in God. Islam means surrender to God.

A real Christian would believe in Muhammad. But I cannot say whether someone is going to hell or heaven. It's up to God. Muhammad said no one will enter heaven with his work, only God accepts you. Let's not ask who is going to hell or heaven. Let us talk about what we agree on. We believe in one God and believe we should do good works unto others. This is our obligation as a person.

Carl: What is your favorite thing or teaching from Jesus?

Mufti Al Bizem: He's a prophet from God. He ordered the people to obey and worship God. What Jesus sent was the same message that Muhammad came with. The teachings are the same. This is our belief.

Ted: Jesus' greatest teaching was that we should love our neighbors as we love ourselves. That we should love our enemies. What does this mean to you?

Mufti Al Bizem: This is a beautiful teaching. But the original has been changed by the Christians, so we must look to Muhammad. We should treat our neighbor so great. The meeting at Yale was about loving your neighbor. But let me remind you that Christianity started here and it is not only for the American people. It is used for the government. If we gave you light, don't give us fire back. Don't give us war and killing. We are human beings.

But if your enemy attacks you, you must defend yourself.

Ted: Most Christians think Muslims believe it's okay to kill your enemies. What do you say?

Mufti Al Bizem: Yet it is Christians who are killing us in Iraq and killing us in Palestine. They have become the enemy. If we kill one person, it is like killing all human beings. Muhammad said never to kill a child, a woman, an old man, or disturb a house or a church. But if someone attacks you, defend yourself.

Muhammad said to treat all your neighbors well, not just your Muslim neighbors. A good Muslim is someone who does not hurt others by his tongue or by his hand. We are ordered to be useful to all humanity on earth. You should give to anyone who mistreats you and forgive anyone who mistreats you.

The Cab from Hell

With nowhere but city central to change into jeans and a T-shirt following our engagement with the mufti, I ducked behind the Jeep and quickly slipped into the more comfortable duds, feeling elated. We'd made it, see?

We'd survived the Hezbollah and Syria and were headed down into Jordan. For the moment, my fears were gone of being the next poster child for the American policy of not negotiating with terrorists who'd kidnapped Westerners.

"See you, my friend," Samir said in farewell, offering me a hug. "Don't worry, it will be safe. A million times a million safe. No problem, not even a teeny, tiny bit."

This was likely what Samir told Carl before he was kidnapped near Fallujah—Carl surely wouldn't have taken the trip into Iraq without consulting his close friend. I had no doubt that Samir believed dropping us off at a cab station to navigate our own way across the border was safe. Samir is the eternal optimist, and his genuine smile made me want to handcuff him to my wrist and force him to accompany us.

"Thank you, friend. You have opened my eyes to a new world."

Ten minutes later, Carl and I had successfully negotiated a fair rate for the three-hour ride south to the border and then on into Amman, Jordan, where we would spend the night in a Marriott before heading west into the West Bank.

Turned out, the cab on the corner was not ours. No, we were given the special cab designed for special guests. The proprietor hurried off and soon returned, driving a red rust bucket on whose grille some joker had glued a Nissan medallion. It looked like a cab from hell. Perhaps the medallion was authentic; if so, we had some hope—Nissans were built to last.

As is often the case, the gentleman we negotiated with in English wasn't our driver. A seedy-looking character smoking by the wall snaked his way over, stuck his Marlboro between his lips, and began shoving our luggage into the Nissan's already half-full trunk as coils of smoke wrapped around his head.

"He's crushing our bags," I observed.

"No, it'll be okay," Carl said casually.

"No, he's practically jumping up and down on them to get it all in!"

Carl frowned and said a word in Arabic. The fellow looked up from his prying, surprised to hear his native tongue from our mastiff. He sucked down the last dregs from his smoldering herb, flicked the cigarette onto the ground, and plopped the rest of the luggage in the backseat. And we were off.

I recall a few things from that ride. I recall the air conditioning as being either all or nothing and the driver grumbling that we Americans were softies who got cold too easily.

I remember discussing the balance of the trip with Carl. He'd finally solidified meetings with both the mufti of Jerusalem and with the Hamas leadership in the West Bank. Physically finding the seven hundred Samaritans who still lived in northern Israel was still up in the air; Carl's contacts were working on it. And when it came right down to it, they hadn't really solidified any meetings with anybody, because with the kind of people we wanted to see, nothing gets nailed down until you are there, outside the door and stripped of all weapons and electronics.

"The bottom line is, it's taken a year to get maybes. But that's pretty good."

"No guarantees," I said, a tad hopeful that at least the meeting with Hamas would fall through at the last moment.

"No guarantees. But our reputation precedes us, buddy. It's looking good."

"They know about us?"

"Of course. They've probably been listening in on us for the last two weeks. At least someone has."

Thanks for the reminder, Carl.

We pulled into a gas station, filled up, then watched as the driver got into a yelling match with the station owner over the price. Not just an argument, mind you. This nearly escalated into a fistfight. What kind of driver would go ballistic with two passengers watching?

What if, just what if, this was one of those out-of-the-frying-pan-into-the-fire situations? You can say what you want about Saudi Arabia's rather special arrangement with its citizens; you can lump Hezbollah into the axis of evil; you can call Syria the devil's playground. But with all three claims, you would get much disagreement throughout the world.

Hamas, on the other hand . . . Even they will agree with the broad consensus that desperation has driven them to open and relentless acts of terrorism. Crap. That was our next stop. And this time without Samir, our ever-present guardian. He has never entered, nor ever could enter, Israel. He's an Arab Lebanese and thus not allowed to enter Israel for any reason.

These thoughts were drumming through my mind when the cab suddenly veered off the highway and sped down a narrow paved road that headed into the country. For a few minutes I shut off the small voice whispering that something was wrong.

"Isn't the border south?" I asked Carl.

"Yep."

"Why are we headed west?"

"I don't know, maybe just a shortcut."

"Or maybe not."

We drove on for a few more minutes and I began to grow increasingly nervous.

"Seriously, Carl. Ask him where the heck we're headed."

"It's fine." But with his tale of his own kidnapping fresh on his mind, Carl's smile was gone. For the first time on our journey, he looked truly sober.

"Ask him!" I demanded. "I'm telling you, this is how it happens. What are we doing off the main road?"

"Okay, okay, settle down." Carl waited a full minute, staring out his window, choosing his words. Then he spoke to the driver in Arabic and received his answer.

"Well?"

"He says the border is closed. He's taking us to another town."

"That can't be."

"I've never heard of such a thing."

Now I was sweating despite the frigid air blasting forth from the air conditioner.

Carl spoke to the driver again, asking why he hadn't mentioned the border closing when we'd rented the cab.

"He said he's going to a meet a friend. The border doesn't open till nine P.M."

"Nine? Whoever heard of a border opening so late?"

"It doesn't sound right, does it? But there's nothing we can do. We can't just jump out. And he doesn't seem eager to explain himself. We're along for the ride now."

We rode in silence for a good half hour, both as somber as two drugged cats. I whispered a hundred prayers and unsuccessfully tried to shove images of kidnapping and executions from my healthy imagination. What scared me more than anything else was Carl's silence.

TRANSCRIPT

Ted: What is the greatest concern in your life?

Syrian cab driver: To find a fare. (Blows cigarette smoke and smiles) To make money.

Ted: What do you think of Jesus' teaching that we should love our enemies?

Syrian driver: Isa was a great prophet. The best prophet, who was without fault, as Muhammad has said. We should listen to the prophet Muhammad. There is great injustice in the world. Great, great injustice.

The old Nissan finally rolled into a small town and the driver pulled over beside two men waiting on a motorcycle. He rushed around, pulled a box out of the trunk, set it on the motorcycle, and approached the window.

In Arabic: "Now my friend, he will take you to the border. I must go."

A new driver piled in, gave us a toothless grin, and sped down the road, leaving our old driver to motor off on his cycle.

The new driver offered an explanation, but not until we arrived at the border did I really believe we'd escaped certain death or at the very least a few months in someone's basement reading statements for a video camera.

Odd thing: I had just finished writing a novel called *BoneMan's Daughters,* which begins with an intelligence officer named Ryan being taken by insurgents near Fallujah, Iraq, very close to the spot where Carl himself was taken, of all things. Following Ryan's harrowing and debilitating experience in the desert, the novel looks at his harrowing encounter with a serial killer in Texas called Bone-Man.

By sheer coincidence, my imagination had already prepped me for the taking.

Nevertheless, we were not kidnapped. Instead, we arrived at a closed border with no place to wait but in a huge duty-free shop loaded with luxury items. The best we could figure out, a friend of some friend had convinced the government to close the crossing so that rich travelers would be forced to spend some time in their shop.

There hadn't been an ounce of foul play in the mind of our driver. Our imaginations had put us in trouble, not him. Oops. Good thing we weren't politicians armed with bombs.

The crossing took us two hours, following a thorough sweep of the vehicle as we slowly drove over open grates through which subterranean inspectors examined the undercarriage. Our bags were emptied, inspected, then thrown back together.

We rolled into the relative safety of Jordan at eleven that night.

"This border brings back some crazy memories," Carl said.

"Oh yeah?"

"Oh yeah."

The Saudi Samaritan

It was hot, they were tired, and all three kids were screaming. Typical scene you might find on any highway in the United States. But this particular scene was at the Syrian border after a Medearis family vacation in Amman, Jordan. After a week of rest and relaxation, they were headed home to Beirut.

Returning home, they simply did the usual—went to the taxi stand with their three little munchkins and purchased a taxi ride all the way back to Beirut. With a promise to take very, very good care of them, the driver sped toward the Syrian border.

The first clue that they might be in trouble came on the Jordanian side of the border crossing when the guard asked if they had a Syrian visa.

No, not this again. Carl assured him they didn't need one since they were residents in Lebanon and since Lebanon and Syria had a border agreement. The Jordanian let them pass. And for the hundred or so meters in no-man's-land between borders, all was well.

Then they hit the Syrian border and it all went to hell in a handbasket. The man behind the glass windows was evidently having a bad day, and that was before he met Carl. He nonchalantly informed the family that they'd have to go back to Amman and apply for a reentry visa.

Carl, having learned the finer points of border crossings in the airport prison in Saudi Arabia, turned a deaf ear to his three screaming kids and spoke calmly, using all his persuasive skills in explaining to the guard that indeed he was wrong, even though he thought he was right.

Naturally, the guard became furious. Fortunately, Chris was present and managed to talk the official down. She was less successful with the kids, who were now crying. The border guard ordered them to the side and said he'd make some calls.

Three hours passed without any news. The taxi driver lost his patience, placed their bags on the side of the road, explaining that he'd already spent the money for the fare on groceries for his eight children, and sped off.

To make matters worse, the border guard casually informed them that their request had been denied and they would still have to go back to Amman. At this point Carl began to lose his cool. The notion of loving Arabs now far from his mind, he stormed over to the main office and unleashed his full fury, explaining that he had no money, no car, no visa, no way back to Amman or on to Damascus. He had a wife who was questioning his sanity and three toddlers who were waking the whole desert with their cries of hunger. He even tried to bribe the colonel in charge with his last few coins.

Surprisingly, the colonel didn't respond well to his not-so-subtle tirade and near threats. The next thing Carl knew, he and his family were being escorted by two guards to the other side of the street, facing back toward Amman. They plopped their two suitcases down and said, "Ma'a Salameh," which means "Go with God" in the vernacular.

There they stood, stranded on the wrong side of the border, broke, lost. Chris broke down and joined her children in their tears. Stripped of his dignity and power, Carl raged. In so many ways this was worse than his Saudi prison cell. Welcome, Carl, to the world of refugees.

Carl claims that his prayer of desperation went something like this: "God, we're pretty upset. Furious. And embarrassed. I don't like Syrians or border guards, and I don't like living in the Middle East. We have no money and no options. So . . . *help!*"

A black Mercedes with tinted windows pulled up. The rear window rolled down and an Arab man asked them in broken English what was wrong. They told him.

"Very well. I'm Saudi and I'm going back to Saudi Arabia now, and I have room in my car. You may ride with me."

Carl explained that they had no money and needed to go back to Amman to get visas and . . .

"No problem. We'll take you right to Amman and pay everything that you need. We're wasting time talking."

Stunned, Carl threw the bags in the trunk, crawled with his family into the backseat of the leather-padded Mercedes 600 Series, and sped off.

The Saudi kept his word and more. He took them to Amman, paid for their trip back to Beirut, and gave them some spending money. He gave Carl a card with his phone number and e-mail address and bid them farewell, insisting they call him at any time.

In the months following, Carl repeatedly tried to make contact with the Saudi, but his number never would ring through and his e-mail account never accepted mail. The city he claimed to come from doesn't show up on any map or Google search.

"So you're saying what?" I asked. "That this guy was some angel?"

"I'm not saying anything. But I'd forgotten about that crazy night until now, crossing the border. There's our Samaritan, buddy."

He had a point.

"So let's hope the Hamas are as good-natured."

12

Nicole

FIVE OF SEVEN

OUR SOURCE FOR Nicole's story had laid out the events of May 5, 2008, with meticulous detail. Nicole was to meet the three men whom she was convinced held the answers to all of her questions that afternoon at the hookah bar. They were Walid, the Muslim proprietor; Father Stephen, the Christian priest who'd fallen in love with her mother; and Naum, the old Jew whose connection to her mother was still a mystery to her.

Nervous and needing to expend some energy, Nicole did what she always did under pressure—she took a long ride. What better destination than to the central post office to make arrangements for her brother's laptop.

In order to minimize the chances for unpleasant encounters, Nicole had forsaken her bike shorts for loose khaki pants. She had even draped her head and shoulders in a dark blue *hijab,* or head wrap. It was hardly conducive to cool riding in the early summer heat, but in some neighborhoods it was good "foreign policy," as she had come to call the intricacies of life in such a multicultural city.

What Nicole did not know, despite her increasing ease with life in Beirut, was that the long-brewing political crisis between Lebanon's

Hariri government and the militant Hezbollah was about to break out into warfare.

In fact, that very day.

Nicole noticed an unusual volume of army trucks on her way downtown, but this was Beirut. Weaving her way along the streets in the heart of the city, she came upon her first barricade within two blocks of the post office.

As swiftly as possible, Nicole traced a detour around the obstacle. Walking into the large postal building, it seemed like she was the only person entering. Everyone else seemed to be scurrying away as quickly as possible.

She quickly secured a post office box, paid a month's rental, and left. Climbing onto her bicycle, she heard a helicopter throb overhead and low concussions rumble beneath her feet. Was that bombing? Her veins ran cold. She had to get back!

She allowed fear to speed her feet, fueling them to pedal as fast as she dared. Reaching a large boulevard, she paused to look for traffic, glanced westward, and gasped.

A wall of burning tires was sending flames and jet-black smoke curling into the sky.

WITHIN MINUTES of the first explosion, the Bekáa House's tables and booths were filled with chatting, animated people, talking vigorously about the sudden violence between their government and their nation's most powerful militia.

There wasn't much to be seen as of yet, beyond thin columns of smoke snaking heavenward and the occasional thump of distant explosions. But there was plenty to see inside the Bekáa House. The bar erupted in vigorous debate on all sides, as was customary in Lebanon, war or no war.

The three men waiting for Nicole Wagner—Naum Sareel, Father Stephen, and Walid the Bekáa House owner himself—all took a table and tried to remain reasonable. Each had his private reluctance to share the things he had come to say. But with the city thrown into chaos, thoughts of Nicole were momentarily lost.

Walid, who knew more than almost any civilian about the failed negotiations that had led to the conflict erupting around them, could not tolerate Hezbollah taking total control of his country. The power they already exercised in the parliament, controlling roughly one-third of the seats, was good. But he feared they would not rest until they had a controlling majority. He received little disagreement from his tablemates.

They huddled around the radio in animated discussion for half an hour, running to the window repeatedly to see what was new on the horizon. But communication was sketchy, and apart from a stream of tanks rolling down the street on the way to fighting in Hariri neighborhoods, nothing changed. They seemed to be in a pocket of relative peace.

A barrage of machine-gun fire close enough to shake one's chest changed that. The sound of slapping feet and frenzied voices filled the silence that had seized the bar. Two young men ran past the windows wearing keffiyehs, the traditional Palestinian battle scarves.

Father Stephen muttered a quick prayer. "God help us. God save us."

But God seemed to have had other ideas this day. Machine-gun fire in the distance sent the two young gunmen racing back. They stormed into the Bekáa House, shouting at the top of their lungs, wildly aiming their weapons into as many faces, and as quickly, as humanly possible.

"Down!" the tallest one shouted. "Down on your faces! Akram, keep them down."

Walid recognized the two Druze militiamen immediately. Akram, the younger, had made an appearance at the hookah bar on the same morning Walid had first talked to Nicole. They'd likely been assigned to hold the bar because they saw it as a potential threat. They'd already scouted the exterior and were now set upon their objective.

"Hands on your tables!" Akram shouted in a thin, nervous voice. "And silence!" The young man was in his early twenties at the most, but this in no way eased his bitterness. Both young men waved their AKs around in wild, amateurish swaths.

Walid swallowed hard. This pair was more likely to hurt someone by accident than through intention. Walid made a critical decision. He would set aside his disdain for the Druze and do what was necessary to survive any foolishness on their part.

"Please," Walid called out to the patrons cowering under the guns. For once, he was prepared to hide his hatred of the Druze. "We will be fine, thanks be to God and our friends who advise us to keep us safe—"

"Shut up!" interrupted the older one, clearly unhinged. "There's talk of possible combat at the airport. If so, we could be in its path. No one is going anywhere until we see what happens. Stay down. Akram, if they get up, shoot them."

THE ONLY CIVILIAN going anywhere fast in that part of Beirut, just then, was Nicole Wagner. She struggled through its dangerous streets on her bike, heading for Shatila.

Even more alarming than the obstacles were the groups of people now starting to clog the street and aim hostile looks at her attempts to weave through them.

Slowly, at half her normal speed, Nicole was closing in on Shatila. Thank God for the GPS. Aggravated by fright and stress, however, her lung power was starting to give out. Her legs were starting to ache, starved for oxygen, which wasn't reaching her at the usual rate through the now tightly pulled hijab.

At last, nearly exhausted by the ordeal, she began to recognize the streets surrounding Shatila. Before she could reach the end of the boulevard, a tide of humanity spilled out, shoved forward by some invisible surge of mass anxiety.

Nicole swerved, trying to avoid the closest walker, and lost control of the bike. Its front wheel toppled sideways and slid into the side of a middle-aged woman in Islamic garb. The woman shouted, grabbed her knee, and crumpled forward.

Nicole shouted her apologies but then made the worst possible mistake. Instead of stopping to at least try to render aid, she struggled back into the saddle and rode shakily away.

The woman's grown son, a thickly built young man in a white shirt and slacks, flew into a rage at the audacity of his mother's attacker. As Nicole rode away, he broke into a sprint behind her. Then he began shouting wild pleas for assistance.

In an instant Nicole found herself surrounded by a gauntlet of would-be attackers. She was now swerving wildly to avoid not only groups of people standing around but also runners intent on tackling her.

She felt something hard—a thrown rock or stick—strike her left shoulder. Pain shot across her whole upper body and she buckled, almost losing control of the bike. Wincing through the agony, she forced herself to look back and assess her pursuer's location.

He was twenty feet away and gaining on her!

She turned the corner. Bekáa House awaited down at the far end, beyond a low barricade. An engine whined in her right ear. She turned. It was her pursuer again, only this time pulling up alongside her on a Vespa motor scooter.

The barricade, perhaps two feet in height, was coming up. She pedaled even faster, hoping against hope, testing her aching deltoids with the intention of jerking the bike over the boards. The barricade loomed close, higher than she'd reckoned. This would be awfully close.

She willed her feet into a frenzy, tensed for liftoff, then saw two male figures launch themselves toward her from the left. The impact burned through her like a ball of fire. She felt herself launched airborne, then struck pavement on the wrong side of the barricade with a sickening crunch. Pain seared her whole left side.

She heard the Vespa sputter to a stop, then the patter of feet. Voices surrounded her, not just angry but enraged. Fists struck her face. Feet smashed cruelly into her stomach, her arms. She felt her pack viciously yanked from her back. The bike pulled out from amid her legs and feet. Her pursuer was upon her now and clearly had been joined by others.

A vicious crunch struck her head. Merciful darkness enveloped her.

AKRAM SHAKIRI was only twenty-one on that day, yet the events that would fill its twenty-four-hour span clearly marked his coming of age. The young Druze had never before been granted such latitude and respect within the militia. Never before had he been issued a gun without close supervision. He and his older brother, Rajab, had never before been assigned a sector to secure by themselves.

They had been where they always were—the back of their father's modest bakery—preparing the next morning's batches when the phone rang. Rajab had grabbed it first. One look at his brother's eyes and Akram knew that this was no bakery order.

Militia business. Within minutes Rajab had fumbled his way into their gun cache and tossed Akram a machine gun. "We've been assigned the hookah bar. Our time has come, little brother."

All of his life, he and his Druze brethren had been treated as outsiders, as virtual lepers by the larger Muslim communities they'd inhabited. No matter how much shared geography bound them in common, the two factions were socially and culturally miles apart. As a result, being transformed into an authority figure was a sensation completely alien to him and his family.

It's important to reiterate that the Druze are Islamic, but not quite. Over the centuries the sect has evolved its own divergent version of the Qur'an surrounded in secrecy. Druze considered themselves Muslim, but most Muslims did not extend them the same courtesy. They were seen as heretics, like Mormons in the eyes of many Protestants, or Samaritans in the eyes of Jews. To Akram and his family, this alienation meant depending on only their fellow Druze for support.

Akram had another problem, however. Despite the thrill of holding a gun and feeling empowered by its presence, he did not aspire to become a soldier. He only wished to do his duty and not fail his people in time of crisis. Nothing more.

Such were the feelings of many militia members, family men who spent months without cradling a weapon yet came out to fight when necessity demanded it. Akram was a poet, not a fighter—a condition his brother seemed determined to correct.

So now his day of reckoning was upon him. Akram strode up and down the Bekáa House and felt the thrill quickly fade for holding a powerful weapon and ordering around the unarmed. This was why he hated the cowardice of the little man with the big firearm who did whatever he wanted to whomever he wanted simply because he *could.*

He focused on watching his older brother for cues on how to act like a righteous warrior. He bore down on the requirements of the situation. *Control the group. Assess the threat. Wait for orders.*

"Nothing is happening here," came the voice of a man at a

crowded table, a Maronite priest. "And I need to return to my flock. They will be coming to church, seeking comfort. Please let me go to them."

A much older man beside the priest joined his plea. "I live downtown. I have a long and dangerous ride home ahead of me."

"Look, can't you just let them out one at a time?" asked Walid, the bar owner.

Rajab waved his rifle. There was no love lost between the Druze and the Maronites, and Akram's older brother was hardly inclined to risk anything to curry favor. "Quiet!" he shouted.

Akram peered out of the windows, trying to gauge the danger outside. Again, he saw only ribbons of smoke, heard only the occasional rattles of gunfire.

"What are we doing here?" he whispered to Rajab.

"Following orders. Something you need to learn."

"So . . . what do we do?"

"Wait for orders. If they run, shoot them."

THIRTY MINUTES LATER, nothing more had happened. Rajab had received no orders on his cell phone. No tanks or gunmen had passed outside. The only change seemed to be a greater sense of pent-up tension and nervousness among the hookah bar patrons themselves.

"Rajab, we should let them go," Akram said. "One at a time out the back. We were ordered to hold this bar, not the people. There's no reason to hold them!"

His brother looked outside one last time, then finally nodded. "One at a time. The priest first. Perhaps he'll catch a bullet on his way."

Akram walked over to the table where the bar owner, Walid, sat with the priest and Jew. "One at a time. The priest can go. Out the back, quickly. You'll remember that we've been kind to you today."

"Of course," Walid answered. "As God wills." Akram opened the Bekáa House's back door, shot glances up and down the alley, and nodded for him to leave.

Father Stephen took one step forward. The ground began to pass beneath him, and he breathed in relief. A block flew by.

Out of the corner of his eye, he saw a shape lying still upon the ground, almost completely concealed by the shadow of a deep alley. A body, breathing in shallow pulls.

He slowed and peered at the sight. A woman whose face was concealed by a twisted hijab now stained with blood. Another day in Beirut, another wounded soul. Just like the seventies and eighties, when more than a hundred thousand citizens, mostly civilians, had perished during the civil war.

Just go. He had neither the time nor the inclination to involve himself with this. His life already featured plenty of drama and heartache. He had seen civilian do-gooders stop and help the wounded during times of war before, earning nothing but a bullet in the head for their troubles. It only compounded the tragedy.

Father Stephen wasn't a courageous man—he'd proven that on more than one occasion. He was simply the dispenser of God's word to the faithful.

Embracing his limitations, he looked away and stepped over the blood trail to avoid soiling his shoes. The last thing he needed was to leave a blood trail all the way to Saint Thomas.

He resumed his sprint, breathing a sigh of relief. Within a minute, he was gone from sight, leaving Nicole Wagner with only minutes to live.

To be continued . . .

13

Ground Zero

JERUSALEM

AS STATED EARLIER, trying to steer clear of political ideology in the Middle East is nearly impossible, but in keeping with our primary objective of searching out the spirit of the Samaritan in the Muslim world, we have focused almost exclusively on the humanity and spiritual ideology of Christianity's perceived enemies. Much was said that would accomplish nothing except to inflame opponents of various political positions, particularly when it came to the war in Iraq and even more when it came to the region's greatest perceived enemy: Israel.

Make no mistake, to a man, everyone we'd spoken to thus far shared the perspective that the current Middle Eastern policies of both Israel and the United States were deeply offensive. The hatred was so raw that on numerous occasions I was quick to point out that I was Canadian. Carl, the American, spoke Arabic, and that earned him a special respect. So between us, we were good.

Still, in our many lengthy discussions, not even Carl and I could agree on what was politically right or wise. And this isn't because we held radically opposing viewpoints on the Middle East. Indeed, depending on the hour and the day, our own opinions seemed to shift.

There was little hope for consensus between even us, much less among those who live in the region.

Nowhere was this hopelessness more dramatic than during the time we spent in Israel.

Honestly, so much depended on perspective. When I was in the West Bank with Palestinian Christians, hearing stories as I gazed upon the massive concrete wall that separated Bethlehem from Jerusalem, I felt one way. When I crossed into Jerusalem and had dinner with an Orthodox Jew, looking back at the wall, I felt another way.

Each party views the other as the occupier. Each has been terribly wounded. The rifts seem to run deeper than the human heart can plumb.

I couldn't shake the similarities between the various factions in Lebanon, nor the near freakish parallels between the conflicts in the region today and the conflicts that had badgered the land two thousand years earlier. Jews, Samaritans, Romans. Muslims, Druze, Christians, Jews.

If the teaching of the Samaritan has not survived as a practical reality since Christ's death, the impetus for conflict that had motivated Jesus to give his teaching surely had.

The only common opinion shared by everyone we spoke to was that there was no political hope. We couldn't find a single soul on either side of the conflict who could suggest an amicable solution to the ideological gulf that divides the hearts of all who live in this small corner of the world.

Perhaps there is none. And perhaps there was none in the time of Jesus, an era in which the Romans were the occupiers, the Samaritans were the heretics, and great suffering was commonplace.

Instead of leading a revolt, as was expected of the coming Messiah, Jesus delivered a scandalous teaching that culminated in his story of the Samaritan. If a soldier demands you carry his bag a mile, carry it two, he taught. Love those who persecute you. Turn the other cheek. Love your neighbors, even if they are enemies, as you love yourself. And what of those of differing religious persuasions who follow a different god and deserve to have fire called down upon them, as James and John said of the Samaritans?

He who loves his neighbors is following God. Loving your neighbor as the heretical Samaritan did is the only solution to the hopeless strife that divides and destroys.

But based on what we'd seen thus far, following this teaching is hardly easier now than it was then.

We weren't in the Middle East to discover the elusive missing link to political policy or to set straight the path of the Arabs and Israelis. In fact, we really weren't in the Middle East to speak to Jews at all. We were there to meet with America's perceived enemies, primarily Muslims, whom Jesus suggested we love.

So let's get back to the harrowing tale of our final days at the table of our enemies.

THERE WERE only two occasions during which I saw Carl break a serious sweat. The first time was sitting in the red Cab from Hell, as recounted a couple of chapters ago. But this was only because the memory of his own very real kidnapping in Iraq was still on his mind.

The second time was crossing the border into Israel.

Here I became the mastiff and Carl became the nervous little puppy dog, though "little" is a misleading word to describe our farm boy from Nebraska. Approaching the border after a wonderful day of relaxation with Carl's friends in Jordan, I was eager and ready to lead the charge. You might even say that in the deepest folds of my conditioned mind, I was leaving the land of enemies and stepping onto the next best thing to U.S. soil. It's no wonder the Middle East throws the United States and Israel in the same bucket.

Carl, on the other hand, having been conditioned by more than a decade of life among the Arabs he loves, was feeling anything but safe and secure. After a while, the psyche of those you live among bleeds into your own.

It wasn't that Carl shared anyone's disdain for Israel. Heavens no. But you can sit through the telling of only so many horror stories about how this small nation called Israel has ripped the food from the mouths of babes and butchered whole villages before you begin to fear her as her neighbors fear her, regardless of how true or untrue said horror stories might be.

Honestly, I enjoyed seeing Carl sweat. This was, after all, a partnership, and the time had come for him to feel a little of what I'd felt for the last two weeks while he hummed his way over familiar ground.

We stopped on our way out of Jordan and gazed over the Promised Land, from high atop a mountain offering the same view Moses might have had millennia earlier. I saw no milk and honey, only bare hills that might make for a perfect desert race for a powerful dune buggy or motocross bike. I remember staring, wondering what all the fuss could possibly be about. Clearly it wasn't the land itself that so many had fought and died for. There was a much deeper magic at work here.

We crossed the Jordan River, nothing more than a strip of green reeds and some water if you look just right. We were close, so very close. And Carl was quiet, so very quiet.

The crossing took us three hours, most of which time was spent being interrogated by female Israeli security agents young enough to be my daughters. They couldn't seem to accept the outrageous notion that we, two Westerners, had actually been to Saudi Arabia, Lebanon, and Syria at all, much less within the span of two weeks.

This was indeed a rarity and it took them a long time to assure themselves that we were really there to write a book rather than blow something up. Maybe if Carl would have stopped sweating over all the documents they would have let us through sooner.

But finally we were through and, with a driver Carl had arranged for, headed toward Jerusalem. From there we would head to Bethlehem.

Which is in the West Bank. Home of the Palestinians and the political parties—Fatah and Hamas.

Carl was soon his usual cheery self, and I once again became the puppy dog. But I was hopeful. The final arrangements to meet with the Hamas hadn't been finalized. There was still a good chance they would fall through and I would be spared my worst fears.

Temple Mount

Visiting the Old City of Jerusalem is a daunting experience for anyone searching for truth. I'd been there once before, when I was in the fifth grade, and then I was more interested in fending off the verbal spars of my younger brother, Danny, than in absorbing history.

Now, thirty years later . . . The deluge of history flooding any open mind that enters this small patch of antiquity in the desert is enough to set the heart spinning. Like a top, the longer your head spins, the more unsteady it becomes, until it's in severe danger of toppling.

Carl's friend of a friend of yet another friend (because that's the way it works in the Middle East) had arranged for the "perfect" English-speaking guide to help us. We met him just inside one of the gates and knew immediately that he was not the perfect guide.

It wasn't that he was a Muslim—in fact, that was a bonus. It wasn't that he didn't speak good English. It wasn't his breath or his attitude. He was a good fellow in all respects.

But from the first few sentences recited in a near monotone for the thousandth time in his career, I knew we were going to get the same story everyone got. We'd climbed to a high point from where we could see all four quarters that divided the old city, and Ahmed was telling us the way it was and when what was built.

"This isn't going to work," I said, facing Carl.

"No?"

"We didn't come to see what a thousand other books have so eloquently described. Can you ask him in Arabic for the story behind the story?"

Carl tried. The guide said, "Yes, yes, of course." But within a minute, we both knew that he had no idea what the story behind the story was or even that there was one.

The Old City is half-mile square, divided by endless alleyways that cut back and forth between four quarters: a Christian Quarter, a Muslim Quarter, a Jewish Quarter, and an Armenian Quarter. The three monotheistic world religions hunker over this small chunk of city in which Jesus was convicted and put to death for his outrageous teaching.

Had the spirit of the Samaritan been snuffed out here, along the Via Dolorosa? Everywhere we went in the Old City we saw icons from every imaginable religious sect, all laying claim to a part of this city. Do they also lay claim to the teaching behind it all?

Do they embrace the parables that personify the life and death of him whom they claim to worship?

Pilgrims. Everywhere there were pilgrims in Orthodox black, lying at the foot of a relic erected in honor of Christ's trial, weeping. Pilgrims in Muslim white, paying homage to the third most holy of all Islamic sites.

Pilgrims dressed in Bermuda shorts like Chevy Chase in a Holy Land vacation, with thousands of dollars of electronics hanging off their hips and shoulders, come to walk where Jesus walked.

But what about his greatest teaching? Any takers?

"No, no, we need the guts," I said to Carl. "What the heck happened here? It's surreal. What makes it so surreal?"

At this point I'm not even sure that Carl knew what I meant. I certainly didn't. And then it hit me. The real story of Jerusalem can't be contained in either the mind or in a book. No guide could tell the way it was, because Jerusalem isn't about the mind; it's about the heart.

It's about the spirit of the Samaritan, not the Samaritan.

It goes beyond time, beyond religion, beyond policy, and no one quite knows what to do about that. So they force it back into the boxes of time, religion, and policy and then walk around shaking their heads, admitting that it will never work.

"What should we do?" Carl asked. "We have"—he looked at his watch—"six hours before we get picked up. We can come back tomorrow after we meet with the Hamas."

"Assuming we're still alive."

"Yes, there's always that. So, what do you say?"

I didn't know what to say, so I sat on a broken wall, stared out at the sun glinting off the gold Dome of the Rock on the Temple Mount, and let the world fade into a swirl of yesterday.

JERUSALEM'S TEMPLE MOUNT embodies such a tightly wrapped bundle of holy sites, religious tension, and historic magnitude that the whole package is truly mind-bending. You couldn't have made up a place so explosive and convoluted if you tried, not even with a simulation-building software capable of whipping up a "Global Religious Core" right out of a programmer's wildest imagination.

With its patch of intact temple wall, its bullet-pocked gates, its layers of antiquity underfoot crowded with mythology and lore, the place is dangerously overstuffed. Your simulation program, if it had survived this long without crashing, would probably take one look at the Temple Mount and flash an alert box warning of ideological overload.

It's nearly impossible to imagine this now, but there was a time when the site now occupied by Jerusalem's Temple Mount was just a Judean hilltop like countless others, sparsely studded with Aleppo pine and Syrian juniper, inhabited mainly by birds of prey, roving wildlife in search of food and water, or maybe the occasional stray lamb from a shepherd's flock.

What caused this spot, among so many on earth, to attract attention? Was this patch of earth upon which has been extracted so much sorrow and blood and sweat and tears chosen by deity?

Or did *we* choose it? We fallible human beings, through the paths of our errant feet and the places upon which we've happened to make some of our very best and very worst and most consequential choices. We choose it with every fervent prayer to God, wept aloud or chanted in supplication or scribbled on a piece of paper to be nestled among the stones of the Western Wall.

What defies human explanation is how so many of those choices, those prayers, and those footsteps just happened to intersect so precisely. So finally, the tangle of conflicting claims provoked by that intersection brings us face to face with the most explosive question of all . . .

Whose Holy City is this?

In some way, Jerusalem reminds one of ancient Baalbek, the ruins of which Carl and I sat upon and asked similar questions.

Since half the world seems to be fighting over the same hundred or so acres of Middle Eastern real estate, this question begs answering, as it has for millennia. Who does Jerusalem legitimately belong to? Who holds moral, if not literal, title to the land? And what criteria do we use to decide?

What if you decided based on the primacy of the Temple Mount in a religion's worldview? To begin with, the Jewish Midrash (a way of interpreting holy texts) holds that it was from here that the world expanded into its present form. The Torah records that it was here

God chose to rest his divine presence, the *Shekhinah*. Many Jews trust that here will rest the third, and hopefully final, temple. For centuries, the Jewish perennial Passover liturgy ended with "next year in Jerusalem." And rarely was there a dry eye in the house. Even Muslim scholars concede that Jerusalem is to the Jews what Mecca and Medina are to their own people. In one of the most dramatic re-unions ever played out on the human stage, the Jews defied the odds and rallied from the four corners of the earth to return here.

Muslims, on the other hand, revere the mount as the location of Muhammad's journey to Jerusalem and his ascent into heaven. It is home to the Al-Aqsa Mosque and the Dome of the Rock, the oldest extant Islamic building in the world. It is the place where it is said the world will gather for the Final Judgment. It ranks as the third holiest site in Islam, after Mecca and Medina. There are other Muslim claims as well. Moses, David, and Jesus are all considered great Islamic prophets, as is Solomon, who first built his holy temple to the one true God here on this mount. For a time, Muslims once faced Jerusalem during their prayers, before the direction was changed to Mecca.

Christians cling to the birth, ministry, death, and return of Christ as all occurring within five miles of this mount.

A dead heat, I would say.

What if you decided who should control this land on the basis of possession? One Muslim faction or another has controlled the Temple Mount since medieval times—even after that control was interrupted, and altered forever, in 1967. However, the Children of Israel held it as their home and capital for thousands of years, until being violently expelled.

Again, inconclusive.

What if we decided based on comparing the relative amounts of peace and harmony brought by each successive religion? In other words, on the basis of which religion had been the kindest and most beneficial to Jerusalem and her citizens. Oh, what a bloody tale that would be. Muslim, Jew, and Christian have all slaughtered for possession of this piece of land. But Christians have perhaps been the most guilty during the last fifteen hundred years.

When the Muslims conquered Jerusalem in 638, Sophronius, the Christian patriarch of Jerusalem, insisted that his surrender be made to the most senior member of the Islamic state. He put on his full patriarchal robes and rode out to the Mount of Olives, there to meet Caliph Omar of Medina. They agreed, as on other occasions, that the safety and freedom of Christians to worship would be guaranteed. Together, the two rode to the Temple Mount. The caliph was shocked to find it a heap of ruins and junk. Some speculate that the city's Christian inhabitants had done this in order to humiliate the Jews or to perpetuate Christ's prophecy that no stone would be left unturned there.

And the Crusades? Here was their impact on the people of Jerusalem. Raymond of Aguiliers wrote upon entering the Holy City, "Men rode in blood up to their knees and bridle reins." William of Tyre wrote of these Christian warriors, "It was impossible to look upon the vast numbers of the slain without horror; everywhere lay fragments of human bodies, and the very ground was covered with the blood of the slain. . . . Still more dreadful was it to gaze upon the victors themselves, dripping with blood from head to foot, an ominous sight that brought terror to all of who met them. It is reported that within the Temple enclosure alone about ten thousand infidels perished, in addition to those who lay slain everywhere throughout the city."

The Jews were officially barred from entering Jerusalem for centuries, so their religion's impact on the city and its people is of more recent vintage. However, even one who supported their claims on the city would have to concede that it was anything but peaceful. The years since 1948 have hardly been rosy times for the previous inhabitants of the city and its environs.

In all, historian Eric Cline of George Washington University counts at least 118 separate conflicts in and for Jerusalem over the past four thousand years. Jerusalem has been destroyed completely at least twice, besieged twenty-three times, attacked fifty-two more times, captured and recaptured forty-four times, suffered twenty revolts and more riots than anyone could count, and has changed hands peacefully only twice.

The legacy of the last four millennia is one of pronounced love for Jerusalem and her God, accompanied by a coldness and mistreatment of her neighbors. If one looks at the history of Jerusalem since the time of Christ, you would have to conclude that his great teaching has been largely ignored since his death. Today, Jerusalem is the most divided piece of land on earth.

In present-day Jerusalem, the Islamic authorities prevent Jews from coming to the Temple Mount, even though their control over the site is custodial and intended to ensure everyone's free access. And speaking of custodianship, parts of the mount are piled with mounds of rubble, much of it bearing great archaeological value, some bearing actual pieces of the Jewish temple itself.

Likewise, within the Christian community, unspeakable affronts abound. Every inch of ground in and around the Church of the Holy Sepulchre, where Christ laid down his life for his neighbor (Golgotha to many Christians), is fiercely contested by different Christian groups. So fiercely contested, indeed, that the key to the outer door of the church has been given to a local Muslim as a neutral party. His name is Abu Joudea, and we spoke to him briefly as he sucked on a Marlboro and showed us the key.

The fight for the Church of the Holy Sepulchre real estate has been so polarizing that the Coptic Church of Ethiopia, having lost its deed to part of the church in a fire, has been relegated to a rooftop presence by the other groups. There its priests live in squalor and sickness, exposed to the elements, too afraid to leave their perch for as much as a moment lest even that property be confiscated by their competitors.

Apparently no one's hands are completely clean.

So, after all this, you may be expecting a predictably even-handed, egalitarian conclusion, something like "Jerusalem is *everyone's* Holy City."

But that doesn't strike me as right either, certainly not in light of Christ's teaching to love your neighbors, carry their burdens, and if necessary lay down your life for them as he did.

I certainly think that the mountains of earthly evidence, from all sides, amount to something like a highly fascinating and confusing wash. Each side can dredge up a pile of highly entertaining data to support its claim to own Jerusalem. Likewise, all sides can muster a heartening saga of sacrifice and reverence for Jerusalem. We all certainly love Jerusalem—we've nearly loved her to death.

But once you've dug through the mounds of rubble and corpses and incriminating evidence of all kinds, it's also quite clear that all sides have committed enough cruelty and treachery in the name of religion to have clearly disqualified themselves from ever setting foot within its perimeter again. If Jerusalem is a showcase for faith, it is also a clear picture of the utter failure of organized religion to bring peace and harmony to those it purports to love. Faith may have exalted Jerusalem, but religious fanaticism has decimated it time and time again. If God had ample cause to banish Adam and Eve from Eden, how much more does he have for banishing religion from his city!

Therefore, being a bit of a contrarian, I am happy to arrive at the following thought: It's *no one's* Holy City. In the end, like the earth around it, it belongs to God. He is the one who makes it holy. And when asked what was the greatest principle to live and die for, Jesus gazed out over this land and said, love God and love the heretic next to you.

He died for that truth.

TRANSCRIPT

Abu Joudea: I'll introduce myself to you. My name is Abu Joudea. I am the keeper of key of the Church of the Holy Sepulchre. I have inherited the key from my father and my grandfather. It's like the kingdom. We received the key on the tenth day of the entry of Saladin in the city of Jerusalem. Saladin was fighting the Crusaders. On the tenth day, he was invited to the church. He came here with my great-grandfather, who was the chief of the Muslims in Mecca. Saladin knew the chief treated the Christians decently, so we inherited the key. I'm the keeper of the church. We received the key 840 years ago. This is the same key. It's the original. This is the oldest key in the whole world.

Carl: Why would this key not be with a Christian family, because it's a Christian church? Why is it with a Muslim family?

Abu Joudea: Because when Saladin entered Jerusalem there was a big struggle between the Roman Catholic, the Greek Orthodox, the Armenian Ottomans, and the Coptics of Egypt. They all wanted the key, so Saladin took the key and gave it to a neutral person. Not a Christian but a Muslim. So the key has remained in my family for centuries.

Carl: So, do you have a son to pass it on to?

Abu Joudea: I have three sons. And grandsons. But my sons are too interested in other things. We will see.

Carl: What do you think of Jesus' teaching to love your enemies?

Abu Joudea: This is good. I love all men.

The Mufti of Jerusalem

Our driver got lost looking for the house of Sheik Ekrima Sa'id
Sabri, the grand mufti of Jerusalem, appointed by Yasser Arafat.
Technically, his reign as grand mufti had expired, but his influence
has not and he is clearly the most prominent Muslim cleric in
Jerusalem at the time of this writing. To be mufti anywhere is some-
thing very special; to be mufti of Jerusalem is amazing. Mufti Sabri's
pulpit to the world is in the Al-Aqsa Mosque atop the Temple
Mount, below which Jews wail and pray.

The mufti's reputation has been complicated by some statements he made in March of 2000 in which he expressed doubts
about the number of Jewish Holocaust victims, calling it a "fairy
tale exploited by Israel to capture international solidarity." He
then refused to meet with rabbis in honor of the pope's visit to
Jerusalem.

Indeed, Sabri has been at the heart of the more violent second
intifada (uprising) following Ariel Sharon's visit to the Al-Aqsa
Mosque later that same year. Some would go so far as to say he led
the charge to the declarations of violence that resulted.

Naturally, we were eager to speak with him.

TRANSCRIPT

Ted: We've been asking rather unusual questions to help Americans understand Muslims in the Middle East as people. May we ask you these questions?

Mufti Sabri: It's a good subject and I will give you information. Have you visited anyone before me, in Jerusalem?

Carl: No, you are our first. We came last night, and this morning we went around the city. So, what do you think is the biggest misunderstanding that Americans have about the Arab Muslim?

Mufti Sabri: Because the American people are simple, it has been used by the Zionist people to organize this nation because they twisted the American people so that they would be against the Arab Muslims. And as a religion, we recognize all the prophets in the world. We are open and believe in what they believe in.

If the American people have a real idea of Islam, they wouldn't be against Muslims. There are Islamic centers in the majority of the cities in the U.S. who are allowing Americans to get a better idea about Islam. We believe that the media is really playing a role of the understanding of the people, and unfortunately, the media is controlled by the Zionist people of the U.S. And that's why there is a misunderstanding. In all the Muslims, you find a few people who are extremists and point those out. For Christians, there are organizations that are unacceptable, like the Mafia. In Islam, there are some extremists who give America the wrong idea.

Carl: What do you think the Arabs misunderstand about the American people?

Mufti Sabri: The only problem is the influence of the Zionists on the United States.

Carl: What do you enjoy doing with your extra time? Do you have hobbies?

Mufti Sabri: I like to read. I like sports and watching football [soccer] matches on TV sometimes. But daily, I read before I go to bed.

Carl: What do you like to read?

Mufti Sabri: Books concerning history. And I wrote twenty books. Most of the books concern Islam. I also published a weekly newspaper in Jerusalem concerning religion, society, and even medical matters. I get to choose the subject I wanted to publish. As a mufti, I always am concerned with health matters in Jerusalem.

Ted: Do you watch movies?

Mufti Sabri: Rarely. Sometimes I watch historical or classical movies. Have you seen *The Message*, about Islam?

Carl: Yes, I've seen it. Have you watched *The Passion of the Christ?*

Mufti Sabri: No, I haven't seen it.

Carl: What advice would you give my three children if they were sitting here?

Mufti Sabri: First of all, to study till they reach the highest point of studying. Secondly, to look to the other religions and to study them. Those who look at other religions won't be extremists to his religion and they will find mercy in other religions. So they will be more understanding when they try to study or learn about other religions and cultures in addition to their own religion. Thirdly, fill their time with things that are important. Emptiness time is not good. Time is on us.

Carl: What makes you laugh?

Mufti Sabri: When I see other people happy, I am happy. In general I'm serious, but I like jokes. I like to hear jokes, but I can't tell jokes.

Now I have a question from my side. Most of the Muslim Arabs in the Mediterranean countries and Europe hate America. The reason of that is since the war in Iraq. The Congress has been deceived himself and are attacking everywhere just like a cowboy with two guns who doesn't know where to shoot. And that is one of the reasons I don't like the American politics. He is supporting the wrong and the unjust like Israel. That's my opinion. I can't understand how simple Americans have to wait years to find out that they had a bad policy. Why?

Ted: America is very divided, like any other place in the world. There are many who agree with what you said and many who don't. The question is, how can people so divided come together? We are talking about learning to love your neighbor. In order to love your neighbor, you must first understand that they are real people. Laughter is something that unites all people. So maybe you can share with us a story of a time your children or grandchildren made you laugh recently.

Mufti Sabri: I have a four-year-old granddaughter. She watches her siblings go to school in the morning, but she is too young to go to school. So she takes her bag and walks with them as if she is going to school. And she starts singing these songs that her brothers and sisters learn at school. She makes conversations with their teachers, and she acts as if she went to school and returned. She tells me that she went to school and her teacher loves her. But she doesn't go. Her name is Na'ira Sabri, named after her grandmother.

Ted: You see, this one little story can connect millions of hearts.

Carl: What you said to us earlier about the politics—nobody will listen to you. What you just said about your granddaughter—everyone will listen. The story could affect the Middle Eastern politics more than condemning U.S. policy.

Ted: Are there any other funny stories you would like to share?

Mufti Sabri: I think in Egypt you got a lot of jokes.

Carl: That's true. Egyptians like to joke.

Mufti Sabri: There is a bus with two floors, a double-decker. Two couples enter the bus. One takes the roof and one stays on the lower part. The couple on the top asks the other passengers, "Where has this bus traveled today?" The passengers tell them they have been to Ramallah. "But you," the passengers ask, "where are you going?" And the couple replies that they're going nowhere yet because the driver hasn't come yet.

Carl: (Laughs) It's the same bus. (Evidently Carl gets the local humor.)

Mufti Sabri: There are two dogs. One is a big-sized dog and the other is small. The owner carries them and sits on the street. He asks ten dinars for the big dog and twenty for the small. A customer passes by him and asks, "I'm wondering, why do you ask ten for the big one and for the small one twenty?" The owner says, "The big one is dog, but the small one is a dog and a son of a dog."

Carl: (Laughs. Like I said . . .)

Mufti Sabri: You have five more minutes.

Carl: When was the last time you cried?

Mufti Sabri: So many! Well, in 1969 when they burned the mosque, that was really a shock for me. And when my mother and father passed away it was very hard. Last time in the last ten days, I cried because I was missing a friend who passed away. A very good friend . . .

Carl: When somebody asked Jesus what is the greatest commandment of all the Torah, he said, "Love God with all your heart, mind, and soul and love your neighbor as yourself." So how would you advise others to love their neighbors and even their enemies?

Mufti Sabri: Everyone in this world has been committed to his religion. If they are committed to their religion, there will never be disputes or war between nations. We appreciate what Jesus has advised the people to do, and I wish that Christian people would take the teachings seriously and do what Jesus has asked them to do. As Muslims, we appreciate Christianity and appreciate Jesus. We consider him as a prophet and respect him. As Muslims, we are not against any religion, not even Judaism. We are only against the Zionists and politics which cause people to suffer. And we are against occupation.

Ted: Much like the Jews were against the Roman occupation in the time of Christ. You have an infectious smile.

Mufti Sabri: (Smiles)

14

Nicole
SIX OF SEVEN

OF THE THREE MEN who had awaited Nicole Wagner at the Bekáa House hookah bar, and who had been present when the two young Druze militiamen burst in, Father Stephen had already left, and Naum Sareel was released next.

Naum had managed to argue that an old Jew with no relatives or friends anywhere close would be lucky to survive being stranded at night in south Beirut during a military attack.

Walid had given him careful instructions to follow the route Father Stephen had taken, out the back and through the sheltered alleyway. Naum had stumbled out and, thanks to some miracle, followed Walid's hurried directions to the letter.

Two minutes later, he came across the same body that Father Stephen had stumbled upon. The body almost blocked his path to the free sidewalk he was headed for. He stopped and considered another route. But Walid had insisted he go this way for his own safety.

He began to inch his way past the woman's body with his back to the wall. She was still breathing. The scarf obscured her face and blood colored every part of her exposed skin. Clearly, she was alive but badly hurt.

For perhaps only the third time in his life, he felt his heart shut tight as though of its own accord. His once ample capacity for compassion, seared and bruised by years in this city, clamped tight once more. Just as he had senselessly refused his son's pleas to move to Israel, just as he had so many times coldly avoided the smiles of passing pedestrians and small children on the street, now again he willed himself not to care.

It was too much trouble. Too much risk, for no gain. Too much pain, always pain in this accursed city.

Then he was past and hobbling forward as fast as he could on his old legs.

Meanwhile, back at the bar, Walid was plying all of his political goodwill in an attempt to convince the gunmen to let them all go out the back. One at time like this would take all night. They had families to attend to—for the love of God, have mercy!

They all heard the back door slam shut and spun to see a middle-aged man rush in, looking for safety.

"What's going on?" Walid demanded. "What have you heard?"

The new patron glanced at the guns, then answered cautiously. "They've closed the airport and taken over the government. It's bloody hell out there."

"Not nearby, though. In the Hariri pockets, fighting with Hezbollah, right?"

"Yes. But I passed a body in the alley up the street. Nowhere is safe now."

Walid's heart quickened. Had Naum fallen on his way out? He would never forgive himself if he had unwittingly sent the old man to his death. For that matter, neither would the Jew's son, now a leading Mossad official.

He turned to the younger gunman. "I have to go check. It could be one of my—"

"You'll go nowhere!" the older gunman snapped.

But the younger, kinder gunman, this so-called terrorist with baby skin, stepped up to defend him. "Go. Hurry, but come back. Your hookah bar hasn't been damaged; don't give us a reason to change that."

Spurred by the threat, Walid hurried outside and fairly ran to the alleyway's entrance. His heart beating wildly, he bent over the body. Even though he, too, was jaded to the sight of death, another part of him hated to see someone in bad shape so close to his establishment. He knelt forward, hands on his knees, and stared harder.

It's not Naum, he realized with a rush of relief. It was a woman. Barely alive. Either way it wasn't Naum and it wasn't one of his patrons. Just another neighborhood ghost, taken before its time.

Not his responsibility.

He sighed, inwardly blaming it on how cruel Beirut could be sometimes. Then he shook his head against a renewal of pity and walked away.

AKRAM HEARD the twin explosions, tried his best to guess their location, and spun to his brother. "Those sounded near our house!" he whispered frantically. "Didn't it sound like that?"

Rajab turned in the same direction, thought for a moment, then frowned. "Maybe."

"Mother's still at home!"

Their father, a higher-ranking militia member, was out securing one of the entrances to Shatila. But their mother would have been left alone to fend for herself during the crisis.

"She'll be fine," said Rajab. "She's survived a lot worse than this."

"But those explosions seemed close," Akram insisted.

Rajab closed his eyes in derision and shook his head. "Only my brother sits here worrying about his mama while Beirut goes up in flames."

"The city isn't going up in flames. Only our street."

An outer door slammed open. Both brothers turned as one, weapons instantly ready to fire. But it was only the bar owner, Walid, holding up his hands and heaving to regain his breath.

"How are things out there?" Rajab asked.

"Fighting, but it's sporadic," the bar owner replied. "Nothing right here in our neighborhood. At least, until those last two explosions, which sounded close."

Akram grabbed his brother's arm. "I have to go! I'm going to check—"

"Fine," his brother said. "Check on her. Tell her I'll be back soon."

Akram ran out the back of the Bekáa House, almost tearing the rear door from its aging hinges in his haste. He sprinted down the alley and veered into a second alley that led to the main street.

He was so focused on images of his house leveled by the bomb blasts that he nearly stumbled over the obstacle that suddenly appeared before him. He jumped over it, deftly landing at midstride beyond it.

Then an awareness struck his brain. The obstacle was a body.

He turned, his concern for his mother's safety still pounding inside him. He couldn't tell much from the body's position, but somehow the woman struck him as young. And she was alive.

Akram bent over and pulled aside the hijab from her face. She was beautiful, young, and had blond hair. More than likely a foreign girl. European.

He bent closer and gently pressed her mouth open. Her breath was incredibly weak, but it was there. She was lying at odd angles and bleeding profusely.

But what he could do? The street was empty. No ambulance would come out here right now, in the middle of a conflict. Even the nearby camp clinic would be battened down tightly, protected by neighborhood snipers who would shoot anyone they didn't know.

Especially a cursed Druze.

He had no choice. He had to check on Mother, but he couldn't leave this person here to die. The very thought of it formed a knot of bitter refusal inside him. God had made him a better person than that.

Pulling off his keffiyeh, he bound it tightly around the worst-bleeding wound, at the top of her left shoulder. He threw his AK-47 into an old fifty-five-gallon barrel for later retrieval, bent down, and hefted the girl over his shoulder. Breathing twice as loudly and emphatically as before, he headed toward home.

Akram had feared in vain. As he neared his street, he saw flames licking the sky almost a quarter mile to the south. His mother and his home were safe.

And when he came running in huffing like he was about to pass out, carrying a body in his arms, the fifty-eight-year-old matriarch of the family flew into action. His mother led him into his bedroom and bid him lay the body down on his unmade bed. Then she sat against the bedside and started pulling back clothes.

"She's weak. Very weak."

"But she'll live?" Akram asked.

"I doubt it," his mother said softly. "Either way, this was a good thing you did. Now leave us. I have to undress her."

To be continued . . .

15

Living Among Enemies

THE WEST BANK

FOR SOME REASON, I'd never before realized how close Bethlehem is to Jerusalem. Only five miles separate Manger Square at the center of Bethlehem from the Old City in Jerusalem. Take out the Israel Defense Forces checkpoints and the clogged traffic, and the journey would be like running down to the Best Buy to buy a PlayStation 3.

We stood in the middle of Manger Square staring at the Church of the Nativity. Behind us stood our hotel, a converted monastery. The walls that surround the square are still pocked with bullet holes from the infamous standoff between Hamas fighters and the IDF in 2002.

This is the birthplace of Jesus, the one who died with a cry for love and forgiveness on his lips. "Father, forgive them for they know not what they do."

At no time during the last three weeks had I felt so disembodied, so confused, so discouraged, so lost as I felt standing there in the square of Christ's birth, five miles from the Church of the Holy Sepulchre, where he was reportedly crucified. Oddly enough, the Hamas hold the keys to Bethlehem, and a Muslim named Abu Joudea holds the key to the site of Christ's crucifixion. Both are in a Jewish state, left bloody by Christians in years gone by.

For the first time, Carl felt as discouraged as I. We had come to learn what had become of those cutting words that divided history—"Love your neighbor"—and we were staring at the face of death on all sides.

The problem I have in writing this today is that there is simply no way to appropriately parse the condition of this land without infuriating one group or the other. The situation is complex and it's bathed in centuries of blood. It's almost as if humanity, being enraged by the outrageous teaching of love, killed the teacher and then went on to wage war against all who set foot on the land where he walked. Throughout history, all hands have been bloodied.

I felt like a small bird on the edge of a great chasm. Should I fly in? Should I fly off? Should I stop flying altogether? God knows, the wings of all who live in the Holy Land eventually get clipped.

"We need some money," Carl said, glancing at his watch. "We could get some on our way to meet Sami. But we can't be late."

Sami. If there was one person whom Carl demanded I sit with, it was Sami. Sami, we must meet Sami.

"How do we get money?" I asked.

"ATM."

"ATM? They have those here? This is where Jesus was born."

Carl smiled. "Give unto Caesar what is Caesar's. Money, dude. There's always money."

"We're walking?" I asked.

"We're supposed to meet Sami at the Holy Land Trust about a quarter of a mile from here. We should go."

We left Manger Square and all of its history behind, like two lost children, walking along the streets of Bethlehem in search of the ATM someone had told Carl was at the bottom of the hill on the way to Holy Land Trust.

We passed two American youths, maybe in their early twenties, idealists who had braved the ocean to study peace and nonviolence under the tutelage of Sami Awad, they told us. We were in Bethlehem to meet with the Hamas who used violence to be heard. But in their midst walked this one man named Sami who defied violence and cried for peace through love. The contrast could not be missed, even by reputation alone.

"How many volunteers come here for Sami?" I asked.

Carl shrugged. "I don't know. Hundreds each year."

So, then, who was this man on the lips of babes, speaking a new language of love in a land filled with so much violence? I suddenly felt a sense of history. The scene from the movie of Gandhi's life, in which a journalist goes to meet a wizened old man at his ashram in India, filled my mind. The journalist had left a changed man.

What if without knowing it we had stumbled on this land's Gandhi?

Sami Awad

Half an hour and two ATMs later, Carl and I were ushered into a small complex on the edge of a cliff. The Holy Land Trust. We found Sami reclining in a room full of cushions at the back of the complex.

The man who stood and greeted us was no wizened old man with round spectacles. He was dressed in gray cotton slacks and a white shirt that needed ironing. Maybe midthirties, with smiling brown eyes.

"Sit. Tea?"

Tea with Gandhi, I thought.

After fifteen minutes of exchanged pleasantries, Sami nodded at me. "So. You are writing a book, I understand. You want me in this book?"

"I don't know. It depends."

"And what is this book about?"

"We plan to call it *Tea with Hezbollah: In Search of the True Samaritan.* We have come to the Middle East to speak to our so-called enemies about the greatest commandment of Jesus."

"Which is?"

"To love your neighbors as yourself," Carl said. "Some say it's essentially an impossible teaching."

A sparkle brightened Sami Awad's eyes. "To love your enemies," he said. "Not an easy thing."

I pulled out my little white Sanyo recorder and turned it on. "So, do you think you can shed some light on the subject?"

"I can only tell you my story. But perhaps it will help."

We were reclined on the pillows, but now Sami stood and paced with one finger against his lips, deep in thought. Behind him was a framed, blown-up photograph of a man being dragged by Israeli police. The name Mubarak Awad was inscribed on the frame. Flags of all the Middle Eastern nations hung on the walls.

"Do you know," Sami said, "there was a baby born in this very town two thousand years ago, and when the authorities heard about him, they thought he would rise up and become a terrorist to lead a rebellion that would overthrow the government. King Herod fought against this coming violence with his own campaign of violence. He killed thousands of children, hoping that the one baby terrorist would be killed in the campaign."

Sami lifted one finger and faced me with his bright eyes. "But that one child grew to be a man, and that one man did not bring the terror of violence. He brought a message of peace and love. And in the end this message was far more dangerous and powerful than any kind of violence. Now I live to make that message known in a land that has forgotten it."

"They killed him for it," Carl said.

Sami offered Carl a faint smile. "It is a dangerous thing to speak about peace when everyone around you wants violence. Or to speak of love when there is so much hate."

"Has your life been in danger?" I asked.

I immediately knew that it was a foolish question, the kind only a Westerner would ask. But Sami was gracious.

"All of our lives are in danger here," he said. "At this very moment. I am surrounded by enemies on all sides. Every morning when I kiss my wife, we both know it could be our last."

Not eager to rush into another foolish question, I waited, then continued when the silence grew heavy.

"So tell me, why would you put your life on the line?"

Sami eased himself to a pillow, crossed his legs, took a deep breath, and told me.

TRANSCRIPT

Sami: My story started before I was born. During the war that led to the creation of Israel, my father's family lived in Jerusalem, a neighborhood called Mousrarah where Jews, Christians, and Muslims lived as neighbors for decades at least. As the war broke out in 1948, that neighborhood was right in the middle of the exchange of fire between the Israeli troops on one side and the Arab troops on another side.

Ted: And you were Christian?

Sami: Yes, Christian.

My grandfather had seven children. Their home was just outside the neighborhood, so it was very nice with gardens and two stories, but it was right in the middle of that exchange of fire. Everything was happening around it. He realized at one point that his whole family would be killed. His only thought of how to protect them was to raise a white flag on top of the house to show both sides that a family lived there. So he climbed to the roof, but as soon as he placed the white flag, he was shot and killed by a stray bullet.

It took a few hours for the children who were at the bottom of the house to even leave the house and to get to their father, and they found his dead body on the top of the roof. They brought him down into the house and actually had to move tile and dig a hole inside the house itself to bury him.

A few days later, after that happened, the Israeli troops took over that whole area and kicked our whole family out of the house. So they moved into the Old City of Jerusalem, which was under Jordanian control, then moved to Bethlehem, where they had other relatives.

My grandmother, now single, wasn't able to care for all seven children and had no choice but to send them to an orphans' home. So my father, uncles, and aunts spent all of their years growing up in an orphanage. It was very difficult in the '40s and '50s. They went from living peacefully in a large home to being orphans and outcasts with little to eat or wear.

Each Christmas my grandmother would gather all of her children and give them a message of forgiveness for the Jews. The philosophy of peace and love that my grandmother placed in their hearts stuck with them. She would say, "The soldier who shot your father did not know who he was; otherwise he would not have shot him."

Ted: If you know them, you won't hate them.

Sami: Exactly. This was her message to my father and uncles.

Now, my father eventually found his way to the United States, a long story that I won't go into now, then returned, found my beautiful mother in Gaza, returned to Kansas City, in the U.S., and it was there that I was born. The family moved back to Bethlehem when I was six months old. My father took a job as the principal at a Mennonite orphanage school, having a heart for orphans, as you might expect. I grew up in that school, and always, always, I heard a message of love and peace towards all people. I was a Palestinian and I was a Christian living in military occupation, but my world was a world of love and peace to others despite the terrible conditions around all of us. Growing up, I saw my kind father mistreated so many times, but always he would say nothing and only smile. The images will never leave my head, you see?

So, when you ask why I would risk my life now for peace, I would point back to my childhood and say that seeds of love and peace were sown into my heart. Now they bear fruit. I owe the land my life.

Ted: When did you first take up nonviolence as the path to peace?

Sami: Ahh . . . The rest of the story, as they say. (A mischievous smile plays on his face.)

My father's brother, Mubarak Awad, was also deeply impacted by my grandmother's message of forgiveness. In 1984, when I was fourteen, he opened a center in Jerusalem called the Palestinian Center for the Study of Nonviolence. As a young teenager, I loved going to the center. For the first time there was something I could do. I felt that this is what Jesus would do. Jesus would not just sit back and allow injustice to happen, but at the same time, he would not carry the sword and start killing everyone who was doing this injustice. So I joined the center as a volunteer when I was fourteen years old. We did many simple things to express ourselves, like planting on lands that were threatened to be confiscated for the building of settlements. We would go with internationals, Palestinians, and sympathetic Israelis to a piece of land that had Israeli bulldozers on them and we would just go plant trees and have sit-ins. Then the Israeli army would come and uproot the trees. And we would come back and plant more trees. (Sami chuckles.) So simple, yes? But it's a voice and there is only love in our hearts.

Ted: Did it work?

Sami: Of course it worked. We were living the commandment of Jesus—that is a measure of success no one can measure. But, like Jesus himself, my uncle was misunderstood and rejected by those on all sides, including our own Palestinian people. His message of peace confronted the rhetoric of the freedom fighters, which has always been that this land will only be liberated through violence inflicted by freedom fighters here and in Lebanon and Syria. But Mubarak, my uncle, stood against them all and spoke of nonviolence.

Then, in 1987, the first Palestinian uprising broke out, the Intifada. A lot of what Mubarak had been teaching up until that point became adopted by the people as legitimate and he gained acceptance to a measure. The—

Ted: Can you tell us what kind of activities—

Sami: (Lifting a hand) Please, be patient. (Smiles) The underground leadership at that time was issuing leaflets that instructed people to do things at different times, but all unified across the occupied territories. So, for example, they would call for a general strike next Thursday. Everybody in the community closed their shops at that time and no one went to school. Or they would call, saying that on Wednesday evening at seven everybody go out and whistle and blow your horns or trumpets and stand on your roof. So at seven that Wednesday night you would just hear waves of whistling and shouting and yelling across Palestine for five minutes. The Israelis heard them as well. This was very empowering to the people, you see?

One of the best examples, which was very powerful although it was very small in terms of its value, was when the underground leadership said at one point during the month, when Israel changes its time [during daylight savings], we'll wait one week after they change their time. So let us work on Palestinian time. This idea of empowering and separation, and that the people can make their own decisions, played out well. It was not threatening. So during that week, you could see children going to school and asking each other what time they had. They were asking when they should go to school. Do they go at eight or at seven? Even some of the teachers, being empowered by that, said they would go on Palestinian time. That happened all through the West Bank, Gaza, and even East Jerusalem.

The military saw this action as so threatening, so they were ordering the Israeli military to stop and to check people on the streets just to see what time they had on their watches. They would give an option to that person that they would either have five minutes to go back to Israeli time or they will pay the price. The price was they would break the watch and the wrist of that person. In many cases, even the arms were broken. Hundreds of arms were broken.

It was during this time, in 1988, that my uncle was arrested. The Israeli army came to his house in Jerusalem and took him to prison. He was put on trial with much media attention. Human rights organizations in Israel and around the world were calling Israel to release my uncle, Mubarak. But he was ordered to be deported from the country, never again to be returned. In 1988, after the judgment came out, he was put in handcuffs and taken to the airport and put on a plane to the U.S. Now he lives in Washington, D.C.

Those days influenced me, sixteen at the time, heavily. With my uncle gone, I stepped in, committed my life to nonviolence, and began to lead demonstrations in Bethlehem. It was now me, instead of my uncle, negotiating with the soldiers to allow us to march peacefully.

But as I became more engaged, my father became very worried. He knew that I wouldn't simply be deported as my uncle had been; I would likely be arrested and put in jail. So my father sent me back to the U.S. to continue my education. At the end of 1988, at the age of seventeen, I returned to Kansas City.

Ted: May I ask a question?

Sami: Yes, yes of course. I didn't mean to make you shy.

Ted: Of course not. But help me understand this, because I, too, grew up in another country and came to the United States when I was eighteen. American Christians tend to think differently about the Middle East than Christians who live in the Middle East. How did your time in America influence you?

Sami: Every day I woke, I longed to go back and heal the wounds of my people. I visited for a short time in 1994 while the Oslo peace process was in negotiations, and we had very high hopes. But I knew I had to further my education, so I returned to the United States and in 1996 acquired a master's degree in international relations with a focus on peace and conflict resolution.

So you see, at this time after many years in the United States, I was quite optimistic, thinking that politically things were moving forward. But when I went back in 1996, I quickly realized that the reality on the ground was different from what the politicians were talking about. The situation for the Palestinians had actually become worse during the years of the peace process.

So at that time, I felt it was important to bring back the work of my uncle. I dug all of the books, including those on and by Martin Luther King and Gandhi, out of storage and started reading them yet again, doing my own research. With three others, I began a new work of nonviolence with a radio station.

Ted: If there was one iconic teaching or event on which you hang your ministry, what would it be?

Sami: I'll give you two. One event and one teaching. First the event. (He sips some tea, thinking.) You know, I've always been fascinated with the birth of Jesus; living here in Bethlehem, it's hard to escape. Millions come to honor the birth of the Prince of Peace. They line up to kiss the ground where he was born, here in the heart of violence to this day. In 1996 I met a couple, the Wainwrights, who had a great love for the Palestinian people. Together, in the year 2000, we embarked on a long journey to follow the path of the Magi who came to pay homage to the child.

They started in Iran, on through Baghdad to Syria, down to Jordan, where I joined them, on across to Bethlehem on camels. The twelve-hundred-mile journey took ninety-nine days and it was beautiful. The journey was a path to peace. But in October of 2000 the peace process collapsed and the second Intifada started. The whole area fell into an abyss of violence that we live in to this day.

There was another journey that is even dearer to me: Mary's journey from Bethlehem to save her child from Herod's soldiers. This story became very real to me in April of 2002 when I was trying to take my nine-month-pregnant wife, Rana, out of Bethlehem. Rana was due to have our first child at any time. If we stayed in Bethlehem, we knew we would have been under curfew, probably for many days, and would be unable to reach the hospital when the time came. This would have put the lives of Rana and the baby in grave danger. If it were any other time, we would have ignored the requests and pleas of our friends and family to leave Bethlehem, but the life of my child was at stake.

I was not able to take the story of Mary out of my mind as we were driving on dirt roads around Bethlehem and Beit Jala trying to leave Bethlehem in a car with big "TV" letters taped to it, passing by Israeli army tanks and army personnel carriers.

At that time, due to the violence, Israeli army troops were being brought from all corners into Bethlehem. Curfews were being imposed and shooting and shelling were heard in the distance as we continued our drive. As the army troops entered Bethlehem, we were trying to escape to Jerusalem. After traveling for almost an hour on a very narrow and rough dirt road, we reached the first army checkpoint to Jerusalem. I made an effort to show my pregnant wife to the soldiers. One of the Israeli soldiers ordered me out of the car and demanded that I take my jacket off and open my shirt to reveal my skin. The other two were pointing their rifles at me, one from a hilltop and one standing next to the soldier making the orders. I told them that I was an American citizen and my pregnant wife was with me in the car. I showed them my passport and told them that my wife did not yet have one. He told me that I could pass but she could not. With the guns pointing at us, there was no way to argue with them.

We returned to Bethlehem to find a different path. The second checkpoint was full of other cars and trucks, and we were lucky to have the soldiers become busy with the car in front of us. One of the soldiers simply waved us through, as tens of cars were now behind us. We were in Jerusalem. At this point, the Israeli army troops were in Bethlehem heading towards the Church of the Nativity in the center of the city where Jesus was born. I can see the tears coming down Mary's cheeks as she began to hear the screams and the cries of the Bethlehem mothers whose children were being slaughtered. On that same night, we received a report of a pregnant Palestinian mother forced to have her child in a car near a new army checkpoint established within the borders of the city not far from the Bethlehem children's hospital. The Israeli soldiers had refused her passage. The child died. We cried.

On the fifth of April, a baby girl was born to our family in a Jerusalem hospital. It was wonderful to have the care of the doctors and the nurses, but we were never able to take our thoughts away from Bethlehem and the rest of the Palestinian cities being attacked, away from the many mothers who were forced to have their babies in their homes or cars, some making it, some not. We dedicated our child in memory of all children killed in both Palestine and Israel.

Ted: I can see how that would make a lasting impression. It's very difficult for both sides, no?

Sami: Violence always makes things difficult for all.

Now the teaching, which is from Jesus. A hundred times a day his words pass through my mind. "Love your enemy." This single teaching is a pillar in all we do. But we must understand how they translate today, yes? What does Jesus actually mean by saying, "Love your enemy"?

First of all, if you're a believer in the words of Jesus, Jesus doesn't give us a choice. He doesn't say we should think about loving our enemies. He doesn't just say "negotiate" or "talk" to our enemies. He says we must love our enemies. It's very clear. It's a commandment. There are no excuses.

Second is the act of love itself. What is the purpose of love? The power of love is creating something new. As with the union of marriage, you go from two separate identities, and in this act of marriage and unifying through love, you become a new identity. So when Jesus talks about loving the enemy, he is talking about working to create something new. Creating a new identity through unity. When you have this new identity, the concept of "the other" is completely eliminated. There is no Palestinian and there is no Israeli in this love. There is no Jew and no Samaritan and no Roman. There are no enemies anymore, you see?

Jesus could have said, "Resolve your problems with your enemy." But he said, "Love your enemy." He wanted to create a real unity within the human body. Their sorrows become your sorrows, their history becomes your history, and their future becomes your future.

So now, a big part of Palestinians loving Jews, and Jews loving Palestinians, is understanding their wounds. As Palestinians, we cannot belittle the Holocaust, which is often hard with many. They understand the Holocaust, but then they say we are the victims of the victims. The only way to deal with this is through healing. Any act of violence done by Palestinians is perceived by a wider Jewish psychology that will understandably be interpreted as an act to annihilate the entire Jewish community.

So on a communal level nonviolence becomes the tool of love to break down the barriers that have been created. Now there is a physical cement wall between Palestinians and Jews, but the real walls were built decades ago, during the Holocaust. And when did the world give healing to the Jewish community after the Holocaust? The only thing we offered the Jews when they cried was to either burn or gas them or throw them into this jungle called the Middle East. And every time they cried about it, the world just gave them money. There has been no real healing for them.

Knowing this, I recently traveled to Poland and visited Auschwitz-Birkenau, the Jewish concentration camp. I needed to feel the pain of my neighbors, the Jews. So I spent the night in an open grave. It was a small casket, for a child. I lay down and I curled up and I wept. After several hours I slept.

To heal someone, you must meet them where they are, you see? This was what the Good Samaritan did. We serve them by understanding them and speaking to them in love, not by shooting at them.

Ted: And how do they react, the Israeli soldiers?

Sami: We frequently engage soldiers at settlements or in peace marches. I speak to the youngest soldier and to the highest commander at the same level, so there is no difference. It's about talking to them in a way that shows respect and love. The soldiers are ordered not to respond, but you can tell that they are thinking. I have often seen Israelis break down and cry when I speak to them.

Recently the Israeli army came in to demolish two Palestinian homes because the Israelis had chosen to build a road that went right next to these homes. These homes became a "security risk." Families had lived in those homes for many, many years, and none of them had engaged in any act of violence. When we heard about this, I led twenty volunteers into three cars and went up to them.

The soldiers had created a block, so we couldn't get through to where the houses were being demolished. I started talking to one soldier and got no response, but I could tell that he was listening by the look in his eyes. We could all hear the people behind him crying as their homes were being destroyed. I calmly asked him to describe what was going on over there, to make him think about it. The soldier suddenly fell to his knees and started weeping. He was pulled away by his commander and thrown into a jeep. After the whole thing happened, we went up and saw the de-stroyed house. As we were walking back down, I saw this solider sitting on the guardrails, so I spoke to him. "I don't need to know your name or anything, but today you gave me hope for humanity," I said. Then I thanked him and walked away.

You see, if you can succeed at showing people the humanity of the situation, then you can expose that injustice, and I would say that to both sides in this conflict. Sometimes they break down and cry because they cannot handle it anymore. Sometimes they grow furious and swear bitterly. And sometimes they use sound grenades and tear gas. Tear gas is not fun, you know. It burns all over your body. You cannot breathe . . . it's choking, you feel like throwing up.

Ted: I've never been gassed. Have you ever been shot at or faced death?

Sami: I try not to think about this question. I may or may have not come close to being killed as a result of engaging in nonviolent actions. But yes, of course. I have been in many situations where live ammunition was fired against me by Israeli settlers, bullets buzzing over our heads as we hit the ground. Other times trapped in my house for many hours while tanks stood guard.

I've stood in front of moving bulldozers and Israeli army jeeps many times to try and prevent them from destroying farmland. I've been physically assaulted more times than can be counted by Israeli soldiers who used their rifles, boots, and batons.

Ted: For example?

Sami: Of course, you want all the details for your book. Is that it?

Just a week ago, hundreds of Israeli settlers gathered on a Palestinian hill known as Ush Ghrab, located in Beit Sahour, or Shepherds' Field. Their intention was to take it back from Palestinian control and build condos on it. These condos are not lived in but sold to rich people who use them for vacation homes on occasion. It allows settlers to expand their control, you see? At any rate, we went up in a show of solidarity with the Palestinians who would suffer as a result of this incursion.

As we stood there, some settlers began to taunt and curse us and wave their machine guns at us. We made our intention of not disturbing them clear, but the commotion provoked the soldiers and they attacked us, instead of controlling the settlers and asking them to leave the area, which they could have easily done. It began with immediate pushing and shoving, and before I knew what was happening, I was being choked by a very large policeman and had my arms twisted by another Israeli soldier. I was thrown to the ground, arms pulled behind me and tied with handcuffs that only become tighter with any movement. With this, and even though there was no intention on my part to move and I informed them of this, the same police officer seemed to have felt that he had just hunted down a big game in the jungles of Africa and wanted to show off to his friends and settlers, so he put his foot on my side as a sign of victory. Am I giving you enough detail? (Smiles)

Ted: I'm sorry, I don't—

Sami: It's okay. Maybe your readers should know what we face every day here in Bethlehem.

I was then thrown to the side of the road where the settlers were walking, and eventually six others, one Palestinian and five international, were thrown down beside me. After a few hours in the same position and with the same handcuffs, one captain who knew me from previous nonviolent actions came and told me of their intention to let us go. At the end of the day, they released most of us because they truly had no reason to keep us. They kept one of the international volunteers and drove off with him in a police car. The reason was never made clear to us.

A moment before, that same captain came to me to inform me of their decision. The sun began to set behind Bethlehem and the beams were breaking through some white and gray clouds. There was a slight and beautiful chill from the autumn air. I gave thanks for that beautiful day and for the fact that the sun does not know Palestinian from Israeli, Christian from Muslim or Jew, and Asian from American or African, and I asked myself: If the sun shines on all of us as one, how much more does the sun's Creator see and love us all as one?

This is my life of nonviolence. And I experience absolute calm and peace in every single one of these moments. Fear, even of death, completely disappears.

Ted: How do the Hamas respond to you?

Sami: Well, as I said earlier, this is the great challenge, because they believe that violence is the only way out. I recall an incident in 2001 a few months after the second Intifada had started. There was a village south of Bethlehem called El-Khoudr where there was tremendous shelling from nearby Jewish settlements and from the Israeli military outposts. At night you could see a barrage of light for hours. So we decided to create a huge human shield that would prevent this bombardment of the poor villagers, who were huddled in their homes.

We went to the village and met with the Palestinian council. We were given a piece of land and brought tents with about forty international volunteers, mostly American, and brought flags that said to the Israelis that there are internationals here, so if you want to kill, you won't just be killing Palestinians. The problem I faced with this incident wasn't from the Israelis but from the Palestinian militant factions in the area who did not understand what I was talking about when I spoke about nonviolence. These factions were committed to engage in armed resistance against the occupation. So I was called in for an emergency meeting that morning organized by all the political factions in Bethlehem.

I went and they were all sitting in a room—each of the heads of all the different factions. I didn't know many of them at that time, and they didn't know me too well. I was nervous but thought I would simply make a very logical argument for nonviolence and tell them how incredible it was that internationals were willing to help. I told them that I was ready to sacrifice my life for this.

But in this meeting it wasn't interrogation; it was accusation. I couldn't make my argument over the anger. I was accused of being a part of the CIA. The last person to speak was the head of the Hamas in Bethlehem. I respected what he had to say. He told me that he did not doubt our patriotism and our nationalism and commitment to the cause. Neither did he see us as spies or CIA agents. He said he just thought we were naive and that nonviolence would not work. The only way was if we treat Israel the way they were treating Palestinians.

So this leader suggested a compromise. Our group could create our human shield but we could not sleep overnight. The problem with that is the shelling usually took place during the night. The mayor of the village was also put under pressure by the militant leaders, so he had to pull back the invitation. We went for a few days during the daytime, but there was nothing that happened during the daytime, so we ended up dismantling the whole project.

So you see, we are caught in between here. Turning the other cheek is never the human norm.

Ted: You speak a lot about volunteers. What was the largest operation involving volunteers, particularly internationals from the United States?

Sami: Perhaps the march on Palm Sunday, 2005. Palestinians, Christian or Muslim, are not permitted to go to Jerusalem for any reason. We organized a massive nonviolent procession to trace the path of Jesus from Manger Square in Bethlehem to Jerusalem on Palm Sunday to pray. There were about one thousand people. There were children with palm leaves and balloons. We had donkeys to symbolize how Jesus rode into Jerusalem two thousand years ago.

As soon as we crossed the section where they were building the wall, we were stopped at the checkpoint behind that section by the Israeli army. They had at least a hundred soldiers. There was a lot of media attention given to this action. And of course the army always gives you an ultimatum. Five minutes and we'll start shooting. So when they gave their ultimatum, everyone sat down. Then we started singing.

The soldiers stood there and said they were going to use force, but we sat there for thirty minutes. Then I gave a speech I had written and we walked back Bethlehem victors in the spirit of love and nonviolence.

Ted: Are you a pacifist?

Sami: So many say that I am a pacifist. But I am not. In fact, I would say that I am the farthest thing away from that. A pacifist verges on doing nothing. My work is about engaging in direct action. Nonviolence is not simply about dialogue and talking about feelings, although of course I dialogue with soldiers often. The real power of nonviolence addresses the problem head-on. This is the true man of peace.

Ted: Having lived in both the Middle East and in America, what does being a Christian mean to you?

Sami: (Smiles) Well, I'll tell you what it doesn't mean. It doesn't mean that you follow Christ or his teaching, now does it? Many very ugly things are done each day in the name of Christianity, yes? The term has lost much of its meaning worldwide; it is mostly a designation of political or social affiliation rather than a confession of faith. As such, to call yourself a Christian carries very little positive connotation and comes with some ugly baggage that is in direct contradiction to the teachings of Christ.

Ted: So then, what does the term *Christian* mean?

Sami: It means what it is understood to mean, like all words. Unfortunately, that meaning isn't what most American Christians think it is. Perhaps it is time we find another term to identify those who follow Christ's teachings.

Carl and I spent several hours with the voice of nonviolence in the Middle East, Sami Awad, and when we finally walked away, we felt as though we'd been bathed in grace. Regardless of one's political or religious persuasion, time spent at Sami's feet is unquestionably time spent with a prophet. And as with so many prophets who have preceded him throughout history, Sami's rhetoric has been fashioned in the face of daily pain.

So many simply can't accept his voice of love, because loving one's enemies, as Christ did, is dangerous business. Sami told us that many Palestinians are outraged to learn that he would express his solidarity with the pain of Holocaust survivors by putting himself in a grave for a night.

Nonviolence is empowering to those who take up its cause. But following the teaching to love one's enemies by embracing their pain adds a new and far more contrarian dimension to the teaching.

It was strange, because where Jerusalem and Bethlehem had burdened us both with the heaviness of so much blood, this one man had risen above the death and oppression of centuries and was appropriating the love of the one who'd preceded him by two thousand years.

"Did we just meet with someone following the teaching?" I asked, walking away from the office complex on the cliff.

"He's like Martin Luther King." Indeed, Sami's bookshelves had been overflowing with the works of Gandhi and Martin Luther King, Jr. "He puts me to shame. This one man could change the Middle East."

But to do so, he would have to live. Sami had spoken to us about his wife's fears. He might not fear death, but his wife warned him frequently.

You read about people like Sami from time to time, but meeting with one while he is still so young is nothing short of cheating history by walking onto one of its pages early, before it gets printed for the world to digest.

"The meeting with Hamas has been confirmed," Carl said, snapping his phone shut. "A car will pick us up in one hour at the hotel."

My pulse surged. I fought a sudden urge to spin around and rush back to the safety of the room where Sami's gentle voice had coaxed us into a world of mystery and power. I'd forgotten the Hamas.

"Wow. You sure it's safe?"

"I sure hope so. They're going out of their way for us. We're committed now."

Mohammed

I tried to put on a brave face as I climbed into the small green sedan with rusted wheel wells and missing hubcaps, and I did so by thinking of Sami as we headed down the hill. But the prevailing knowledge that Sami lived with the threat of death hanging over his head compromised my attempts.

Our driver seemed friendly enough, but neither Carl nor I knew him—the arrangements had been made by a friend of Carl's in Jordan. If I can just get past today, I kept telling myself, I will be fine. We had passed through six countries, looked into the eyes of terrible danger, both real and perceived, and lived to tell. So why should this invitation to tea be any different?

Because this was Hamas, and Hamas openly embraced violence as the means to political reconciliation. Carl, the mastiff whose trail I'd dutifully followed, had lost his swagger. You see, even he was nervous. Or was that my imagination kicking in again? No, no, he really was out of his element.

We wound our way through impossibly narrow streets and came to a stop at the bottom of a steep alleyway no more than five minutes after leaving Manger Square. So close?

I climbed out and faced the stares of dozens of onlookers. Clearly they were unaccustomed to seeing Westerners here. Not a good sign. Our driver motioned us to follow, so we did, up the path past shops that sold local wares—clothing, water, food. No trinkets here. This was no tourist district.

An older man missing one eye followed us unblinkingly as we passed by. He might have been smiling for all I know, but I was seeing the secret, hidden meaning behind every look, and none of it was good. Every gesture could be a signal, every whisper an instruction passed on to unseen men with guns: "Target approaching;

we have them. Don't spook them. Whatever you do, don't tip them off."

You know those scenes of the Mob operating out of meat shops and dry cleaners in which all appears normal until they take you to the back? I felt like the victim being led to the back to meet the big guy, and I was a nervous wreck.

The impression only solidified when we came to a narrow street shop that sold clothing and large bolts of material. "Come," our driver said. "Here."

I followed Carl inside and then toward the back where two metal chairs had been placed. "Wait," the driver said.

"Here?" I whispered to Carl. "You're sure about this?"

"I guess." He turned to the driver and confirmed his instructions. "Wait here?"

"Yes. Wait here. I will get him." He vanished through a curtain and we sat.

My heart was hammering. *Please, please, please, God, let this be okay.*

The man, whom we will call Mohammed for his and our protection, wore a green shirt with two pens in the pocket and a warm bearded smile. No sidearm. And no AK-47 strapped to his shoulder. Neither did he possess rope with which to bind us.

Which made sense. After all, he was among the top leaders with Hamas, not a sniper.

He took our hands, greeted us in English, and pulled out a third chair. My mind was spinning, but his casual nature had disarmed me. Okay, so far, so good. It had taken months of planning and oceans of travel, but here we were, in the lair of one of America's greatest perceived enemies.

"You would like to speak to me?" Mohammed said.

I fumbled for my trusty recorder.

"Yes," Carl said. "We would like to ask you some questions. Is that okay?"

"Yes." He wore a silver Seiko watch and was well fed but not overweight. "That is why I have come. You are writing a book?"

"Yes. We would like you to be candid."

"Of course." He dipped his head. "So ask your questions."

Carl: Can you tell us a little bit about who you are?

Mohammed: (Some details have been changed.) My name is Mohammed. I'm over forty, am married, and have eight children—five girls, three boys. I finished high school in 1981, and was in Italy for three years, and finished in Bethlehem University from '84 to '93 because I was in prison for the first Intifada. My parents are dead. So we love to live and we like others to live, because we are human beings. Islam asks us to love others and live with others as humans, not as animals. That is the idea of all the messages of God. As we agree now, God is for all human beings in this life. So this is my life.

Carl: How do you speak English so well?

Mohammed: I studied in the Franciscan school. I speak English, a little French, and Italian. I was born in Bethlehem. And I hope I will die here.

Ted: How old is your youngest child?

Mohammed: My oldest is twenty years old. We teach our children well and benefit others. My oldest, she studies in medicine and pathology. I love my family and children and I like to be home, always.

Ted: And your youngest?

Mohammed: Three years.

Ted: You know, when children are three years old, they do a lot of pretty funny things, so maybe you can remember one of your children's funniest moments.

Mohammed: I always laugh when I see them laugh. The funniest thing of my littlest one . . . He asks me, "Do you like God?" and I always say, "Yes." So he says, "Then give me this thing."

Ted: Do you all gather together for dinner?

Mohammed: Friday we all sit together for breakfast and lunch. Lunch is at two P.M.

Ted: Do you mind if I ask you a question about your wife? What is her name?

Mohammed: Elisa.

Ted: What makes your wife special?

Mohammed: She has stayed with me for twenty years and had eight children. (Laughs) She manages to raise them well. So she is special to me. A good mother and good wife.

Carl: I have to say, it embarrasses me to say that if most of my friends right now in America knew we were talking to someone from the Hamas, they would be shocked. They would be worried that at any time you might kill me. (Laughs) It's embarrassing.

Mohammed: Well, this idea . . . our enemy tried to put it in their minds.

Ted: What do you think the Americans' greatest misunderstanding is of the people who live in Bethlehem or the Palestinians in general?

Mohammed: Well, about a week ago, there was a group from America here. They are afraid for no reason. They think we are terrorists and have guns. In their movies, for example, they always think there is a huge power behind us and we're always fighting. And they think we worship the devil. They relate us to what they see in the movies, but we are not like that. If you lived in Bethlehem, you would not see one kill another for no reason. We fear God. We fear that when we die we will stand in front of God and he will ask, "Why did you kill this man?" So we are afraid. We live to be human because God wants us to be human.

Ted: What do you think the people in Bethlehem's greatest misunderstanding of Americans might be?

Mohammed: We know that people are different from the government. The government is made up from about fifty thousand people, but the other 250 million are victims of that government. So we believe that America should free itself before freeing any other country.

Carl: Do you think that your friends have any misunderstandings of the American people?

Mohammed: As people, they know that most of them do nothing. They like other people. But the face of America is a bloody one.

Carl: Do you have any hobbies?

Mohammed: Before, I did, but not anymore. I used to play basketball and was good. But I don't think I can anymore. (Laughs) I watch TV and movies. I also like to learn.

Ted: What is your favorite American movie?

Mohammed: Any action movie. Like *Rush Hour* and *Rush Hour 2*.

Ted: We were talking to a Bedouin prince, and his favorite actor was Jim Carrey. It's strange for an American to hear that a Bedouin prince's favorite movie is a Jim Carrey movie because we don't even think that Bedouins watch TV.

Mohammed: (Laughs) We all have TV here. And we all like to learn about other countries.

Ted: Did you see *Gandhi*? If so, what did you think?

Mohammed: Yes, it's a long one. He's a great person.

Carl: You have a Gandhi here. His name is Sami Awad.

Mohammed: Yes, but I don't know if he's great or not.

Ted: Do you watch sports?

Mohammed: I like to play, but I don't like to watch.

Ted: The teenagers in the United States love music or play video games. As parents, we try to get them to go outside and play and do something healthy. What do your children do?

Mohammed: Is the same way. And I also want them to study. My son who is five likes to stay in front of the computer for many hours on games. I tried to play for one or two minutes, then I leave. It's something else.

Ted: When was the last time that you cried?

Mohammed: As Muslims, we always cry, but only in front of God when we are alone. It's something mixed with our crying. It's not shameful. So I cry when I do something wrong and I ask God to forgive me.

Ted: When was the last time outside of your prayers that something happened that brought you great pain that you would like to share with us?

Mohammed: I don't have something in mind. Well, this life is full of pain. Two weeks ago, I have a cousin, seventy years old, who always went to the mosque. Then one day he didn't come, so we went to his house and he was dead. It was a painful thought that you could die and no one would know. I put myself in his shoes and it was painful.

Ted: Do you think death is more common here?

Mohammed: Someday everyone will die.

Carl: Most Americans know that Muslims believe in God, but they don't realize that Muslims believe that Jesus is a great prophet. When I say Jesus, what's one thing that comes into your mind?

Mohammed: That he is a prophet. And we believe in all other prophets. And we believe that Muhammad was the last prophet. But I believe many of the Christian people don't believe that Muhammad was a prophet.

Carl: What do you think is special about Jesus?

Mohammed: In the Qur'an we say we don't differentiate between the prophets.

Ted: How do the Christians and Muslims get along in Bethlehem?

Mohammed: As people. There is no conflict.

Ted: So, do you believe a Christian, if he wants to go to heaven, should become a Muslim?

Mohammed: Religiously, we believe in different things, but at least we believe that we should not force you to become a Muslim. It's your opinion. But I will tell you about Islam if it's your choice. Our ancestors did not force anyone to become Muslim.

Ted: Yet in the past, humans have taken religion and distorted it for their own use, like Christians did during the Crusades. All Christians are offended by the Crusades. In Islam, there were times in history when Islam was forced on people or taxes were forced on them if they did not convert.

Mohammed: I think it's a different viewpoint. They didn't force people to be Muslims; it was to free people to have a choice. In history, it never says Muslims forced people to convert.

Ted: So you would say to the American people, you aren't interested in forcing them to believe in Islam?

Mohammed: I believe in Islam and will say what the Qur'an says.

Ted: I ask this because in the United States people believe they were attacked by Muslims. Some believe that Al-Qaeda and other extremists are punishing America because they are evil and they want America to feel pain so they will convert to Islam. What do you say?

Mohammed: I think for every action, there is a reaction. What happened in the U.S. was a reaction of the hurt felt in other countries. This is what I think. It's not a war between Muslims and Christians. I think we can live together better than before because we are more intelligent. We read more and know more about each other. We should all be humans. We can communicate. We can agree and live in peace.

Ted: Is it good for a Muslim to love Christians?

Mohammed: It's good for a Muslim to love everyone. We have Christians and Jews and Muslims, and we have no problem to live together as religions, not as governments.

Ted: Jesus taught that the greatest commandment is to love the Lord your God with all your heart, mind, and soul, and the second most important commandment is to love your neighbor as yourself. By "neighbor," he went on to give the parable of the Good Samaritan. So, what do you think about this teaching as it relates to Americans loving Palestinians, Americans loving Muslims, and Palestinian Muslims loving Americans?

Mohammed: I have a story. It's at the time of the Prophet Muhammad. He had a Jewish neighbor. This neighbor hated Muhammad. He took his garbage and put it on Muhammad's door. Muhammad said nothing and took these things at his door and threw them away. So one day Muhammad goes in the street and didn't see the garbage, and he went to see what happened to his Jewish neighbor. He learned that he was sick. So he went to visit him. Because our religion says to love everyone, even if they had hurt us in some way. So the neighbor was surprised.

We like to live with them in peace, but if they take their gun and begin to shoot at us, we will not stay. I believe in Jesus, but I do not believe that if one slaps me on my cheek, I should turn my other cheek. It's not right to be slapped on the face. We must be human at the end.

Carl: So, do you think Jesus was wrong?

Mohammed: No, he was not wrong, because he has his thoughts too. But here now, if you turn the other cheek, they will say that you are weak and they will do more harm. So we believe that what Jesus said applies to some situations but not to ours.

Ted: Your story of Muhammad made me think of the wall. Last night we walked through the security into Bethlehem. There's an immediate difference from the outside to the inside. You see garbage on the inside. Much like in your story, you might say it's like your neighbors are putting garbage in Bethlehem, on your doorstep. What would Muhammad's teaching say, then, about this situation and how to treat the Jews? If you follow the story, you should do what Muhammad did and go visit the Jew, yes?

Mohammed: But it's different. When you say they put their garbage, they aren't only doing that; they are killing us. As I said before, I will not turn my cheek. I will fight back. I will be patient with the neighbor and teach him to be good to me. Now, they are doing bad and they insist to do this. So, what can I do except fight back? And the story I told you about how to be human. If the other part is not human, you will be forced to act as not a human being.

Carl: Tell us something new about Hamas.

Mohammed: Hamas is from this country. In one family you can find one brother who is Hamas and one is Fatah. It's not wrong. Different ideas will have different solutions. Sometimes we agree and sometimes we don't, but we don't hate each other. We still have the power to be good brothers. We are all Palestinians. If Israel came to us and said I will give you a government if you all agree on one party only, I would say no.

Carl: I've always heard that the Hamas believes that Israel doesn't have the right to exist. Is that true?

Mohammed: I would like to ask you this. Do you believe Israel has the right to exist in our country? Because sixty years ago, there was no Israel. Then the next day, they had their rights and government and we had nothing. Do you believe this is right and what we do is wrong?

Carl: I think it's the wrong question, because they do exist.

Mohammed: But do they have the right to exist? And we exist too and they took our country.

Ted: In your opinion, do you see the solution as two states? Or do you see the solution as being one state? Or do you see the solution as being Israel leaving?

Mohammed: Why don't they let all the Palestinians return here and let us have elections? If they elect the Israeli government, so be it; and if they elect the Palestinian government, so be it. One big election. That would help us, because there are many more Palestinians than Jews if they let Palestinians return to their country.

Carl: Right now, is it about even, Jew and Palestinian?

Mohammed: Yes. At some point there will be many more Palestinians. There was Saddam, then there was no Saddam; now it's Iran, but tomorrow there might not be Iran. So after time, everything changes. In Palestine also it will change in time.

Carl: So time is on your side.

Mohammed: Yes. You never know.

Ted: Is there any one last thing you would like to say to Americans?

Mohammed: I say love yourselves and you will love others. Live in peace with yourself and you will live in peace with others.

Ted: Good. You know I have to say, while I don't necessarily agree with everything you say, you don't look so scary to me. You smile very much. So here's my last question. Do we look like monsters to you?

Mohammed: No. (Laughs) You are good people.

Carl and I returned to our hotel in one piece, and that night we slept with some relief. But a new sense of hopelessness had settled over us. The gulf between neighbors *within* Bethlehem seemed nearly as great as the gulf between them and their neighbors over the wall in Jerusalem.

We had become more convinced by the day that the wisdom found in the parable of the Samaritan two thousand years ago was perhaps even more appropriate today than it was back then. But truth is always timeless.

If only it were truly possible to follow this wisdom in the real world.

Tomorrow we would wake and travel by cab to meet with an Israeli Jewish contact who had agreed to take us to the seven hundred surviving Samaritans in northern Israel. Our long journey would end there. With any luck, our final cup of tea would be with the survivors of the very people Jesus singled out in his story so long ago.

What would they have to say after all this time? Would they understand the gulf that divides neighbors? Have they learned the lessons of love that cost Jesus his life? Would they offer us new hope?

We would know tomorrow, assuming no war broke out overnight.

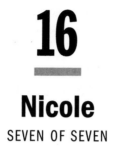

16

Nicole

SEVEN OF SEVEN

NICOLE WAGNER spent a total of three days on the brink of death, unconscious and wounded in the home of Abdul and Shenia Shakiri. Her wounds were serious. It would be counted as almost a miracle that Shenia was actually a former nurse, trained both in modern medicine and in the folk medicines of her mountain-dwelling ancestors. In all, the young woman suffered a shattered shoulder blade, a severe concussion, bruised internal organs, and severe shock.

Her first moment of awareness came late on the second day. It lasted only a few seconds, but it would forge an emotional link that would alter her life from then on.

When her eyes opened, she saw a face. Light brown skin, dark brown eyes, and nearly black hair. It was the face of an Arab woman. It appeared almost identical to the face of her own Momma. This face seemed to blur with that of the Momma she remembered and become one.

"Momma, I miss you," she whispered.

The face stared at her, then leaned forward and kissed her softly on the forehead. Then whispered in a tongue whose literal meaning she could not understand.

A moment later, Nicole smiled blearily and drifted off again.

She opened her eyes several more times that day and every time saw the same maternal face above her. Each time, she smiled identically and drifted back into a deep and health-restoring slumber.

Early on the third day, she awoke for good. The older woman was next to her, sponge-bathing her face when it happened.

"My name is Nicole," she said slowly.

"Good morning, Nicole," the older woman replied. "I cannot tell you my name. It is for my safety and perhaps yours as well."

"I've been calling you Momma, haven't I?"

The older one's face softened. "It is no problem." She continued sponge-bathing in silence for several moments. "You have a mother, back in America?"

Nicole shook her head. "She's gone. Passed away."

Saying it just then made Nicole feel the grief afresh, as though she was just learning it herself for the first time. Another gentle moment passed between them as the nurse finished bathing her.

"What exactly happened to me?" Nicole asked at last.

"I do not know exactly. You were lying almost dead on the street, and someone brought you here."

"But this isn't a hospital."

"It's a home. There was no help for you that night. There had been fighting and everyone was inside. There was no way to the hospital."

"I remember. Everyone was inside except me."

The woman brushed hair from her forehead. "You are a very brave girl."

"Very stupid, I would say. So you found my backpack? To know all this?"

"You wanted to help the Shatila girls."

"And the computer?"

"Do not worry. Once they discover you are in good health, a dozen computers will be given."

Nicole hesitated. "Who brought me here?"

"He's in hiding. His life's in danger now."

"For helping me?"

The woman offered a kind smile. "This is Beirut," she said simply.

"Will I meet him?" Nicole asked.

Her caregiver stood and turned toward the door. "Get some rest, child. Leave what is God's in God's hands."

THREE DAYS after being beaten on the streets of Beirut and left for dead, and two days after awakening from her brutal beating in the care of a Druze home, Nicole Wagner awoke from a deep sleep, feeling a strange sense of close human presence.

She looked at the foot of her bed and blinked at a figure standing out of focus. A young man, roughly her own age, stood smiling gently. Dark hair, smooth brown skin. His likeness to his mother . . .

Nicole froze. She knew this man. He was the one who'd walked into the hookah bar and earned Walid's rage not so long ago. The Druze heretic. He was the one who'd saved her?

Except for when she'd turned to see him, her back had been to him that day—he likely didn't recognize her.

Seeing she was awake, the young man held his hands together nervously and stepped lightly around the bed to her side. But he didn't speak. His broad smile seemed to prohibit him from doing anything but smile at his handiwork.

"So . . . ," Nicole said. "You're the one."

"Hello," he said, his voice quavering and nervous. "My name is Akram. Your caretaker is my mother. You are in our home."

She didn't know what to say. To most back home, and to so many even here in the Middle East, her savior would quickly be called the enemy. Even a terrorist. Yet here she was, facing his nervous smile and wide eyes.

"I am very grateful for your family's kindness," she finally said.

The mother stepped through the curtained doorway. "Akram is the one who found you. He is the one who brought you here."

Nicole looked in his eyes. Something about his demeanor had told her that the meeting was more than mere courtesy. All she could think to say was, quite simply, "You saved my life. Thank you."

"You are most welcome. I am so sorry I could not take you to a real hospital. I simply had no strength to carry you that far. Besides, it would not have been safe."

"I received better care right here."

"Yes, my mother is a wonderful nurse." His eyes darted about the room. "I'm sorry about all the nonsense on the walls."

The walls had been lined with sheets of handwriting, most of it in Arabic and some in English. They were poems, exquisitely penned. Lying in bed, she'd read all of the ones written in English. They concerned nature and the beauty of Lebanon and unrequited love. So delicately written that Nicole had assumed they'd been written by a girl.

"*You* wrote these?" Nicole asked him.

He blushed.

"You're an incredible poet," she said.

"Thank you. I never intended for them to be read. Not like this."

Nicole stared into his eyes, now keenly aware that she was looking at the kind man who'd saved her life. How could she ever repay this man? She had no clue, so she simply said what was on her mind.

"You saved me. There had to be others. But you were the only one who stopped."

He glanced at his mother. "That may be true, but no one would believe it. I am Druze and we have many enemies in Beirut."

"I will tell the truth. I will stand up and tell anyone."

He flashed her that wondrous smile again, but his mother spoke for him.

"The safest thing for all of us would be for Akram to take you back with a hood over your head and simply release you. I apologize for the uncomfortable suggestion. But it would save you from knowing where we live. This is for your safety as well as Akram's, you understand."

"But . . . Of course, but—"

"Then maybe someday we can meet each other on the street, just friendly neighbors out for a walk. And we can talk together, share some tea."

Nicole felt like crying. "I would like that."

Akram stepped forward, lifted Nicole's hand, and kissed it.

E-MAIL FROM NICOLE

Dear Doug,

I'm so sorry for the worry and stress I've probably put you through this last week. I'm sure everyone has assumed I was dead. Knowing Beirut, that would have been a safe assumption.

You're going to think I've lost my mind, given that I almost died, but the coolest thing has happened. I'm going to tell this to you, but you've got to promise never to repeat it to anyone. In fact, destroy this message as soon as you read it. I know I can trust you, or I'd never even write this much.

I know the media has said I woke up in captivity and was brought back with a hood over my head. That's a common Beirut scenario, and it's all true. But it's not the whole truth.

I asked for the hood. And I know the people who held me. They had nothing to do with harming me. In fact, they were the ones who saved my life. I would have literally died alone that night if it wasn't for them. I wasn't saved by any of the people on the news. They're all claiming to have rescued me, but all they did was find me walking safely along a sidewalk and took me into protective custody.

By the way, I'm sorry for losing your laptop. But we've received over a dozen computers since. Less than two days later, Fahima, the young Palestinian girl I'm trying to help, came to me from a session on her very own laptop and asked for my help in registering for a foreign scholarship. I think I told you that there's plenty of grants and financial aid waiting for any refugee child who shows enough promise.

So I took her into the Palestinian Youth Center, asked for this scholarship register, and as they handed me a thick, aging book, it just hit me like a load of bricks. Mother's name could be in this very book!

I started flipping those pages like someone about to die of heatstroke. There it was, registered August 18, 1986. An entry on behalf of scholarship applicant Muna Dawhi. And then the name of a sponsor, Rahm Bernet.

I had a name. Two names: the surname of our family (Dawhi) and quite likely the full name of my biological father (Rahm Bernet). Within a day, I had my answers, courtesy of the American Embassy worker who's been helping me with paperwork and Walid, the hookah bar owner.

Our mother's family survived the Shatila Massacre, but three years later, in May 1985, they disappeared from the camps altogether. No trace. It happened during the so-called "war of the camps"—yet another flare-up of violence to overtake this sad refugee settlement.

They're gone, Doug. Melted into thin air.

And my biological father, Rahm Bernet? I've learned he has served for decades in the Lebanese Parliament, always defending himself against charges that he was responsible for the deaths of thousands of innocents. But when I talked to Walid, he admitted that Rahm Bernet was the name that he and Father Stephen and Naum Sareel were planning to give me.

So there it is, my father a mass murderer.

Now I know who he is, but I'm not planning to contact him. I'm quite de-cided on this. It's better for him that he never meet me, and I know now that I can go through the rest of my life never having a part in his life. It wouldn't be safe even if it were desirable.

It's better to let the past and its secrets be, the way I figure it. In fact, I've burned Momma's letters, the proof of my father's guilt. You should have seen Walid's face fall when I told him that.

I have a feeling that the other two would be just as disappointed. They were hoping to use me for their own purposes, and that's another reason I can't confront my father.

You'd think I'd be devastated, learning what I have. After all, I came here looking for family. For my blood. For a connection to my own people.

What I found was something very different.

I've met some fascinating people who I could count as friends, I sup-pose. A hookah bar owner, an old Jewish survivor, and an influential priest who loved Mother. Sandra, Fahima. And that's cool.

But I've also met someone counted as an enemy who's managed to put all that to shame. A man who was willing to put my life ahead of his own.

I came looking for my family and instead found a Good Samaritan, a man and his mother who saved my life when others left me to die.

Did I mention the fact that Akram and I are going for tea on the board-walk next Monday? He's a beautiful person, Doug. I'm sure you would like him. (Please don't read anything into that ☺.)

Then again, you never know!

Kisses, Nicole

17

The True Samaritan

LANDS UNKNOWN

CARL AND I stood on the corner of a town in Israel that could easily pass for any suburban neighborhood in the United States. Micah (name changed for security), an Orthodox Jew, stood next to us, pointing past a teenager in tight jeans on a skateboard. An iPod dangled from the boy's hip and a dark-haired girl walked beside him, hugging an armful of schoolbooks. The contrast between this neighborhood and Bethlehem was astonishing, and to be perfectly honest, I felt giddy.

I was home.

Carl, on the other hand, was anywhere but home. He's spent too much time in the desert, see? Here, there were manicured lawns. The streets were freshly paved and a small boy swung from monkey bars in the adjacent park. They sold Rockstar energy drinks in the gas stations, for crying out loud! Give me a Light Vanilla Rockstar any day and I am at peace.

Evidently Carl was more comfortable being stranded at the border between Syria and Jordan, waiting for his Saudi Samaritan to drive up in a big black limo and . . .

I caught myself. For a moment it became clear to me that my thoughts were somehow inappropriate. I had looked into the stare of a beautiful clerk at the Rockstar gas station, saw bitterness and pain behind glassy brown eyes, and was thankful I didn't share her life. I had walked the streets of Bethlehem and thanked God I did not live in that prison. I had looked out across Damascus, seen the poverty, and been tempted to turn my back. And here, in southern Israel, the scantiest signs of normality had me begging to be home. Fine, all fine, but I was here to step into the shoes of enemies, not flee from them at the first signs of pain.

There is a teaching in the New Testament that defines love as participating in the suffering of our fellow man. How many times have I written about suffering and death in my novels, only to have Christians in America express disapproval? Too many to count. Many American Christians would rather turn a blind eye to the ugliness of real life, preferring to think only about what is "good and pure" because they forget that they are first admonished to think on what is "true," which certainly includes the suffering of others. Like the Crusaders and some caliphs, and so many misguided Christians and Muslims throughout history, they use religion to serve their preferences rather than challenge them to do the right thing. In doing so, they perpetuate the suffering of others, like the Pharisee who walked by the beaten man in Jesus' tale of the Samaritan.

But, in my own heart, was I not doing the same now by reveling in the similarity of Israel and America? I am the chief among all hypocrites.

Micah was speaking. "I had just come up the street from the gas station. You can't see it now; it was around the corner. But the blast . . ." He shook his head. "So far away, but the concussion from the blast came first, like a fist." He pressed a hand against his chest and swallowed. "I still have nightmares."

"It was a bomb?" I asked, having missed some of the discussion.

"A suicide bomber, yes. What disturbs me most is the thought of what that kind of blast must have done to her. To the suicide bomber."

"What did you do?"

"I was shocked. I panicked. So I jump into the nearest taxi, and people are running to help them, and I just think I need to get out of here. It was only my second week in the country, and I was bombarded by hate around here. On the Jewish side, I'm hearing racist comments about the Arabs, and vice versa. So I jump in the taxi and tell him I want to go back to the other side of town. Then the taxi driver says, 'Ah, the Arabs are all animals. They aren't human beings.'

"At that time, I just was so angry. And I just blew up in his face and yelled, 'That's part of the problem! It's because we treat them like animals. That's why we're in the state we're in!' And then he just starts yelling at me. I'm yelling at him. We were yelling at each other as if we ourselves were responsible for the whole war. He's calling me an Arab lover, and I'm saying I do love Arabs and God loves Arabs, and we're all created in the image of God. It was just plain crazy. War makes everyone do crazy things."

Micah opened the door to his van, shaking his head. "We have to leave if we are going." We climbed in and headed north toward Tel Aviv. Carl continued the discussion with Micah, but my mind was in stasis. The trees passed by in a surreal blur like the other images in my head. Names and faces.

Mohammed the boat pilot in Egypt. The bin Laden brothers in Saudi Arabia. Samir Kreidie (if only he was with us now!). A Bedouin prince who loves Jim Carrey. Baalbek. Ayatollah Fadlallah. The Hezbollah sheik, Nabil. The mufti of Damascus. Straight Street. The key keeper in Jerusalem.

Carl's kidnapping in Fallujah. Sami Awad, a new kind of Martin Luther King. The Hamas, smiling in resolution to gain back what was once taken.

And now stories of suicide bombers down the street.

I turned my attention to Micah, who was speaking in the front seat. "The problem is, if I tell my story of pain, then people could take that in the wrong way. So there is the problem. Things polarize so quickly. If I tell you a story of pain, it is used to draw some people into your story, so that's good. But at the same time, it makes people hate the other side."

Carl shifted in his seat. "Maybe. Or maybe people just need to hear the truth. This isn't a book about Middle Eastern politics; it's a book about learning to love embittered enemies. That could be Muslims and Christians, Israelis and Palestinians, or Republicans and Democrats. I mean, I think that's what the story of the Samaritan is all about. Before you can administer healing, you have to first begin at least to understand their wounding. Sami Awad, you've heard of him?"

"Of course; who hasn't? Many Jews also support his cause of non-violence. He's an example for all mankind."

"He told us about sleeping in a Jewish grave in Auschwitz—"

"He told you that? You can't be serious. A Palestinian visiting Auschwitz and . . ." Micah breaks off, either too emotional or swept away in thought; I couldn't tell through his sunglasses.

"Crazy, huh?"

"That's what we need. That's exactly what we need. I hadn't heard; when did he do this?"

"In the last few weeks."

"Dear God, the man is blessed." He took a deep breath. "The problem is, the West won't even hear about it."

"Why?"

"Because they don't care. Their mind is on gas pump prices."

We headed down a long stretch of highway that cut through the desert, headed north. I wanted to know more about Micah's story of pain.

"So tell me, as an Orthodox Jew, you've felt the pain of other Jews?"

"Yes. Yes, of course!" He stared ahead and gripped the wheel with both hands. "I was just so crazy for a long time here, trying to understand. Then one year later, March of 2003, I was downtown running errands, and I was coming back to where I lived, and I had just missed my bus. Bus 32. The bus driver saw me running towards the bus, but he drove off anyway. I got mad. So I couldn't decide if I should wait thirty minutes for the next bus or just get on the subway. I finally walked over to the subway and said I would take that. In the subway, I hear of this terrorist attack right where I was going."

"No."

He nodded. "I get off the subway and everything is blocked off. And the whole top of Bus 32 was blown off. Windows alongside the street were shattered. Cars on either side were damaged. And if you were on that bus, I don't know if anyone survived. . . . People were even killed at the bus stop. I'm just shaken up."

"So that's the same bus—"

"That I tried to catch. I would have been killed. But it wasn't me; it was a bus full of children. The bomber intentionally got on a bus after school and blew himself up."

We sat in silence.

"I went home in shock and opened my e-mail. And there was an e-mail from a friend of a friend. 'Dear Abigail is going home with the Lord.' "

Micah turned to his side window, visibly shaken. "This fourteen-year-old girl was the daughter of missionaries in Israel. I had met her parents once. She was killed on that Bus 32. Her brother did martial arts with her, and she would hang out with her youth group, and her friends were Jews and Arabs and everything. She wasn't even Jewish. I was absolutely devastated. Dear God, why couldn't it have been me who got on the bus instead of her?"

Neither Carl nor I could say anything.

"I went through periods where I just got mad at everybody. I just have to take days alone with God. I just pray and sit in silence. I just cannot be with people. Because no matter who I talked to, I couldn't get an understanding. They would try to sympathize and then say something about Arabs and then I would get mad. It just didn't work. I had to be alone."

"What happened to the girl's parents?" Carl asked.

"I went to the funerals of every child on that bus. There was only standing room at those funerals. Most responded with anger, but Abigail's parents didn't speak that way. They talked about the love of God, and they talked about how Abigail loved Jews and Arabs and insisted that to teach hatred against the Arabs would go against everything Abigail believed."

We rode along the way without speaking for a while. There didn't seem to be anything appropriate to say. In moments of clarity the best response is sometimes to hide away and meditate or pray. We settled for turning our minds to the hum of rubber on asphalt beneath us.

"Which brings us back to the parable of the Good Samaritan," I said. "I'm considering telling a similar parable about a girl named Nicole in Beirut."

"Funny you say that," Micah said. "I was invited to speak to a gathering in another country recently, and when I arrived, the leader discovered that I believe in loving Muslims. He was like many Christian Zionists who go way overboard. Very upset. So angry he asked me not to share my views. But of course I had to say what I believed."

Naturally, I had my recorder out and on. It seemed we had inadvertently stumbled on a gold mine in this Orthodox Jew. I had known he was a scholar, thus the connection arranged by a friend of a friend in searching for the right party to take us to the Samaritans. But I hadn't expected this. Micah, who, as it turned out, has several doctoral degrees, was providing far more than an informed ride to tea with the Samaritans.

"I used the Bible," he said. "I read from John 4, where Jesus spoke to the Samaritan woman at the well. I explained from my point of view how the Palestinians of our day are like the Samaritans. How we have to love them. So the leader stood up and stormed out. Half the audience was furious with me."

"Seriously?"

"So, what's the context of the Good Samaritan story? How did Jesus start the story? He started with the great commandment. Love God, love your neighbor. Now, in Judaism, that is a burdened question. In the Mishnah, which is the summary of all interpretation of Jewish law, 'neighbor' is a technical term for a friend. It basically defines a neighbor as a practicing Jew, which was how the Pharisees in Jesus' time interpreted it. They were trying to trap Jesus so they could condemn him to death, you see? 'Who is my neighbor?' But Jesus refused to get into the law; his answer was the story."

"The Good Samaritan."

"Exactly. The Good Samaritan. The lawyer trying to trap Jesus asked him what he should do to inherit eternal life. Jesus gave his famous teaching, saying that you should love God and you should love your neighbor as yourself. The real question in Luke 10 came then. Who is my neighbor? *Who* should I love?"

"So this was a trap? The lawyer *wanted* Jesus to say Samaritan?"

"So it seems. All Jews knew that a Samaritan by definition could *not* be good. It would be like a Christian preacher praising a Muslim cleric today. And vice versa. Would Christians stand for that?"

No answer needed.

Micah was in high gear, and his eyes suddenly brightened like a child's. "You mentioned the Druze in Lebanon, right? A parable you plan to tell in which the Druze is likened to the Samaritan."

"That's the plan, yes."

"We're heading north now, to visit the Samaritans. But did you know that there are many more Druze in northern Israel than Samaritans? Seventy-five thousand, roughly. A splinter group of Islam considered as heretics, just like the Samaritans were a splinter group of Judaism, considered as heretics."

I turned to Carl. "You knew this?"

"Well, yeah, but honestly I hadn't considered the irony of both groups living in northern Israel."

The connection was a clincher for me. Nicole's story, which had come from the deepest reaches of my imagination, was more relevant than I could have possibly guessed.

Micah was nodding. "Like the Druze today, Samaritans in history were enemies in part because of their heresy. Worthy of death."

"And the same could be said about Muslims and Christians," Carl said.

"Exactly. In the Christian mind-set, they should look at Muslims and see them as modern-day equivalents to the Samaritans in Jesus' day."

Carl and I looked at each other. Bingo.

Back to Micah. "And the conflict between Jews and Samaritans was violent?" I asked. "Like this conflict is today?"

"Yes, of course! Nehemiah." Micah said the name Nehemiah as if it should turn the lights on for us all by itself.

I revealed my ignorance. "Sorry. What about Nehemiah?"

"If you go back to Nehemiah, you can read that the Samaritans opposed the rebuilding of Jerusalem and the temple, so the Jews had to build with a working tool in one hand and a spear in the other to defend themselves. Sound familiar?"

"Yeah"—Carl raised an eyebrow—"but seriously, making the connection between Samaritans and Muslims is a bit of a stretch for Christians, trust me."

"Okay, fine, I get that. But it's clear-cut." Micah waved a finger, excited now. "We are to love our enemy because they are our neighbor, regardless of their offense, be it heresy or violence. Jesus implied that the Samaritan, a wicked defiler of God, was the one following

God by loving the wounded man. This was the kind of teaching that got Jesus killed."

Which begged our overarching question, which I then asked: "So, is this an impossible teaching to follow?"

Micah shook his head and remained silent for a full thirty seconds. "Loving someone who's blown up a bus? Or stolen your land? The so-called evil enemy? I can tell you this: it's as hard today as it was for the Jews who first heard the parable of the Good Samaritan. It's a very dangerous teaching."

THE PARABLE OF THE SAMARITAN

On one occasion an expert in the Law stood up to test Jesus. "Teacher," he asked, "what must I do to inherit eternal life?"

"What is written in the Law?" he replied. "How do you read it?"

He answered: " 'Love the Lord your God with all your heart and with all your soul and with all your strength and with all your mind; and 'Love your neighbor as yourself.' "

"You have answered correctly," Jesus replied. "Do this and you will live."

But he wanted to justify himself, so he asked Jesus, "And who is my neighbor?"

In reply Jesus said: "A man was going down from Jerusalem to Jericho, when he fell into the hands of robbers. They stripped him of his clothes, beat him and went away, leaving him half dead. A priest happened to be going down the same road, and when he saw the man, he passed by on the other side. So too, a Levite, when he came to the place and saw him, passed by on the other side. But a Samaritan, as he traveled, came where the man was; and when he saw him, he took pity on him. He went to him and bandaged his wounds, pouring on oil and wine. Then he put the man on his own donkey, took him to an inn, and took care of him. The next day he took out two silver coins and gave them to the innkeeper. "Look after him," he said, "and when I return, I will reimburse you for any extra expense you may have."

"Which of these three do you think was a neighbor to the man who fell into the hands of robbers?"

The expert in the Law replied, "The one who had mercy on him."

Jesus told him, "Go and do likewise."

The Samaritan Survivors

As we wound our way north, Micah began to fill us in on the history of the Samaritans from the time of Jesus' teaching up until the present. We knew there were roughly seven hundred alive today, but very few people seem to know much about them. In fact, Micah himself has never seen a Samaritan. This, it turns out, is one reason he, the consummate scholar, agreed to take us.

As for me, I couldn't take my mind off a Druze fighter named Akram who was going to show mercy to a young woman named Nicole.

We've already rehearsed the origin of the Samaritans in chapter five. How the Talmud, 2 Kings, and the renowned historian Josephus alike claim that the evil Assyrian ruler Sargon II sent back a diverse and piecemeal bunch of pagans to repopulate the land. And how these heathen idolaters became the Samaritans, essentially immigrant foreigners who mixed Judaism with their own religions to form a witches' brew of half-baked, synchronistic heretical beliefs, which is why the Jews in the time of Christ so despised them.

But what became of them after the time of Christ?

Despite Jesus' generous spirit toward the Samaritans, his followers were not so generous. With the coming of Christianity as a formal religion, Samaritan fortunes were shattered. A Christian Byzantine emperor massacred a large number of Samaritans and destroyed their temple for good. They, in turn, rebelled under a charismatic, messianic figure named Julianus ben Sabar, only to see the revolt crushed by Emperor Justinian I. His retribution was devastating. Tens of thousands of Samaritans died or were enslaved. Their faith was virtually outlawed. In a single event, the Samaritans dwindled from a population in the hundreds of thousands to near extinction.

Under the ensuing Islamic rule, the remaining Samaritans lived under the typical non-Muslim, or *dhimmi* status, expected to pay special taxes. Their last high priest claiming kinship through Eleazar son of Aaron died in 1624 without children, ending the family line. In 1919, an illustrated *National Geographic* article on their people stated their numbers as fewer than 150.

Today, approximately seven hundred Samaritans remain in

Palestine, their numbers bolstered by the recent practice of seeking brides from outside the dangerously inbred community. Some live in Holon, near Tel Aviv, where we would meet them. Most inhabit a village perched high on Mount Gerizim called Kiryat Luza.

Although they openly continue their ancient rites atop the mountain, it is the only community so far north where full Israeli citizens live without fences around their houses, barriers guarding their perimeters, or the need to carry guns.

This is certainly not due to any fortunate accident of geography, for in fact Kiryat Luza lies deep within the Palestinian Authority, smack between the Palestinian city of Nablus and Israel Defense Forces positions higher up the mountain's flanks. Many a sniper's bullet or artillery shell has shattered the peace of a Samaritan family's dinner.

Instead, the town's geographical layout perfectly mirrors a precarious policy of neutrality, as the Samaritans have tried to steer through the minefield of the world they inhabit. It now seems the Samaritans have mastered an ability to live at peace with their neighbors, Palestinians and Jews alike, which is unprecedented anywhere in their land.

The Game of Backgammon

THE FATE OF THE MIDDLE EAST AT A ROLL OF THE DICE

"What makes a Jew, a Jew?" I asked Micah as we slowly rolled up to the Samaritan synagogue, distinguished in subtle ways from typical Jewish synagogues that excited our host but left me tapping my foot.

"You mean the Chosen Ones? Who gets the promises made to the Jews?"

"Basically. Assuming you interpret prophecy the way so many Christians do, how do you know if you're one of those people promised this land and all that comes with it? What makes you a Jew? Do Samaritans qualify?"

Micah chuckled and opened the van door. "Well, yeah. . . . You don't know, not really."

"I noticed a lot of black Jews from Ethiopia. They're converts, right? They're not Semitic by blood. Or are they?"

"No. And what's really crazy is that many Palestinians kept out of

Israel proper are more likely the descendants of the people who sat and listened to Jesus at the Sermon on the Mount than many Jews living in Israel. The whole blood thing gets crazy."

"So, when Christians say the Jews have certain rights and privileges, are they talking about Israeli citizens?"

"No, because Israel could decide to allow anyone to be a citizen. Christians believe those promises belong to the bloodline."

"But there is no pure bloodline. Half the Palestinians are in that bloodline?"

"Not half, but you get the picture." Micah turned his eyes to the synagogue. "Like the Samaritans. Are they true Jews, or are they from Assyria? Recent DNA analysis proved that they are a mix."

"So, who's right?"

"Yes, well, that's the question, isn't it? God knows."

We walked into the synagogue but could find no one there. It looked quite rundown, hardly the kind of temple I imagined after thinking so much about the status of these people in the courts of history.

Then again, Samaritans were the forgotten ones—the outsiders without rights—which is why Jesus seemed to favor them.

We approached a young man on the street and told him we were looking for the one man most respected for his understanding of all things Samaritan. Their leader. He immediately directed us down a side alley.

"At the end you will find him. In the house on the left. He knows everything."

So we trudged down the alleyway, which was barely wide enough to squeeze a single car through. Two-story stucco houses rose on both sides, bordered by a fence with old concrete fence posts. The typical paraphernalia littered the porches—clay-potted plants, wind spinners, laundry drying on clotheslines.

In addition I noticed round, wooden game pieces, each the size of a quarter, sitting on top of half the posts. Checkers or backgammon pieces? Black and white. Odd.

We rounded a slight bend in the alleyway and walked up to a covered carport at the end. In this most inconspicuous of spaces stood a single table, and around that table sat two older men. They were leaning over a backgammon board, focused on the play at hand.

Paying them little mind, we followed our directions and ducked into the porch of the last house on the left. A younger man wearing an undershirt answered the door, wiping sleep from his eyes.

When we told him who we were looking for, he yelled out to the carport we'd passed and a scratchy voice called back.

"This way." He led us back the way we'd come.

As we approached, one of the older men engaged in the backgammon match stood, eyes still fixed on his last roll. "What is it you want?"

Micah told him.

He eyed us through droopy eyes, as if trying to judge our sincerity, then motioned for his son, the younger man in the white undershirt, to take his place at the board.

We had found our Samaritan. At a rickety card table in a carport outside of Tel Aviv. He yelled something at the house and then invited us to sit in three folding chairs next to the card table.

In slow, halting English, he addressed us. "So . . . you wish to know about the Samaritan?"

I pulled out my recorder, and for a moment he looked like he might perk up. But he cast his eyes back to the backgammon board, where his son had begun to roll the dice in his stead.

"There are seven hundred Samaritans today?" I asked.

"Yes. And we are growing, some here, some on the mountain."

"Many young people?"

"The youth? The youth have their minds on other things." He glanced at the board and pulled out a pack of Marlboro Reds. With shaking fingers, he dug out a single cigarette and set the pack on the table. His wife came out and offered us lemonade, which we gratefully accepted.

Lemonade with the Samaritans.

This was it. We had traveled so far, through so many countries, and shared tea with so many teachers in search of the Samaritan. And here we were, three travelers face to face with that Samaritan.

I felt like the Magi having come so far to pay homage to the king at the manger. But I had not expected to find him sipping lemonade at a folding card table, digging out a cigarette.

"Can you tell us about the Samaritans and what distinguishes you from the other Jews?" Carl asked. Micah translated.

"We worship God where God is to be worshiped—on Mount Gerizim, where Jacob worshiped, not in Jerusalem. And our Torah is not defiled."

The old man put his cigarette between his lips, lit it, and drew deep. Smoke poured out of his nostrils and hung in the still air. I started to ask another question, but there was no need, because he continued, casting a lost gaze over my shoulder.

"I will tell you this story . . ." And he began to retrace the whole story of how this prophet said this and came to this mountain and spoke this truth about this doctrine, which meant they should call the name of God this and not that.

Not to sound harsh, but it was the most trivial parsing of truth and opinion that I have ever heard, complicated by the fact that it was all spoken in Hebrew and interpreted by Micah, the man with many doctorates who alone seemed fascinated.

It was like hearing a Presbyterian explain just why God didn't like what the Pentecostals were doing. Like hearing an Episcopal priest explain why the Baptists were all wet.

Trivial detail to most of the world. Differences ignored by Jesus in his day. Meaningless to all but seven hundred in Israel today and those like the disciples James and John, who were so offended by this doctrinal difference that they begged Jesus to call fire down from heaven to kill them.

Jesus rebuked the two disciples. He would surely rebuke Pentecostals and Baptists and Episcopalians and Catholics and Muslims and Jews and any other group that suggested the same fate for their heretical enemies as James and John did.

What I found more interesting than the Samaritan's convictions was his complete sincerity. I looked deep into his brown eyes and for some time wondered if he believed a word he was saying, but I could see that he did.

I found his explanation tedious, and after such a long journey, I found my interest in the prize waning. All this for *this*?

But then something strange began to happen. Setting aside the Samaritan's precise division of truth and doctrine, I began to focus on the man before us. The balding human being with slightly bloodshot, brown eyes, likely in his early seventies.

He wore gray slacks with a small tear along the right pocket seam, and his buttoned-up shirt had thin blue and green stripes on it. A trimmed gray mustache graced his upper lip between two bulging cheeks that gave him something of the look of a walrus. His skin was very clean and unblemished and his nose was small. A good-looking man, our balding Samaritan.

Even more interesting than his appearance was the cigarette. He'd lit it up as he launched into his long exposition of utter truth, taken one long drag, then seemed content to let it burn. And burn.

Soon the ash was longer than the unsmoked tobacco, and my eyes kept glancing down to see if he was going to drop the ash in some unseen tray.

But he was too engaged in parsing words.

And in the clatter of dice on the backgammon board.

He let the cigarette burn, but the game between his son and the other older fellow was heating up, and our Samaritan kept sneaking peeks to see if white or black was going to win.

The ash fell from his cigarette at about the point in his monologue where some temple was selected above another temple as the true place of worship. It landed on his lap and he brushed it onto the floor without a missing a beat.

I was suddenly caught up in the perfect microcosm of all things Middle Eastern. Carl nudged me and I looked up to see that he, too, was seeing what I was seeing.

Here we were speaking to the great enemy of those in Jesus' audience two thousand years ago, and nothing had really changed. Religion was still being parsed by ordinary people who drank lemonade and smoked cigarettes. But our Samaritan's fullest attention wasn't on either his doctrine or his cigarette. Or for that matter, his guests.

His attention was on the roll of the dice to his right.

A sudden cry of victory and a growl of disapproval, and all eyes fixed on the backgammon board. The battle between the white and the black pieces had come down to one final roll.

I laughed with Carl, right there at the Samaritan's table. We both saw it. It was as if we were looking at the game of Middle Eastern life in which the fate of so many came down to a roll of the dice. Who was right, who was wrong, who would live, who would die? The headiest challenges in the Middle East were no better off in the hands of crafty theologians or shrewd politicians than in the hands of a player in a back-alley game of backgammon. Neither inspired much agreement or hope.

A simple teaching made two thousand years ago, on the other hand, might bring both agreement and hope. A message of love in the face of impossible and arbitrary odds. Rather than roll the dice to see which enemy might win today, enemies should put down the dice and love each other.

Scandalous.

As it always has been, so it was now before our very eyes.

The son rolled the dice. A three and a two. He slapped the table and swore. His white chips had lost this battle to the black chips.

"Another one," he growled.

Yes, another one.

Our Samaritan finally took another drag on his nearly spent Marlboro and launched back into his explanation of who was right and who was wrong regarding true worship of God.

Feet in the Sand

It was nearly midnight, and Carl and I sat across from each other at a table in the sand. Our flight from Tel Aviv would leave at six o'clock the next morning. The restaurant had been recommended by the Hilton in which we would spend our last night.

We were both spent. There seemed little to say. Too much to say in the space of so little time. A book could hardly contain all we had gleaned from our short journey of discovery.

We had started in the heart of Islam at Al-Azhar, unquestionably the greatest authority on Islamic thought and law in the world. Then on to Saudi Arabia, the land of Mecca, where Islamic law is lived.

North to Beirut and Baalbek, then south to the stronghold of the Hezbollah. All the way, we met with figures whose names would launch the eyebrows of any agent in Homeland Security or the CIA into his hairline.

Then across to Syria, that distant land of mystery and muftis.

And south into the Holy Land. Jerusalem. Bethlehem. The Old City, Manger Square, the Hamas. Sami Awad.

Finally to northern Israel to meet the Samaritans with tales of suicide bombings ringing in our ears.

And along the way I'd reached into my most reliable source, my own imagination, to relive the parable of the Samaritan, which today might be called the parable of the Druze—or as you've come to know it, Nicole's story. I needed to experience what the characters from Jesus' Samaritan parable had experienced so long ago, and I wanted to experience it with the reader, as if it were happening today. At the risk of leaving the reader feeling tricked, I have left numerous but subtle clues that Nicole's story is a parable. I assure you, it's the only part of this book that is fictional.

"So," I said, "what did we learn?"

"Boy."

Yeah, boy. What could be said?

"That, like Walid the Muslim, Naum the Jew, and Father Stephen the Christian, all the world is a hypocrite," Carl said.

"As am I."

"And I."

It was a good time for a drink, and we sipped in silence, lost in thought.

Carl cleared his throat. "After this, I'm not sure I will ever be comfortable calling myself a Christian again. The label means little of what Americans think it means and a whole bunch of what they don't think it means. At least in this part of the world."

Hmmmm . . .

He continued. "This all started out with a question in Denver: What do Martin Luther King, Gandhi, and Jesus all have in common? So let me ask another question: What do Christians, Muslims, Druze, Samaritans, and Jews all have in common?"

"They all worship the God of Abraham," I said.

"None of them seem to be following the teaching of Jesus."

I hesitated. "So it seems."

"They're all guilty, regardless of religion. Over here Christians are known as much for violence as the next guy. Heck, the Christians are the ones pulverizing the terrorists and all those who happened to be nearby with shock and awe these days. That's the way the world sees it, right?"

No lie there. It was exactly how much of the world understood the war in Iraq. "Right." I took another drink. "And what about our primary question?"

"Whether Jesus gave the world an impossible teaching?" Carl's brow arched. "What would you say?"

"I would agree with Sami Awad and Dr. Micah. It's as hard today as it was two thousand years ago. They should know."

He nodded. "As hard as it is, Martin Luther King, Gandhi, and their mentor, Jesus, all knew one thing. It's the *only* solution."

"You're now a pacifist?" I asked.

"No. I don't know what I am with respect to governments' use of power. But one on one, love is the only solution, and nobody does it well. Not Christians, not Muslims, not Jews, not me."

"To love your enemy, you have to sit and have tea with them, so to speak."

"Carry their burdens."

"Lie in their graves."

"Forgive them on a television broadcast."

"Pick them off the street, take them home, mend their wounds, and pay for their food, like our good Druze, Akram, did."

The waves washed up on the white sandy shore carpeted with moonlit foam. It made me think of a bomb going off in a crowded tourist district, like this one, still bustling with people. A small amount of fear reared its ugly head, and I reminded myself that in— I glanced at my watch—ten hours I would be safely in the air, bound for Denver.

Unless someone had chosen our particular flight to be the next one to fly into some tall building.

"So, what do we tell them?" Carl was asking.

I considered the question. Then lifted my glass.

"The truth," I said.

Carl lifted his glass and smiled. "To the truth."

Glossary

The **ABAYA**, *cloak* in Arabic, is an overgarment worn by some women in parts of the Islamic world. It is the traditional form of the hijab, or Islamic dress, for many countries of the Arabian Peninsula such as Saudi Arabia, where it is the national dress for women. Traditional abayas are black and cover the body from shoulders to toe.

ALIYAH, a Hebrew word meaning *ascent*, is a complex term used to signify the calling of a Jew to read the Torah in the prayer service, the obligation of Jews to make the pilgrimage to Jerusalem three times a year in the centuries before the destruction of the Temple, and the ongoing religious recognition of the holiness of the act of immigrating to the Land of Israel.

AYATOLLAH (literally means *Sign of God* in Arabic) is a high-ranking title given to certain Shiite clerics. Those who carry the title are experts in Islamic studies, such as jurisprudence, ethics, philosophy, and theology. They usually teach in Islamic seminaries.

A **BURQA** is an enveloping outer garment worn by women in some Islamic traditions for the purpose of cloaking the entire body. It is worn over the usual daily clothing and covers the face.

The **CALIPH** is the head of state in a caliphate and the title for the leader of the Islamic Ummah (community), ruled by the Shariah. It literally means *successor* or *representative* in Arabic. The early leaders of the Muslim nation following Muhammad's (570–632) death were called "Khalifat Rasul Allah"—meaning Representatives of the Messenger of God

The BYZANTINE EMPIRE or Eastern Roman Empire, was the continuation of the Roman Empire during the Middle Ages, centered on its capital of Constantinople and ruled by emperors in direct succession to the Roman emperors.

A COPT, or Coptic, is a native Egyptian Christian. A major ethno-religious group that has ancient origins, Copts are Egyptians whose ancestors embraced Christianity in the first century. The word *Coptic* was originally used in classical Arabic to refer to Egyptians in general, but after the bulk of the Egyptian population converted to Islam, it has undergone a semantic shift over the centuries to mean more specifically Egyptian Christian.

The DRUZE are a religious community found primarily in Lebanon, Syria, and northern Israel whose traditional religion began as an offshoot of Shiite Islam in Egypt around 1000 A.D. but is unique in its incorporation of Gnostic and Eastern religious traditions—such as a strong belief in reincarnation. Theologically, Druze consider themselves "an Islamic reformatory sect," while most Muslims consider the Druze to be a heretical sect and not true Muslims.

A FALUKA is the classic Egyptian boat traditionally used for fishing in the Nile River.

A FATWA is a religious opinion concerning Islamic law issued by an Islamic scholar. In Sunni Islam any *fatwa* is nonbinding, whereas in Shia Islam it could be binding, depending on the status of the scholar. Western media frequently uses the term incorrectly to specifically mean an Islamic law pronouncing a death sentence upon someone who is considered an infidel or a blasphemer, whereas the term's correct definition is significantly broader and simply meaning a declaration of any kind.

HAMAS—an acronym meaning "Islamic Resistance Movement"—is a Palestinian Islamic socio-political organization that includes a paramilitary force. Since June 2007, after winning a large majority in the Palestinian Parliament and defeating rival Palestinian party Fatah, Hamas has governed the Gaza portion of the Palestinian Territories. The European Union, the United States, and three other countries have classified Hamas as a terrorist organization.

Hamas was created in 1987 by Sheik Ahmad Yassin, Abdel Rantissi, and Muhammad Taha of the Palestinian wing of Egypt's Muslim Brotherhood at the beginning of the First Intifada, an uprising against Israeli rule in the Palestinian Territories. Hamas launched numerous suicide bombings against Israel, the first of them in April 1993. Hamas ceased the attacks in 2005 and renounced them in April 2006. Hamas has also been responsible for Israel-targeted rocket attacks, IED attacks, and shootings, but reduced those operations in 2005 and 2006.

In January 2006, Hamas was successful in the Palestinian Parliamentary elections taking 76 of the 132 seats in the chamber, while the previous ruling Fatah party took 43. After Hamas's election victory, violent and nonviolent infighting arose between Hamas and Fatah. In June 2007, elected Hamas officials were ousted from their positions in the Palestinian National Authority government in the West Bank and replaced by rival Fatah members and independents. Hamas retained control of Gaza. On June 18, 2007, Palestinian President Mahmoud Abbas (Fatah) issued a decree outlawing the Hamas militia. Israel immediately thereafter imposed an economic blockade on Gaza, and Hamas launched rocket attacks upon areas of Israel near its border with Gaza. After the end of a six-month ceasefire the conflict was escalated, and Israel invaded Hamas-controlled Gaza in late December 2008. Israel withdrew its forces from Gaza in mid-January 2009 but has maintained its blockade of the Gaza border and airspace.

RAFIK HARIRI (1944–2005), a self-made billionaire and business tycoon, was the prime minister of Lebanon from 1992 to 1998 and again from 2000 until his resignation, October 20, 2004. He headed five cabinets during his tenure. Hariri dominated the country's postwar political and business life and is widely credited with reconstructing Beirut after the fifteen-year civil war, but also for the widespread corruption that followed the war and the crippling damages done to the economy, with the public debt rising from $2.5 billion to over $40 billion and economic growth slowing from 8 percent to -1 percent during his time as prime minister.

Hariri was assassinated on February 14, 2005, when explosives equivalent to around 1,000 kg of TNT were detonated as his motorcade drove past the St. George Hotel in Beirut. The investigation by the Special Tribunal for Lebanon into his assassination is still ongoing and currently led by the independent investigator Daniel Bellemare. In its first two reports, UNIIIC indicated that the Syrian government may be linked to the assassination.

HEZBOLLAH literally means *party of God* in Arabic, and is a Shia Islamic political and paramilitary organization based in Lebanon. Hezbollah is now also a major provider of social services, which operate schools, hospitals, and agricultural services for thousands of Lebanese Shiites and is a significant force in Lebanese politics. It is regarded as a resistance movement throughout much of the Arab and Muslim world. Many governments, including Arab ones, have condemned actions by Hezbollah, while others have praised the party. Six western countries, including Israel and the United States, regard it in whole or in part as a terrorist organization.

Hezbollah first emerged in 1982 as a militia in response to the Israeli invasion of Lebanon, also known as Operation Peace for Galilee, set on resisting the Israeli occupation of Lebanon during the Lebanese Civil War. Its leaders were inspired by Ayatolla Khomeini, and its forces were trained and organized by a contingent of the Iranian Revolutionary Guard. Hezbollah's 1985 manifesto listed its three main goals as "putting an end to any colonialist entity" in Lebanon, bringing the Phalangists to justice for "the crimes they [had] perpetrated," and the establishment of an Islamic regime in Lebanon. Hezbollah leaders in the past have also made numerous statements calling for the destruction of Israel, which they refer to as a "Zionist entity" built on lands wrested from their owners.

Hezbollah, which started with only a small militia, has grown to an organization with seats in the Lebanese government, a radio and satellite TV station, and programs for social development. Hezbollah maintains strong support among

Lebanon's Shia population, and gained a surge of support from Lebanon's broader population immediately following the 2006 war with Israel. It is able to mobilize demonstrations of hundreds of thousands. Hezbollah has been granted veto power in Lebanon's parliament. In addition, a National Unity Government was formed in which Hezbollah controls nearly 30 percent of the seats.

Hezbollah receives its financial support from Iran, Syria, and the donations of Lebanese and other Shia. It has also gained significantly in military strength in the 2000s. Despite a June 2008 certification by the United Nations that Israel had withdrawn from all Lebanese territory, in August of that year, Lebanon's new cabinet unanimously approved a draft policy statement which secures Hezbollah's existence as an armed organization and guarantees its right to "liberate or recover occupied lands." Since 1992, the organization has been headed by Hassan Nasrallah.

HIJAB is the Arabic word for *curtain* or *cover* meaning "to cover, to veil, to shelter." In popular use, hijab is a head cover and modest dress for women among Muslims, which most Islamic legal systems define as covering everything except the face and hands in public.

The INJIL is Arabic for *Gospels,* referring to the first four books of the New Testament and one of the five Islamic Holy Books that the Qur'an records as revealed by God. Even though Muslims generally believe the New Testament to have been corrupted over time, they still highly respect the idea of the Injil.

INTIFADA is an Arabic word which literally means *shaking off,* though it is usually translated into English as *uprising.* According to a 2007 article in the *Washington Post,* the word "crystallized in its current Arabic meaning during the first Palestinian uprising in the late 1980s and early 1990s." It is often used as a term for popular resistance to oppression.

ISA is the Arabic word for Jesus used in the Qur'an.

The KEFFIYEH *(scarf)* is a traditional headdress typically worn by Arab men, made of a square of cloth, usually cotton, folded and wrapped in various styles around the head. It is commonly found in arid climate areas to provide protection from direct sun exposure, as well as for occasional use in protecting the mouth and eyes from blown dust and sand. Its distinctive woven check pattern originated in an ancient Mesopotamian representation of either fishing nets or ears of grain.

MARONITES are members of one of the Lebanese or Syrian Eastern Catholic Churches with a heritage reaching back to Maron the Syriac Monk in the early fifth century. The first Maronite patriarch, John Maron, was elected in the late seventh century. Although reduced in numbers today, Maronites remain one of the principal ethno-religious groups in Lebanon, and they continue to represent the absolute majority of Lebanese people when the Lebanese diaspora is included.

MIDRASH—Hebrew for *to investigate* or *to study*—is a term referring to the not exact but comparative method of exegesis of Biblical texts.

The MOSSAD, the Institute for Intelligence and Special Operations, is the national intelligence agency of Israel, responsible for intelligence collection and covert operations such as paramilitary activities, political assassinations, and the facilitation of aliyah, where it is banned. *Mossad* is the Hebrew word for *institute* or *institution*.

A MUFTI is an Islamic scholar who is an interpreter or expounder of Islamic law (Sharia).

The MUTAWEEN or MUTAWA means *subjugated people* in Arabic and is commonly used as a casual term for the government-authorized or -recognized religious police of Saudi Arabia. More recently the word has gained use as an umbrella term outside the Arab-speaking world to indicate religious-policing organizations in other Muslim countries.

MUHAMMAD is considered the great and final prophet of Islam. Born in Mecca around 570 A.D., he died in Medina in 632.

The PHALANGE, or LEBANESE SOCIAL DEMOCRATIC PARTY, is a right-wing Lebanese political party. Although it is officially secular, it is mainly supported by Maronite Christians. The party played a major role in the Lebanese Civil War. In decline in the late 1980s and 1990s, the party has slowly re-emerged in recent years and currently plays a role in Lebanese politics once again.

AL-QAEDA (in Arabic: *The Base*) is an Islamist group founded some time between August 1988 and 1990. It operates as a network comprising both a multinational, stateless arm and a fundamentalist Sunni Muslim movement calling for a return to the "base" or "foundation" of Islam according to some radical teachings of the religion.

Al-Qaeda has attacked civilian and military targets in various countries, the most notable being the destruction of the World Trade Center on September 11, 2001. This action was followed by the U.S. government launching the so-called War on Terrorism. As of 2009, the group is believed to have between 200 and 300 members.

The SAMARITANS are a religious ethnic group of the Levant. Religiously, they are the adherents to Samaritanism, a parallel but separate religion to Judaism or any of its historical forms. Based on the Samaritan Torah, Samaritans claim their worship is the true religion of the ancient Israelites prior to the Babylonian exile, preserved by those who remained in the Land of Israel, as opposed to Judaism, which they assert is a related but altered and amended religion brought back by the exiled returnees.

Ancestrally, they claim descent from a group of Israelite inhabitants who have connections to ancient Samaria from the beginning of the Babylonian exile up to the beginning of the Common Era. The Samaritans, however, derive their name not from this geographical designation, but rather from the Hebrew term שָׁמְרִים (Šāmĕrı m), "Keepers [of the Law]."

Although historically they were a large community—up to more than a million in late Roman times, then gradually reduced to several tens of thousands up to a few centuries ago—their unprecedented demographic shrinkage has been a result of various historical events, including most notably the bloody repression of the Third Samaritan Revolt (529 CE) against the Byzantine Christian rulers and the mass forced conversions to Islam in the Early Muslim period of Palestine. According to their tally, as of November 1, 2007, there were 712 Samaritans living almost exclusively in two localities, one in Kiryat Luza on Mount Gerizim near the city of Nablus in the West Bank, and the other in the Israeli city of Holon, near Tel Aviv.

SHARIA is the body of Islamic religious law. The term means *way* or *path to the water source*. It is the legal framework within which the public and private aspects of life are regulated for those living in a legal system based on Islamic principles of jurisprudence and for Muslims living outside the domain. Sharia deals with most aspects of day-to-day life. Islamic law is now the most widely used religious law, and one of the three most common legal systems of the world alongside common law and civil law.

SHEIK is a word or honorific term in the Arabic language that literally means *elder*. It is commonly used to designate an elder of a tribe, a revered wise man, or an Islamic scholar. Although the title generally refers to a male person, there existed in history also a very small number of female sheiks. It may also refer to a man over forty years old.

SHIA or **SHIITE** Islam is the second largest denomination of Islam, after Sunni Islam. Approximately 15 to 20 percent of the Muslim world is Shiite.

Similar to other schools of thought in Islam, Shia Islam is based on the teachings of the Islamic holy book, the Qur'an, and the message of the final prophet of Islam, Muhammad. In contrast to other schools of thought, Shia Islam holds that Muhammad's family, and certain individuals among his descendants, who are known as Imams, have special spiritual and political rule over the community. Shia Muslims further believe that Ali, Muhammad's cousin and son-in-law, was the first of these Imams and was the rightful successor to Muhammad; thus, they reject the legitimacy of the first three caliphs. Shia Muslims constitute the majority of the population in Iran, Azerbaijan, Bahrain, Lebanon, and Iraq.

SUNNI ISLAM is the largest denomination of Islam. The word is derived from the word *Sunnah*, which means the words and actions or example of the Islamic prophet Muhammad.

The **TALMUD** (Hebrew: *instruction, learning*) is a record of rabbinic discussions pertaining to Jewish law, ethics, customs, and history. It is a central text of mainstream

Judaism. The Talmud has two components: the Mishnah (c. 200 CE), the first written compendium of Judaism's Oral Law; and the Gemara (c. 500 CE).

The **TEMPLE MOUNT**, also know as Mount Moriah and by Muslims as the **NOBLE SANCTUARY**, is a religious site in Old City of Jerusalem. Due to its importance for both Judaism and Islam, it is one of the most contested religious sites in the world.

The Temple Mount contains the holiest site in Judaism. Jewish Midrash holds that it was from here that the world expanded into its present form, and that this was where God gathered the dust he used to create the first man, Adam. The Torah records that it was here that God chose to rest His Name and Divine Presence, and consequently two Jewish temples were built at the site. According to Jewish tradition, the third temple will also be located here, and will be the final one. In recent times, due to difficulties in ascertaining the precise location of the Mount's holiest spot, many Jews will not set foot on the Mount itself.

The Noble Sanctuary is the third holiest site in Islam, associated with biblical prophets who are also revered in Islam. The site is the location of the al-Aqsa Mosque and the Dome of the Rock, the oldest extant Islamic structure in the world.

A **THOBE** is an ankle-length garment usually with long sleeves, similar to a robe, worn by Muslim men.

The **TORAH**—Hebrew for *learning* or *instruction*—is sometimes translated as *law*. It refers either to the Five Books of Moses (or Pentateuch) or to the entirety of Judaism's founding legal and ethical religious texts.

The Torah is the most holy of the sacred writings in Judaism. It is the first of three sections in the Tanakh (Hebrew Bible), the founding religious document of Judaism. The names of the five books in English are Genesis, Exodus, Leviticus, Numbers, and Deuteronomy.

The Torah is also considered a holy book in Islam.

When used with an indefinite article, a Torah usually refers to a Torah scroll, written on parchment in a formal, traditional manner by a specially trained scribe under very strict requirements.

ZIONISM is the international political movement that originally supported the reestablishment of a homeland for the Jewish people in Palestine. The area was the Jewish biblical homeland, called the Land of Israel (Hebrew: *Eretz Yisra'el*). Since the creation of Israel, the Zionist movement continues primarily as support for the modern state of Israel.

Zionism is based on the foundation of historical ties and religious traditions linking the Jewish people to the Land of Israel and the concept of Jewish nationhood.

Timeline of the Modern-Day Israeli-Palestinian Issue

1917 | Balfour Declaration
During World War I, Great Britain issues the Balfour Declaration, promising a Jewish homeland in the area called Palestine, which would respect the rights of all native Palestinians.

1922 | Post-WWI Middle East
After the defeat of the Ottoman Empire, the League of Nations confirm a British mandate over Iraq and Palestine, and a French mandate over Lebanon and Syria. Transjordan then separates from the Palestinian area and become an autonomous country.

1936 | Arab Demands
Many Palestinian Arabs ask for a halt to Jewish immigration and plead with their compatriots to not sell any more land to Jews. British troops attempt to control the growing tensions, but violence increases. The Peel Commission recommends the partition of Palestine between Arabs and Jews.

1947 | United Nations Partition
Britain allows the U.N. to decide what to do about Palestine, which is then partitioned into Jewish, Arab, and international areas, with 55 percent allocated to the future Jewish state.

1948 | Israel's War of Independence
When the British Mandate expires in May 1948, Israel declares itself a new Jewish nation, and the British leave the Middle East. Arab states declare war on Israel, but Israel prevails. The U.N. declares, through Resolution 194, that the Palestinian refugees from the new Jewish state should be allowed to return home and that compensation

for their land should be paid. In 1949, agreements with other Arab nations allow Israel to annex more land and now control 77 percent of Palestine. Jordan controls the West Bank area of the Jordan River up to and including the old city of Jerusalem.

1956 | Suez Canal Crisis
Egypt nationalizes the Suez Canal. U.N. forces patrol the Sinai Peninsula to keep the tenuous peace in that region between Egypt and Israel.

1964 | Palestinian Liberation Organization
The PLO is established, committing to do whatever it takes to liberate the homeland of the Palestinian people. Yasser Arafat will lead the movement and the Palestinians until his death in 2004.

June 1967 | The Six Days' War
Following numerous border clashes between Israel and its Arab neighbors, Egypt blocks the Straits of Tiran, the critical sea passage connecting the Red Sea with the Arabian Sea, and Arab forces mobilize for war. Israel launches preemptive attacks on Egypt, Syria, Iraq, and Jordan. Six days later, Israel occupies the Golan Heights, Gaza, the Sinai Peninsula, and the West Bank, including most of Jerusalem. About six months later, the United Nations passes Resolution 242, declaring that Israel must not gain new territory through war and that it should withdraw from the recently acquired territories. This resolution is the basis that Arab nations have since used when negotiating with Israel.

1973 | Yom Kippur War
Egypt and Syria attack Israeli troops in the Sinai and the Golan Heights. After sixteen days of war, U.N. Resolution 338 is passed, simply confirming Resolution 242.

1977–79 | Sadat and Begin
The two key leaders in the crisis—President Anwar Sadat of Egypt and Prime Minister Menachem Begin of Israel—visit each other's countries. President Jimmy Carter hosts the Camp David Accords, and in 1979 the two countries sign a peace treaty.

1981 | Sadat Killed
Israel increases the rate and amount of Jewish settlements on Palestinian lands. Anwar Sadat is assassinated.

1982 | Israel Moves into Lebanon
In response to Palestinian attacks from Lebanese territory, Israel moves to destroy the PLO stronghold in that country. An early version of Hezbollah is established in Lebanon as a resistance movement to the Israeli forces.

1987 | First Intifada
A Palestinian uprising erupts (Intifada, or "shaking off"). The Islamic organization Hamas is founded in the Palestinian Territories.

1988 | Arafat Recognizes Israel

The Kingdom of Jordan gives the West Bank and East Jerusalem to the PLO. Yasser Arafat recognizes Israel's right to exist and renounces the use of violence.

1993 | Oslo Agreement

Israel and the PLO work out a peace agreement that would recognize the other's right to exist, but extremists from both sides undermine the process.

1994 | The Palestinian National Authority

The Palestinian National Authority is formed as the agreed-upon political wing of the PLO. Jordan and Israel sign a peace treaty and begin to open their borders.

1995 | Rabin Assassinated

Israeli Prime Miniser Yitzhak Rabin is killed by an Israeli fundamentalist.

2000 | Israel Withdraws from Lebanon and Second Intifada Begins

Israel withdraws from all of Lebanon except one small piece of disputed land (the Shebaa Farms). Ariel Sharon's controversial visit to the Temple Mount a few months before his election as prime minister triggers the second Intifada.

2002 | Arab Peace Plan

The Arab League adopts a formal plan to normalize relations with Israel if they withdraw to the pre-1967 borders. Israel begins building a wall to separate Israel from the West Bank.

2004–05 | From Arafat to Abbas

Yasser Arafat dies in November 2004 and Mahmoud Abbas (Abu Mazen) is elected President in 2005.

January 2006 | Hamas Wins

Ariel Sharon suffers a stroke. Hamas wins the Palestinian elections by a small majority. Hamas functionally takes control of the Gaza Strip.

Summer 2006 | Hezbollah-Israel War

Hezbollah captures Israeli soldiers, and Israel attacks Lebanon. A brutal one-month war ensues. Over 1,000 Lebanese are killed during the war, mostly civilians; 118 Israeli soldiers and 45 Israeli civilians die.

2009 | Gaza-Israeli War

On December 27, 2008, Israel launches an offensive to stop the Hamas rockets into southern Israel. The nearly one-month war kills approximately 1,500 Palestinians and 13 Israelis.